Measuring the Gains from Medical Research

Measuring the Gains from Medical Research

An Economic Approach

EDITED BY

Kevin M. Murphy

AND

Robert H. Topel

THE UNIVERSITY OF CHICAGO PRESS

Chicago & London

Kevin M. Murphy is the George J. Stigler Professor of Economics in the Graduate School of Business and the Department of Economics at the University of Chicago and a research associate of the National Bureau of Economic Research.

Robert H. Topel is the Isidore Brown and Gladys J. Brown Professor in Urban and Labor Economics in the Graduate School of Business at the University of Chicago and a research associate of the National Bureau of Economic Research.

The University of Chicago Press, Chicago 60637
The University of Chicago Press, Ltd., London

Printed in the United States of America

12 11 10 09 08 07 06 05 04 03 1 2 3 4 5

ISBN: 0-226-55178-4 (cloth)

The University of Chicago Press gratefully acknowledges the generous contribution of The Mary Woodard Lasker Charitable Trust, and funds solicited by and supplied to the Trust by Abbott Laboratories Fund, Bristol-Myers Squibb Foundation, the DeBakey Medical Foundation, and the Robert Wood Johnson Jr. Charitable Trust, toward the publication of this book.

Library of Congress Cataloging-in-Publication Data

Measuring the gains from medical research : an economic approach / edited by Kevin M. Murphy and Robert H. Topel.
p. ; cm.
Includes bibliographical references and indexes.
ISBN 0-226-55178-4 (cloth : alk. paper)
1. Medicine—Research—Cost effectiveness—Congresses.
I. Murphy, Kevin M. II. Topel, Robert H.
[DNLM: 1. Research—economics—Congresses. 2. Cost-Benefit Analysis—Congresses. 3. Health Expenditures—trends—Congresses. 4. Health Status—Congresses. 5. Research Support—Congresses. 6. Socioeconomic Factors—Congresses. W 20.5 M484 2003]

R852.M383 2003
362.1′068—dc21

2002010963

⊗The paper used in this publication meets the minimum requirements of the American National Standard for Information Sciences—Permanence of Paper for Printed Library Materials, ANSI Z39.48-1992.

CONTENTS

INTRODUCTION

The papers collected in this volume study the economics of improving health and the returns to medical research. They address a number of questions: What is the value of improvements in health? Have past improvements in health substantially contributed to economic well-being? Have investments in medical research, both public and private, produced significant improvements in health? What might be gained from future expenditures on medical research, and how can we measure prospective gains?

To motivate what follows, it is worthwhile to review some basic facts about improving health and expenditures on medical research. Mortality data, the most common measure of health "output," show that during the twentieth century the life expectancy of Americans increased by roughly 30 years. In 1900, 18 percent of males born in the United States died before their first birthday; by 2000, the cumulative death rate among males did not reach 18 percent until age 68. These strides, along with similar progress occurring in other developed countries, accounted for the largest and most widespread gain in health in recorded history. This progress occurred on many fronts: infant mortality in the United States fell by 95 percent; deaths from many infectious diseases, such as diphtheria, tuberculosis, cholera, and influenza, were virtually eliminated; mortality rates from heart disease—which remains the most common cause of death—fell by more than two-thirds between 1954 and 2000.

The papers in this volume were presented at a conference on the economics of medical research, convened in Washington, D.C., in December 1999. We are grateful to The Mary Woodard Lasker Charitable Trust and the Lasker Foundation for underwriting the conference. The impetus for our work and for the conference was a question posed by Hugo Sonnenschein, who asked whether medical research spending is worthwhile. We thank Hugo, as well as Sam Silverstein and Leon Rosenberg of the Lasker Foundation, for their encouragement and patience.

Along with progress in the "quantity" of health, Americans' expenditures on health care have increased dramatically, faster than in any other developed country. Between 1960 and 1998, real (1996 dollars) per-capita health-care expenditure in the United States increased from $679 to $4,030, or at an annual rate of 4.9 percent. Over the same period, per-capita incomes grew at only 2 percent annually, so the share of health care in household expenditures soared. By 1998, U.S. health expenditures accounted for 12.9 percent of national income—far and away the highest share in the world and roughly 60 percent above the average (about 8 percent) for other member countries of the Organisation for Economic Co-Operation and Development (OECD, 2001). Yet Americans are not measurably healthier than citizens of other developed countries, which has led many to question the productivity of high health care expenditures and associated methods of allocating and delivering health care.

The United States also spends more—much more—on medical research than any other country. In 1995 health research and development (R&D) spending from all public and private sources totaled $36 billion, of which about $13 billion was funded by the federal government.[1] The federal commitment has expanded rapidly since then: in fiscal 2000 government-funded medical research expenditures in the United States totaled roughly $18.4 billion, and Congress has recently committed to a doubling (to roughly $35 billion) by 2004 of the budgetary appropriations for the National Institutes of Health. By comparison, in the year 2000 government funding for medical research in the entire European Union, which is 25 percent more populous than the United States, totaled only $3.7 billion (OECD, 2002). Evidently, Americans place unusually high collective value on medical research, and they are willing to pay for it.

The central issue addressed in this volume is whether this extraordinary national commitment to medical research is worthwhile. Taken as a whole, the papers collected here suggest that it is—and given the extraordinary value of improvements to health, we may even spend *too little* on medical research. We find, for example, that growth in longevity since 1950 has been as valuable as growth in all other forms of consumption combined (Nordhaus); that medical advances producing 10 percent reductions in mortality from cancer and heart disease alone would add roughly $10 *trillion* (a year's gross domestic product [GDP]) to national wealth (Murphy and Topel); and that the average new drug approved by the FDA yields benefits worth many times its cost of development (Lichtenberg). Focusing on specific treatments and breakthroughs, medical research accounts for most of the extraordinary gains against cardiovascular disease that have occurred since 1950, including behavioral changes that have produced healthier lifestyles (Cutler and Kadiyala), while "informal" medical research that changes medical practice has played a large role in reducing mortality from heart attacks (Heidenreich and McClellan). Despite these obvious gains, much remains to be done in building an economic framework for evaluating the costs and benefits of specific medical treatments and of medical research more broadly (Meltzer).

Our specific research findings are summarized below.

I. The Contribution of Health to Economic Well-Being

National income accounting is the method by which we typically measure economic well-being. If per-capita incomes are higher in Canada than in Mexico, we conclude that the average Canadian is "better off" in some measurable sense than the average Mexican. If incomes grow over time within a country, we take that as evidence of improving welfare for the typical citizen. Since improvements in health and longevity obviously improve welfare, one might well ask how they are incorporated into measures of national income. Remarkably enough, they aren't.

In "The Health of Nations: The Contribution of Improved Health to Living Standards," William Nordhaus explores how measures of national income accounting might incorporate improvements in the health of a country's population. Nordhaus argues that national income accounts would more accurately reflect changes in welfare if they properly measured the *output* of the health care sector. His approach is to obtain direct measures of health quantities and to weight those quantities by appropriate prices, yielding "values" of health. For example, if persons are willing to reduce consumption by, say, $3,000 in each year of life in order to gain one additional year of life expectancy, then an extra year of life is equivalent to a $3,000 increase in annual income. Armed with (rough) evidence of this "willingness to pay" for additional life years, Nordhaus adjusts national income measures to reflect the "value" of increasing lifetimes.

Nordhaus's empirical results are striking. Under reasonable assumptions, he finds that the value of increases in life expectancy is about equal to the growth in all other consumption. For example, between 1950 and 1995, average annual growth in per-capita consumption was a little over 2 percent per year. Expressed as a proportion of measured consumption, improvements in longevity over this period added just under 2 percentage points per year to economic growth in the United States. To put this in perspective, Nordhaus frames this comparison in terms of a choice: Suppose you had to forgo either the health improvements that occurred over the last half century, or the cumulative improvement in all other aspects of life. You could have either (*a*) 1950 health and 2000 nonhealth living standards; or (*b*) 2000 health and 1950 nonhealth living standards. Which would you choose? If you have a hard time choosing, then you agree with Nordhaus: *Over the last half century, improvements in health have been as valuable as all other sources of economic growth combined.*

Kevin Murphy and Robert Topel take up related issues in "The Economic Value of Medical Research." As we noted above, the United States invests more into basic medical research than any other country. Are these investments worthwhile? Should we invest even more? To answer these questions we need a framework for valuing improvements in health and progress against disease, against which we may compare the costs of producing new medical knowledge and delivering health care.

Murphy and Topel develop such a framework, based on individuals' willingness to pay for increases in longevity and improvements in the "quality" of life. They then apply this framework empirically, measuring the value of both past gains in longevity and the prospective gains from progress against various diseases. Like Nordhaus, they find that past gains have been enormously valuable. Improvements to life expectancy alone (ignoring improvement in the quality of life) added about $2.6 trillion per year to national wealth between 1970 and 1998. By comparison, average GDP over this period was about $5.5 trillion—the *uncounted* value of rising longevity is nearly half the measured national output.

While it is not possible to give a precise estimate of the contributions of medical research to these gains, the evidence suggests that past contributions have been large and that the prospects for future contributions are similarly important. For example, research-generated advances in medical knowledge are known to be important contributors to reduced mortality from heart disease (Cutler and Richardson, 1997; Cutler and Kadiyala, this volume). Murphy and Topel find that progress against heart disease contributes $1.1 trillion of the $2.6 trillion annual gain from increasing longevity. Looking ahead, they conclude that a 10 percent further reduction in mortality from heart disease would have a present value of $5.5 trillion to current and future generations, while a 10 percent reduction in mortality from cancer would be worth $4.4 trillion. By comparison, the present value of the current NIH annual budget, discounted at 3 percent, is less than $1 trillion, or less than one-tenth the size of these prospective gains.

II. Medical Research and Health

While it seems plausible that a large portion of the gains documented by Nordhaus and by Murphy and Topel are due to advances in medical knowledge, existing evidence to support this conclusion is thin. How does medical research affect health? This central issue is taken up in three papers.

In "Pharmaceutical Innovation, Mortality Reduction, and Economic Growth," Frank Lichtenberg examines the effects of new pharmaceutical introductions on a direct measure of health: life years saved. Using data on the number of prescriptions of individual chemical compounds and the diseases for which compounds are prescribed, Lichtenberg estimates the effect of new drug compounds on mortality. He finds that the introduction of new drugs—measured by the share of drugs recently approved by the FDA among all prescriptions for disease—significantly reduces mortality. On average, according to his estimates, the typical new drug approved in the period 1970–91 saves over 11,000 life-years annually. Even imputing a low value of $25,000 per year to life-years saved, and ignoring other health-improving benefits of new drugs, Lichtenberg estimates that the estimated benefits of new drugs have vastly outweighed their costs of development.

Moving from Lichtenberg's broad perspective on a variety of diseases, the papers by Paul Heidenreich and Mark McClellan and by David Cutler and Srikanth Kadiyala provide a sharper focus on the relationship between the production of new medical knowledge and progress against cardiovascular disease (CVD). This focus is important and timely for two reasons. First, by studying a single disease category it is easier to assess the impact of particular treatments on measurable outcomes. Second, though CVD mortality fell by about two-thirds since 1950, it remains the leading cause of death in the United States. It therefore provides a useful laboratory for understanding why such remarkable progress occurred, and what remains to be achieved.

Improvements in health during the first half of the twentieth century have been attributed to improvements in public health—which may well have a research base—and to economic development (Fogel, 1994). But post-1950 increases in longevity are concentrated among the middle-aged and elderly, and occur largely because of a steady decline in mortality from CVD (NCHS, 1999). These gains are widely attributed to improvements in biomedical knowledge (Hunink et al., 1997; Braunwald, 1998). In "Biomedical Research and Then Some: The Causes of Technological

Change in Heart Attack Treatment," Heidenreich and McClellan conduct a detailed review of the literature on how technological advances borne of medical research have affected the treatment of heart attacks.

Heidenreich and McClellan find that formal applied research studies do not explain much of the changes in clinical practice that actually account for declining heart attack mortality. Instead, clinical practices themselves appear in many cases to *lead* the results of clinical trials, and in others to lag the results of trials by many years. They classify the process by which new clinical knowledge is disseminated as "informal R&D," and they argue that it accounts for much of the changes in clinical practice that affected heart disease mortality. As a result, understanding and affecting informal R&D activities may be a critical part of guiding public policies to increase the value of the biomedical knowledge base. And, as this component of R&D is not counted in R&D spending, they conclude that biomedical research activity is much higher than formal spending measures may suggest.

David Cutler and Srikanth Kadiyala also study cardiovascular disease. In "The Return to Biomedical Research: Treatment and Behavioral Effects," they emphasize the connection between medical research and individuals' behavioral choices that affect health. For example, research findings that smoking promotes heart disease and other ailments have caused smoking rates to fall by one-third since 1960, which reduces the incidence of heart disease.

Cutler and Kadiyala estimate that about one-third of the decline in CVD mortality is due to invasive treatments (e.g., coronary bypass surgery or angioplasty), one-third is due to the use of risk-reducing pharmaceuticals (e.g., antihypertensives or antilipidemics), and the remaining third stems from behavioral changes (e.g., reduced smoking and lower-fat diets). Just as new medical treatments are largely the outcome of research, Cutler and Kadiyala find that a large portion of health-improving behavioral changes result from medical research into how people can become or remain healthy. Thus productive "medical research" does not refer solely to investigations of new procedures or chemical compounds, but rather incorporates research into healthy lifestyles as well. Further, because the changes in lifestyle that produce health gains are not obviously cost-increasing, unlike high-tech medical treatments, they may have substantially higher rates of return on basic research investments. Cutler and Kadiyala estimate that the return on producing basic information about disease risk is about 30 to 1—far greater than the 4 to 1 ratio that they estimate for technology-based research.

III. When Are Medical Treatments Worthwhile?

The studies outlined above indicate that public and private medical research is extremely valuable, largely because people place high values on health and longevity. But the high average value of medical care and research does not mean that medical expenditures (for either research or care) are worthwhile on the margin. At a macro level, vastly higher medical expenditures and research outlays in the United States are not reflected in substantially better health outcomes for Americans relative to citizens of other developed countries. At a micro level, quasi-experiments in which expanded health care is extended to groups who already have substantial coverage also fail to show substantial gains in health outcomes (Manning et al., 1987; McClellan et al., 1994). Given that care is unlikely to be allocated by a pure price mechanism in any type of modern health-delivery system, it is important to develop methods for allocating medical resources in an economically rational way. Yet methods of making allocative decisions based on costs and benefits are poorly developed.

In "Can Medical Cost-Effectiveness Analysis Identify the Value of Research?" David Meltzer reviews and extends cost-effectiveness analysis, the most widely discussed method for evaluating the costs and benefits of particular treatments. Treatments are ranked according to their cost per unit of benefit—for example, dollars per life year—and those with the lowest cost per unit are deemed attractive. Meltzer provides a striking example, due to Eddy (1990), of the effectiveness of Pap smears done annually, every 2 years, or every 3 years. A Pap smear done every 3 years increases life expectancy by 70 days; every 2 years by 71 days, and every year by 71 days and 8 hours. Meltzer (1997) finds that the marginal cost per life year of an annual Pap smear, compared with one done every other year, is $833,000.

Clear examples such as this aside, Meltzer shows that the effective use of cost-effectiveness analysis faces a number of methodological and empirical obstacles. These include the measurement of costs and benefits (what is the appropriate measure of benefit for, say, a hip replacement?), and the incorporation of uncertainty and attitudes toward risk in evaluating payoffs from medical care. Meltzer suggests how cost-effectiveness analysis can be extended to evaluate the costs and benefits of individual medical research projects.

IV. Conclusions

Advances in medical knowledge, borne of medical research, are a main source of longer and healthier lives. The value of gains in health over the past half century appears to have far outstripped the comparatively modest investments in medical R&D, and it is plausible that future investments can yield "extraordinary returns." Much remains to be done, however, to understand the path by which medical R&D is translated into valuable gains in health. It is possible, for example, that the costs of delivering new types of medical care that are the fruits of medical research may outstrip the benefits to recipients. This is particularly important when the costs and benefits of specific treatments play little role in treatment decisions—a characteristic of most modern health-delivery and financing systems. While such distortions are important and worthy of further research, they are beyond the scope of the analyses presented here.

Note

1. Source: National Institutes of Health, Office of Reports and Analysis, table 126.

References

Braunwald, E. M. 1998. "Shattuck Lecture: Cardiovascular Medicine at the Turn of the Millennium." *New England Journal of Medicine* 337, no. 19:1360–69.

Cutler, David, and Elizabeth Richardson. "Measuring the Health of the U.S. Population," *Brookings Papers: Microeconomics 1997*, pp. 217–271.

Eddy, David. 1990. "Screening for Cervical Cancer." *Annals of Internal Medicine* 113:214–26.

Fogel, Robert. 1994. "Economic Growth, Population Theory, and Physiology: The Bearing of Long-Term Processes on the Making of Economic Policy." *American Economic Review* (June).

Hunink, M. G., L. Goldman, A. N. Tosteson, M. A. Mittleman, P. A. Goldman, L. W. Williams, et al. 1997. "The Recent Decline in Mortality from Coronary Heart Disease, 1980–1990: The Effect of Secular Trends in Risk Factors and Treatment."

Manning, Willard, Joseph Newhouse, Naihua Duan, et al. 1987. "Health Insurance and the Demand for Medical Care: Evidence from a Randomized Expert." *American Economic Review* 77, no. 3:251–77.

McClellan, Mark, Barbara J. McNeil, and Joseph P. Newhouse. 1994. "Does More Intensive Treatment of Acute Myocardial Infarction in the Elderly Reduce Mortality?" *Journal of the American Medical Association* 272, no. 11 (21 September): 859–66.

Meltzer, David. 1997. "Accounting for Future Costs in Medical Cost-Effectiveness Analysis." *Journal of Health Economics* 16, no. 1:33–64.

National Center for Health Statistics (NCHS). 1999. Mortality series: <http://www.cdc/gov~nchs>.

CHAPTER ONE

The Health of Nations: The Contribution of Improved Health to Living Standards

William D. Nordhaus

I. Introduction

Nations generally measure their economic performance using the yardstick of national output and income. It is not widely recognized, however, that conventional accounting approaches do a poor job of capturing improvements in the health of the population in our gross domestic product (GDP) or incomes per capita. How would standard economic measures change if they adequately reflected improvements in the health status of the population as well as other goods and services? This is the question addressed in the present study.

The first section discusses the theory of the measurement of national income, examines some of the shortcomings of traditional concepts, and proposes a new concept that can be used to incorporate improvements in health status. In the second section, we discuss how the proposed measure fits into existing theories of consumption and valuation. The third section applies the concepts to the United States over the twentieth century.

At the end, we conclude that accounting for improvements in the health status of the population would make a substantial difference to our measures of economic welfare over the twentieth century in the United States.

II. Including Health Status in Measures of National Income

Current Approaches to Measuring the Contribution of Health in the National Accounts

While the GDP and the rest of the National Income and Product Accounts (NIPA) may seem to be arcane concepts, they are truly among the great

William D. Nordhaus is the Sterling Professor of Economics at Yale University.

The present research was supported in part by the National Science Foundation. I am grateful for comments from David Cutler, Angus Deaton, Robert Gordon, and T. N. Srinivasan.

inventions of the twentieth century. Much as a satellite in space can survey the weather across an entire continent, so can the GDP give an overall picture of the state of the economy. Since their first construction by Simon Kuznets, who won the Nobel Prize in economics for his contributions to national income accounting, enormous strides have been taken in developing and improving indexes of economic welfare. Starting with rudimentary measures of national income and output, nations now have a wide range of indexes that not only include conventional concepts but also disaggregate these for industries and regions, use improved techniques for aggregation, and display a wealth of detail.

Nevertheless, since the beginning, there have been concerns that the accounts are incomplete and misleading because they omit most nonmarket activity. To meet this criticism, private scholars as well as official statistical agencies have begun extending the national accounts to include several nonmarket sectors, including natural resources, the environment, transportation, leisure time, and unpaid work.[1]

One question that has been virtually ignored in attempts to extend the national accounts is the need to account adequately for improvements in human health. It is little understood outside the priesthood of national accountants that there is no serious attempt to measure the "real output" of the health care industry. The techniques used to measure the price and quantity of health care are highly defective, and there are *no* attempts to account for improvements in the length of life into current measures of living standards.

It might be argued that including health status is some radical, far-out, and woolly-headed attempt to incorporate intangible, noneconomic, and sociological measures into our social accounts. This argument is wrong, for health care expenditures are already included in measures of national income and output. Indeed, they are a growing fraction of GDP: the fraction of personal consumption expenditures devoted to medical care rose from 5.1 percent in 1959 to 14.0 percent in 2000. What is radical is not the inclusion of health care but the notion advanced here that we should make a serious attempt to measure the *output* of the health care sector and to *value* this output correctly.

Both common sense and recent economic studies suggest that there is little connection between medical spending and the measured economic value of health-status improvements. At a commonsense level, the lack of connection comes because "real" medical care spending in fact measures spending on inputs rather than the results in health outcomes. The current approach is to measure health output primarily by the number of physician visits, the number of hospital days, and similar measures rather than the actual delivery of services or changes in health status. It will come as a surprise to most noneconomists that improvements that come from new products, such as the discovery of antibiotics or the substitution of drugs for invasive surgery, are completely omitted in current measures of real output.

Attempts to measure improvements in the health status of the population—including everything from vaccinations, microsurgery, and new drugs to airbags, exercise, and anti-cigarettes advertising—pose a new and difficult challenge to measuring national income. Recently, economists have begun providing better outcome-oriented estimates of the prices and outputs in this sector. One of the most striking findings comes from a study by Cutler et al. (1998), who estimated that a true price index for the treatment of heart attacks would rise about 5.5 percent per year more slowly than the corresponding component of the Consumer Price Index (CPI). Similar results were found in studies of treatment for glaucoma by Shapiro and Wilcox (1997, 1999) and for cataract surgery by Shapiro, Shapiro, and Wilcox (1998).

Given the likelihood that we are dramatically mismeasuring, and almost certainly underestimating, the contribution of improvements in health care to economic welfare, this raises the question of how to proceed to obtain better estimates. One approach would be to continue the approach just described of constructing better measures of output and prices to reflect the (literal) decline in the cost of living. This approach was adopted by the Boskin Commission and is the thrust of much current research on health economics.[2]

Another, quite different approach, which is used in the present study, is to obtain direct measures of health status, weight them with appropriate prices, and then estimate the value of improvements in health status. This approach treats medical care as an instrumental input and subtracts it from consumption expenditures. We would instead adjust real income to reflect the value of the improvement of health status. This approach is actually much simpler than "fixing" price and output indexes because measures of health status are generally much better than data on the impacts of particular technologies on health status. We will see that following this path has radical impacts on our measures of real income and output.

Alternative Measures of National Income

Before proposing alternative concepts, it will be useful to describe different approaches to measuring national income. The concepts of social income and national income go back centuries. They are largely based on the analogous definitions of individual income, with appropriate adjustments for aggregation and national boundaries. We can distinguish two fundamentally different approaches to measuring income: one based on production and one based on utility. (Utility in this context means preferences, not usefulness.) The former is the basis of modern national-income accounting, while the latter is more appropriate when considering sustainable income and the contribution of improvement in health status.

Production-Based Measures (Hicksian Income)

The modern treatment of social income dates from the writings of J. R. Hicks. When economists and accountants measure national income, they almost universally rely upon the Hicksian definition. The discussion of social income in *Value and Capital* states, "The purpose of income calculations in practical affairs is to give people an indication of the amount which they can consume without impoverishing themselves" (Hicks, 1939: 172). Hicks then goes on to provide his first definition of social income:

> *Income No. 1* is thus the maximum amount which can be spent during a period if there is to be an expectation of maintaining intact the capital value of prospective returns...; it equals Consumption plus Capital accumulation. (pp. 173, 178; emphasis added)[3]

This definition is what is called "Hicksian income"—the maximum amount that can be consumed while leaving capital intact. In practice, this means that income equals consumption plus a generalized measure of capital accumulation.

The Hicksian concept is the standard definition of net national or domestic product used in the national-income accounts of virtually all nations today, where consumption and investment are limited to those legal goods and services that pass through the marketplace. It is *production-based* in the sense that it attempts to measure the rate of production at a given time. Such measures are not concerned with the health status of the population or whether people are enjoying that production for a longer period of time.

Utility-Based Measures (Fisherian Income)

While standard concepts of income are useful tools for measuring current production, it is difficult to extract any welfare significance from them. The shortcoming of the traditional approach is clear when we consider situations where technologies are improving or where people are living longer. An economy in which people have a per-capita income of $20,000 with lives that are nasty, brutish, and short would be ranked as equivalent to one with the same per-capita income and lives that are healthy, civilized, and long. In the context of health, the key point is that the same *annual* income with a long and healthy life should be ranked as a higher living standard than that income with a short and diseased life. Including health status in income is particularly important when a large and growing fraction of our economy is devoted to health care.

An alternative approach is to define income as utility-equivalent consumption.[4] I have called this Fisherian income after Irving Fisher, who defined income as the flow of consumption that could be harvested from the nation's capital stock.[5] Under this approach, income is defined as the level of consumption that would give the equivalent level of utility from consumption and other determinants of utility in different situations. This definition has been used to define the level of "sustainable income" in situations where there is a tug-of-war between resource exhaustion and technological change.[6] In cases where lifetimes are fixed, this is equivalent to defining income as the consumption equivalent of current assets and current and future technologies.

For concreteness, call this utility national income, and define it as follows:

> *Definition.* Utility national income is the maximum amount that a nation can consume while ensuring that members of all future generations can have lifetime utility that is at least as high as that of the current generation.

If life expectancy is unchanging, income is the maximum real consumption annuity that a nation can spend out of its resource endowment. The major difference in analyzing living standards with variable lifetimes is to recognize that people are better off when they live longer, and that this fact should be reflected in measures of their incomes and living standards. This approach measures the increased income from longer life expectancies by the consumption-equivalent of the utility or value of the health or longevity improvements.

III. Integrating Health Status into Income Measures

Consumption and income are traditionally measured as flows of goods and services (or utilities) during a given period of time. Changes in an individual's health status (while alive) pose no terribly deep issues of measurement, for we can treat these as new or improved "goods and services" that can be appropriately priced and included in the consumption basket.

Treatment of shortening or lengthening life, by contrast, poses qualitatively different problems of measurement. I begin this section by considering a simple life-cycle model of consumption in which there are tradeoffs between life and consumption. I then show how this approach might be used to construct a framework for measuring income.

A. Life-Cycle Model with Variable Lifetime

We want to examine the gain in "real income" from improved health and life expectancy. We do this in the context of the life-cycle model of consumption. An individual is assumed to value consumption and health according to a lifetime utility function:[7]

$$(1)\quad V(c_t;\theta,\rho,\mu_t)=\int_{\theta}^{\infty}u(c_t)e^{-\rho(t-\theta)}S(\mu_t)dt,$$

Where $V(c_t;\theta,\rho,\mu_t)$ is the value at time t of the consumption stream now and in the future faced by an individual of age θ; $u(c_t)$ is the stream of instantaneous utility or felicity of consumption; ρ is the pure rate of individual time preference; $S(\mu_t)$ is the set of survival probabilities; and μ_t is the set of mortality rates. The key assumption here is that utility is a function of the expected value of consumption weighted by the probability of survival. As we will see, the utility function has a natural semicardinal interpretation as the value of life extension.

We begin with a simple and tractable assumption about mortality to show the basic relationships; when developing the empirical estimates in later sections we will use more realistic life tables. Consider the simple case where the survival function is exponential. Equation (1) then becomes

$$(2)\quad V(c_t;\theta,\rho,\mu_t)=\int_{\theta}^{\infty}u(c_t)e^{-(\rho+\mu)(t-\theta)}dt.$$

We assume that each individual has a given endowment of expected labor income and can buy zero-cost real annuities that have any desired trajectory. We can further simplify for computational purposes (to be relaxed later) by assuming that the real interest rate faced by the individual is equal to the mortality adjusted rate of time preference, $(\rho+\mu)$. Given these assumptions, the individual will choose a consumption annuity that yields constant consumption during the individual's lifetime, $c_t=c^*$. Integrating (2) yields a particularly simple outcome:

$$(3)\quad V(c_t;\theta,\rho,\mu)=u(c^*)/(\rho+\mu).$$

Equation (3) shows that the total utility value of consumption is the utility of the flow of constant consumption discounted by a discount rate that equals the sum of the force of impatience and the force of mortality.

An individual will often face a tradeoff between "health and wealth." What would be the tradeoff given by (3)? At age θ, changes in consumption and health yield the following:

$$(4)\quad \begin{cases} dV/dc^* = u'(c^*)/(\rho + \mu) \\ dV/d\mu = -u(c^*)/(\rho + \mu)^2. \end{cases}$$

Hence the relative value of consumption and mortality is

$$(5)\quad \frac{dc^*}{d\mu} = -u(c^*)/[u'(c^*)(\rho + \mu)].$$

We make two normalizations that will simplify the discussion without loss of generality. First, we simplify by selecting a goods-metric utility function. This gives us a metric in which utility is measured in terms of goods at the equilibrium, which implies that $u'(c^*) = 1$. In other words, *utility* is defined so that one unit of utility is one extra unit of the good. Second, we choose the units so that 0 is the "death-indifference level of existence." That is, when the utility of consumption is $u(c) = 0$, the individual is indifferent between life and death. This implies that there is zero utility after death.

Given these assumption, (5) reduces to

$$(6)\quad dc^*/d\mu = -u(c^*)/(\rho + \mu),$$

or without discounting,

$$(7)\quad dc^*/d\mu = -Tu(c^*),$$

where T is life expectancy ($T = 1/\mu$). The interpretation here is that a uniform change in mortality rates at every age will produce a welfare change equal to the number of years of life (T) times the goods value of life, given by $u(c^*)$—recall that the utility of years after death is normalized at $u = 0$.

The major difficulty in applying this approach is determining the goods value of life. There have been many studies of this, which are reviewed below. An example is as follows: Most studies of life value examine the tradeoff between current risk and current income, say at age $K = 40$. Consider a decline in the mortality rate of $\Delta\mu(\theta)$ for one period. Then the survival rate is higher by $e^{\Delta\mu(\theta)}$ at the end of the period, $K + 1$. Discounted utility evaluated at age $\theta \geq K$ is then

$$(8)\quad V(\theta) = e^{\Delta\mu(\theta)}u(c^*)/(\rho + \mu).$$

Hence, using this simple mortality assumption, the tradeoff between current risk and current consumption is approximately

$$(9)\quad dc/d\mu(\theta) = u(c^*).$$

Now the decline of $\Delta\mu(\theta)$ leads to a change in life expectancy of approximately $\Delta T = \Delta\mu/\mu$. The value of this change is

$$dV/dT = dV/d\mu(\theta)\, d\mu(\theta)/dT \sim u(c^*)\mu/(\rho + \mu).$$

So the tradeoff between life expectancy and consumption without discounting is approximately

$$(10)\quad dc/dT = u(c^*)\mu.$$

Note that this approach indicates that it is not generally correct to adjust for changes in health status by calculating lifetime consumption, which would be c^*T in the present example. This approach is only correct when $u(c) = 1$. Our numerical estimates below indicate that this approach will generally undervalue improvements in life expectancy.

B. Valuation of Life

Measuring utility income with health improvement requires finding appropriate "prices" to use to value health status. There is a voluminous literature on the value of fatalities prevented.[8] It is generally accepted that the "willingness to pay" to reduce risk is the appropriate approach for valuing risk reductions. Studies of this fall into three general categories: labor market studies, which examine the risk-wage tradeoff; consumer purchase decisions (such as for smoke detectors), which examine the price-risk tradeoff; and contingent valuation studies, which attempt to determine preferences from a systematic examination of individual's stated preferences.

The most weight is generally put on labor market studies, because these reflect actual behavior, because labor force decisions are repeated, and because there are dozens of studies from different periods, countries, occupations, and samples. It is important to note that the tradeoff examined is a *current risk–current income* ($dc/d\mu$) choice between current occupational hazards and current wages. From these tradeoffs (which involve comparing income per year against mortality risk per year) we derive an implicit dollar cost per unit mortality risk. Because the risks are relatively small (approximately between 1/100,000 per year to 50/100,000 per year), the interpretation is the marginal valuation of risk reduction or increase.

Not surprisingly, there is great variation in the implicit price of risk (or price of a statistical life). The serious estimates from a recent survey range from \$0.6 million to \$13.5 million per fatality prevented. The U.S. Environmental Protection Agency uses the relatively high figure of \$4.8 million per fatality prevented in its cost-benefit study of the value of clear air.[9] Tolley et al. (1994) recommend a value of \$2.0 million per fatality prevented for use in health-care decisions. In this study, I settle on \$3.0 million per fatality prevented as a reasonable choice, but the figures are easily modified to reflect different assumptions.

In our analysis above, we calculated the increment to sustainable consumption of an additional life-year, LY (see equation [10]). There is some confusion but little solid evidence on how to measure the value of an added life-year. Most studies derive LY values from the studies of the value of reduced mortality described above.

We can sketch the methodology as follows. In terms of the model used above, almost all estimates concern the value of reductions in current mortality $[dc(\theta)/d\mu(\theta)]$. For concreteness, we assume the following:

$$(11)\quad dV/d\mu(\theta) = \$3 \times 10^6 \qquad \text{(in 1990 incomes and prices)}$$

To convert this to the value of a life-year requires further assumptions. Many of the studies underlying the estimate in (11) concern labor market decisions of working men, for which we can use $\mu(40) \sim 0.025\,\text{yr}^{-1}$ for those age 40. To convert these into value per life-year requires assuming a discount rate, which we alternatively take to be 0 and 3 percent per year. Using these values, we obtain

$$(12)\quad dc^*/dT\,|_{d\mu(40)} = \begin{cases} \$1{,}828 \text{ per LY at } \rho = 0 \\ \$6{,}757 \text{ per LY at } \rho = 0.03. \end{cases}$$

These are the annuity or flow equivalents of the present value of an increase in a LY. That is, they reflect the increase in the constant consumption necessary to compensate for a current loss of a life-year. Taking the present value of the consumption annuity yields a capital value $[dV/d\text{LY}]$ of \$75,000 per LY at a discount rate of 0 and \$162,000 per LY at a discount rate of 3 percent per year. Tolley et al. (1994) recommend a central present value of \$100,000 per LY from their studies, which is broadly consistent with these numbers and analysis.

In the estimates presented below, we use actual survival functions rather than the theoretical ones analyzed above. Using 1990 life tables, we obtain the following estimates:

$$(12')\quad dc^*/dT\,|_{d\mu} = \begin{cases} \$2{,}600 \text{ per LY at } \rho = 0 \\ \$7{,}600 \text{ per LY at } \rho = 0.03 \end{cases}$$

These estimates using actual life tables in (12′) are quite close to the values for the simplified model given in (12), which motivates using that model. (The capital values associated with these numbers are given at the bottom of table 1.2.)

C. Measuring Income with Variable Lifetimes

Next turn to the issue of measuring income or consumption. For this purpose, we take the utility-based measure of income. It will be helpful to start with the case of utility-based income with fixed and certain lifetime. In this approach income is the maximum sustainable consumption consistent with a given expected value of labor earnings and an exogenously given interest rate. Under the assumption of no bequests, note that income is also equal to sustainable consumption, where the latter is defined as the maximum constant real consumption annuity.

More precisely, assume that the consumption discount rate is a constant, r. Once we know the entire path of consumption, given by $C(s)$ for $s \geq t$, we can easily calculate utility income at time t, denoted by $\mathcal{C}(t)$, as follows:

$$(13)\quad \int_t^{\infty} \mathcal{C}(t) exp[-r(s-t)]ds = \int_t^{\infty} C(s) exp[-r(s-t)]ds$$

or equivalently

$$(14)\quad \mathcal{C}(t) = r\left[\int_t^{\infty} C(s) exp[-r(s-t)]ds\right].$$

Note that $\mathcal{C}(t)$ measures the *constant* consumption annuity available at time t. Equation (14) shows that measures of utility income or sustainable income are inherently a wealthlike measure, as was emphasized by Irving Fisher and Paul Samuelson.[10]

The utility definition of income is a natural springboard for considering the measurement of income with varying lifetimes. Start by extending the definition of income and consumption to uncertain, variable, and endogenous lifetimes. To begin with, consider the traditional definition of income. For example, say that in lifetime situation "Short," individuals consume 100 units per year each and live for 50 years, while in situation "Long," individuals consume 100 units per year and live for 60 years. Under the standard flow definition of consumption, there would be no difference in economic welfare or living standards between Short and Long. This is clearly defective to the extent that people prefer to live longer.

An alternative and preferable approach is to convert the combination of consumption and the survival function into the equivalent utility with a benchmark survival function and consumption. Take the Short lifetime situation as the benchmark. Using the example of the preceding paragraph, we ask what consumption annuity using the life expectancy of situation Short would give individuals the same utility as the consumption and life expectancy of situation Long. An individual might consider situation Long (with a constant consumption of 100 and a lifetime of 60 years) to be equivalent to, or have equivalent utility with, a constant consumption annuity of 110 units per year with the life expectancy of situation Short. We would then say that (using situation Short as the benchmark) the income in situation Long was 110, compared with that of 100 in situation Short.

Using the notation of the last section, define $S =$ Short and $L =$ Long. Then let $V[c_t^S;\, \theta,\, \rho,\, \mu_t^S]$ be the utility of consumption stream c_t^S and age-specific mortality rate μ_t^S, while $V[c_t^L; \theta, \rho, \mu_t^L]$ is the utility of consumption stream c_t^L and age-specific mortality rate μ_t^L. We define income $c^*(L, \mu^S)$ as the constant consumption stream that would go with mortality rates in Short, which yields the equivalent utility as the consumption stream and mortality rates in situation Long. That is, $V[c^*(L, \mu^S); \theta, \rho, \mu_t^S] = V[c_t^L; \theta, \rho, \mu_t^L]$.

We then compare incomes in different situations by estimating the constant equivalent consumption annuity with a benchmark mortality function. Say we use mortality rates from situation S as the benchmark. We can then compare situations S and L by comparing $c^*(S, \mu^S)$ and $c^*(L, \mu^S)$, such that $V[c^*(S, \mu^S);\, \theta,\, \rho,\, \mu_t^S] = V[c_t^S;\, \theta,\, \rho,\, \mu_t^S]$ and $c^*(L, \mu^S)$ such that $V[c^*(L, \mu^S);\, \theta,\, \rho,\, \mu_t^S] = V[c_t^L;\, \theta,\, \rho,\, \mu_t^L]$. There will be the usual index-number problems involved in these comparisons because the definitions will differ whether we use the mortality rates of situation S or L. It is to my knowledge an open question whether the usual index-number theorems apply here, but I see no reason they should not.

Because this tangle of algebra is somewhat forbidding, it will be useful to summarize the major points. Traditional income accounting looks at the flows of consumption and income in measuring living standards: consumption of food, purchases of electricity and apparel, airline travel, and so forth. These measures do not consider the length of life or the quality of the population's health. The alternative proposed here corrects for mortality and morbidity by asking how much consumption the individual would be willing to pay to trade for improved health. If, for example, an individual would pay 2 percent of consumption each year to gain an additional life-year, then we use that number to say that an additional life-year is equivalent to a 2 percent increase in annual income. In the estimates below, we use this technique only to adjust for changes in life expectancy, although they could also be used to adjust for changes in morbidity.

IV. The Impact of Improved Life Expectancy on Economic Welfare in the United States, 1900–1995

A. Previous Studies

The literature on estimating the economic value of improved health is surprisingly sparse. Dan Usher (1973, 1980) considered the issue as part of a more general study of the adequacy of conventional national output measures, but his approach was highly stylized and was written before the surge of detailed estimates of the value of life. A number of indexes incorporate life expectancy, particularly the United Nations Development Programme's Human Development Index (HDI).[11] The technique for incorporating health in the HDI is, however, completely arbitrary. Economic historians have begun to compile systematic indicators on various health-related measures, such as height and the body-mass index, and these tend to move with other measures of health status, but it is difficult to put a price tag on these indexes.[12] Important additions to the literature are studies by David Cutler and Elizabeth Richardson (1997), discussed below, and the contribution of Kevin Murphy and Robert Topel, presented in chapter 2 of this volume.

B. Methods

We now implement the ideas in earlier sections for the United States. The calculations here estimate the value of the health component of utility income, or the value of improvements in health status, which we call health income. Table 1.1 shows illustrative data on major health risks in different regions from the study of the global burden of disease by Murray and Lopez (1996). This table gives a rough idea of what economic development means in terms of health status.

The fundamental data for the United States are shown in figures 1.1 through 1.4. Figure 1.1 shows U.S. per-capita consumption from 1900 to 1995. The data are from the Commerce Department for the period 1929–95 and from various private scholars for 1900–1929. The Commerce Department figures are in chained indexes converted to 1990 price levels. Earlier estimates are in constant prices.

Figure 1.2 shows the survival rates for three years, 1900, 1950, and 1995. The most dramatic change came in the early part of this century: the probability of surviving the first year rose from 87 percent in 1900 to 96 percent in 1950. Figure 1.3 shows life expectancy at different ages. Gains in life

TABLE 1.1 Major Health Risk Factors in Different Regions, 1990

	Global Totals		Established Market Economies		Sub-Saharan Africa	
Risk Factor	Years of Life Lost (000)	Percentage of Total (%)	Years of Life Lost (000)	Percentage of Total (%)	Years of Life Lost (000)	Percentage of Total (%)
Malnutrition	199,486	22.0	0	0.0	89,305	39.4
Poor water supply, sanitation, and personal and domestic hygiene	85,520	9.4	8	0.0	28,781	12.7
Unsafe sex	27,602	3.0	1,271	2.6	12,226	5.4
Tobacco	26,217	2.9	7,967	16.0	927	0.4
Alcohol	19,287	2.1	2,537	5.1	3,319	5.9
Occupation	22,493	2.5	2,826	5.7	1,973	3.5
Hypertension	17,665	1.9	3,471	7.0	1,674	3.0
Physical inactivity	11,353	1.3	3,860	7.8	796	1.4
Illicit drugs	2,634	0.3	717	1.4	449	0.8
Air pollution	5,625	0.6	310	0.6	377	0.7
TOTAL	417,882	46.0	22,967	46.2	139,827	73.2

SOURCE: Murray and Lopez (1996), vol. 1, pp. 311–15.

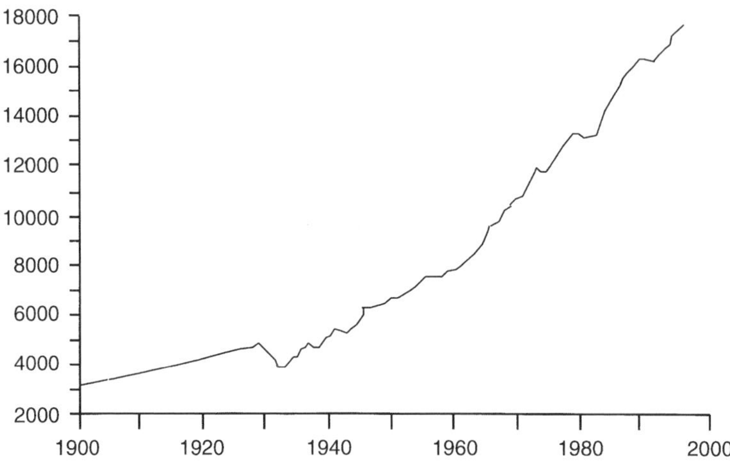

FIGURE 1.1: Per-capita consumption (1990 chained dollars)
SOURCE: Department of Commerce, Bureau of Economic Analysis

expectancy have been substantial throughout the entire century. Figure 1.4 shows the change in life expectancy at different ages over the last four decades.

One preliminary question concerns a parallel between health improvements and the slowdown in conventionally measured productivity. Is the famous "productivity slowdown" found in conventional economic measures mirrored in the health statistics? Figure 1.5 shows gains in life expectancy at birth along with conventionally measured growth in labor productivity for the decade ending in the year indicated by the point. "Health productivity growth" (measured as the change in life expectancy) rose until 1975 and then declined gradually since then. The trends in health and nonhealth productivity appear to move quite differently.

To calculate the value of improved health status, we use the approach outlined above. We use two different approaches—the *mortality approach* and the *life-years approach*. Under the mortality approach, shown for the simple model in equation (7), the value of improved health status is calculated by taking the change in the population weighted mortality rate times the estimated value of lower mortality. Under the life-years approach, shown in the simple model in equation (10), the economic value of improved health is equal to the increase in life expectancy times the value of an additional life-year. In both cases, the estimates are weighted by the share of the population that is experiencing the lower mortality or greater life expectancy.

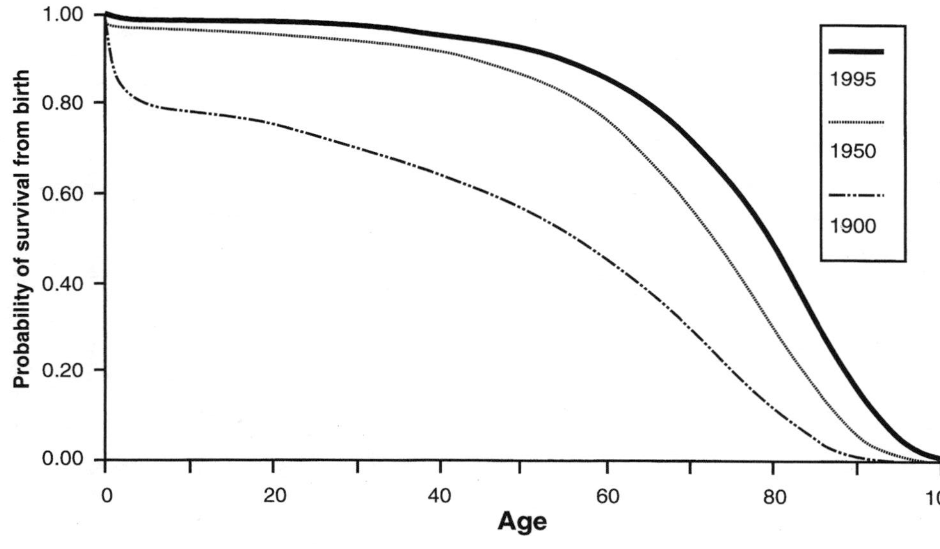

FIGURE 1.2: Survival probabilities

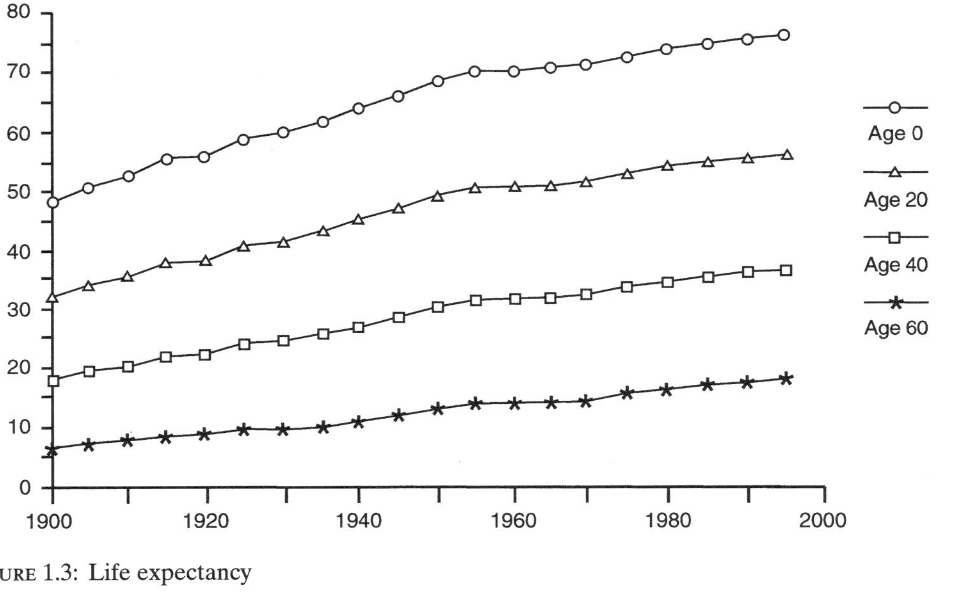

FIGURE 1.3: Life expectancy

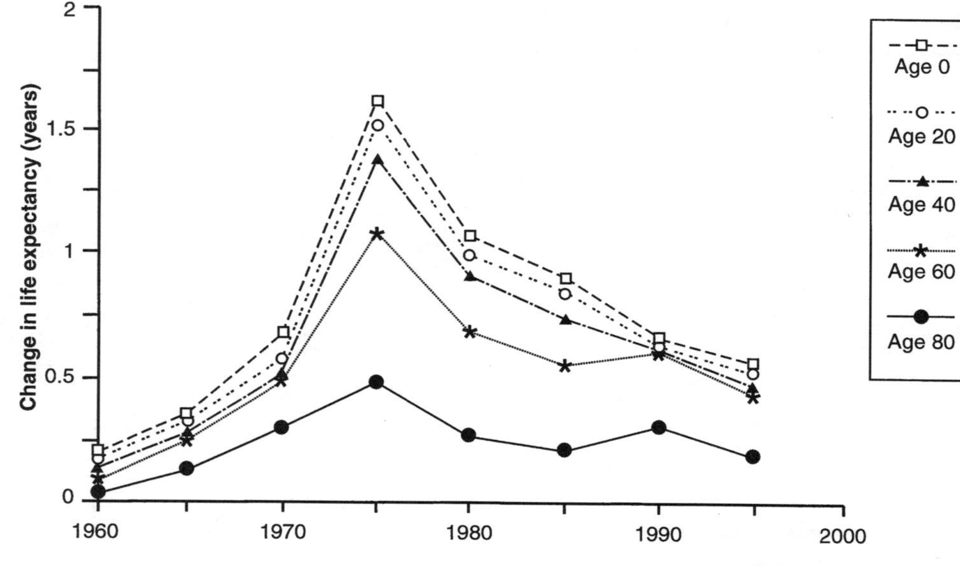

FIGURE 1.4: Gains in life expectancy

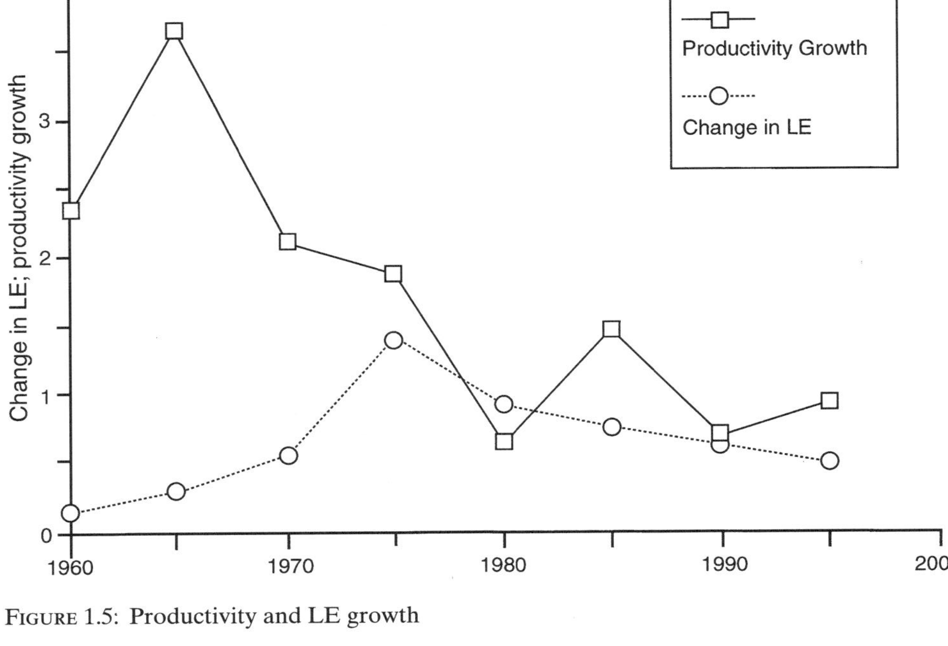

FIGURE 1.5: Productivity and LE growth

TABLE 1.2 Growth in Living Standards from Health Improvements and Consumption*

	1900–1925	1925–50	1950–75	1975–95
Consumption	2.0	1.8	2.4	2.0
Health value: Life-years approach				
Discount rate				
0 percent p. a.	2.3	3.3	1.9	1.7
3 percent p. a.	2.3	3.2	1.8	1.6
Health value: Mortality approach				
Current pop. weights	3.2	4.0	2.6	2.0
1950 weights	2.9	4.2	2.3	1.8
Notes on valuation:				
Value of life: (1990)	3000.0 thousand 1990 dollars			
Value of life-year (1990)				
$\rho = 0.00$	14.5 thousand 1990 dollars			
$\rho = 0.03$	95.3 thousand 1990 dollars			
Consumption (1990)	16.5 thousand 1990 dollars			

*Increase as percent of per-capita consumption; in annualized percentage growth rates

C. Simple Calculations

It may be helpful to work through a simple example to illustrate the methodology. For the period 1975 through 1995, the population-weighted average decline in the mortality rate was 2,249 per year per million persons. Taking the hedonic estimate of the value of fatalities prevented of $2.66 million (which adjusts the $3 million in 1990 for movements in average consumption), this decline in mortality would have a value of $5,980 per person over this period. The average per-capita consumption over this period was $14,700. Hence the economic value of improvements of living standards due to reduced mortality is estimated as 40 percent of consumption over this period, or about 2 percent per year. Table 1.2 shows this calculation using actual 1950 population weights, and the growth is 1.8 percent per year.

The estimate using the life-years method is somewhat more complicated. Because improvements in mortality extend life expectancy in the future (particularly in the case of reduced infant mortality), we must consider the impact of discounting on valuation. The approach taken for this simple example is to calculate the value of a life-year on the assumption that the increase in the life-year takes place through a uniform reduction in mortality. This allows us to use the valuation of mortality discussed above to estimate the value of an additional life year. For example, in 1990, a uniform reduction in mortality of 0.001 per year would lead to an increase in population-weighted life expectancy of 1.16 years. Over the period 1975–95, the increase in population-weighted life expectancy was 2.1 years. The value of an additional undiscounted life-year is, according to the calculations presented above, equal to \$2,600 (see equation [12′]). Therefore the gain in health income over these two decades was \$2,600 × 2.1 life-years = \$5,400. The equivalent of 1.6 percent per year in conventional consumption units, this is the closest to the estimate shown by the actual calculations in Table 1.2.

D. Actual Calculations

The central results of this chapter, showing calculations on the economic contribution of health and nonhealth consumption, are shown in table 1.2 and in figure 1.6. For these estimates, we use only changes in life expectancy and omit any changes in morbidity (we discuss this question below). These estimates differ from the simple calculations in the preceding section because they use actual survival rates and population distributions rather than the simplified ones assumed above.

The major result that comes through using all techniques is that the value of improvements in life expectancy is about as large as the value of

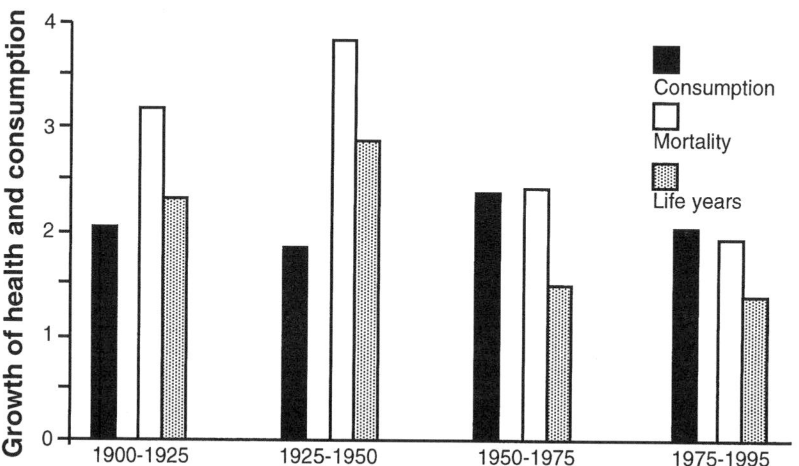

Figure 1.6: Economic contribution: consumption and health status
Notes: Bars show the increase in either conventionally measured per-capita consumption and in per-capita "health income" for the period. In each case, the denominator used in calculating the growth rate is the level of conventionally measured per-capita consumption. The figures are averages for five-year periods. The two right bars use the mortality approach and the life-years approach to valuing increases in longevity.

all other consumption goods and services put together. For example, over the two decades from 1975 to 1995, conventionally measured per-capita consumption grew at an average rate of 2.0 percent per year. Over this period, the annual average improvements in life expectancy had an economic value between 1.6 and 2.0 percent of consumption.[13] Over the entire period from 1900 to 1995, the value of improved health or health income grew at between 2.2 and 3.0 percent of consumption, whereas consumption grew at a rate of about 2.1 percent of consumption. Health income grew somewhat more slowly than other consumption during the second half of this century, while it exceeded the value of the growth in consumption during the first half of the twentieth century.

The two techniques (the life-year approach and the mortality approach) give approximately the same results. This is not surprising, for they are calibrated to yield the same value of life lengthening for uniform mortality rate changes. The mortality approach gives slightly larger numbers because of the distribution of mortality changes.

How do expenditures on health improvements compare with improvements in health income? This is a difficult question because spending to improve health status pervades our market and nonmarket activities. Table 1.3 provides illustrative estimates of the magnitudes. To begin with, the bottom three rows of table 1.3 show the increase in nonhealth consumption and in health income over the 1980–90 period. This shows again that the size of the gains from health and nonhealth consumption are approximately the same.

Market expenditures on conventional health care are reasonably well tabulated. They were in 1990 about one-quarter of nonhealth personal consumption expenditures. Many important items are excluded from these figures. Two exclusions, shown in table 1.3, are pollution abatement and expenditures on sewage and sanitation. In addition, there may be substantial non-market costs, primarily in time use. Our time-use studies are particularly inadequate, but existing estimates indicate that the value of nonmarket time devoted to health is but a small fraction of market costs.

The last column of table 1.3 compares the increases in expenditures with the increases in health income and nonhealth consumption for the period 1980–90. These show that the increase in health income (from mortality alone) is approximately the same size as the increase in nonhealth consumption. The increase in expenditure on health care was approximately one-half the increase in mortality-based health income. It seems likely, however, that a substantial part of the expenditures (such as that on dental, psychiatric, vision-related, and nursing home services) was life-quality-enhancing

TABLE 1.3 National Health Expenditures and Income, 1980–90*

	Time, 1985 (minutes per day)	Value per capita (1990 prices)			
		1980	1990	Increase, 1980–90	
Total expenditures		**2,477**	**3,690**	**1,213**	
Market [a]					
Conventional health care		1,856	3,004	1,148	
Other					
Pollution abatement		378	404	26	
Sanitation and sewage		99	123	24	
Nonmarket					
Time spent on medical care[b,c]					
Child care: Medical	1.0	32	32	0	
Obtaining goods and services:					
Medical appointments	2.0	64	80	16	
Personal needs: Medical care	1.5	48	48	0	
Income and Consumption					
Health income					
Life-year method[d]		*na*	*na*	***2,292***	*1.7 %*
Mortality method[e]		*na*	*na*	***3,120***	*2.3 %*
Nonhealth personal consumption		*12,261*	*15,198*	***2,937***	*2.2 %*

*Per capita, in 1990 prices and incomes

[a] Current dollar figures are converted into 1990 prices using the price index for personal consumption.

[b] Time is converted into current prices using average hourly earnings in 1990 less a tax rate of 30 percent.

[c] From Robinson and Godbey (1997), app. A.

[d] Uses the life-year method with a discount rate of 3 percent

[e] Current population weights

rather than life-year-extending. Suppose that half the increase in per capita expenditures, or $600, was life-extending; this would be a good investment for the increase in health income of between $2,300 and $3,100 per capita over the 1980–90 period.

E. Qualifications

How robust are the estimates provided here? The underlying mortality data are among the most reliable of our social statistics. The most fragile part of the estimates concern life and mortality valuation, as discussed above. One assumption on which there is little evidence is that the premium on reduced mortality is a constant fraction of per-capita consumption over the entire period. More precisely, we assume that the value of a reduction in the mortality rate of 0.001 per year is $3,000 in 1990 prices, and we scale that value over time to the ratio of the given year's per-capita consumption to 1990 per-capita consumption. There are no comprehensive studies of the mortality premium over time, although movements in the wage of risky occupations (such as coal mining) are consistent with this assumption. I suspect, however, that the premium has risen over time. This would be consistent with the rising share of health care expenditures in total consumption. If the premium were indeed increasing over time, then the contribution of health to economic welfare would be relatively smaller in the earlier period and relatively larger in the later period.

A few other assumptions are of some significance but will not affect the major results. One important issue is whether people should be weighted the same at every age. Many health care professionals and some survey evidence suggest that the value of a life-year is higher in the middle of the life span (between 20 and 40 years) than at either end.[14] Most surveys indicate, for example, that infant mortality would receive a lower weight than adult mortality. Figure 1.7 shows an alternative set of weights proposed by Murray in Murray and Lopez (1996) which differ by age. Figures 1.8 and 1.9 show the trend and changes using the two sets of weights for life expectancy for different discount rates. The differentially weighted series show virtually identical growth as the equally weighted series over the period 1900–1950 but have slower growth in income in the 1950–95 period. In the latter period, the growth in health income is between 10 and 20 percent slower with differential age weights, primarily because the Murray weights put a lower value on the increases in life expectancy of older people. Under this alternative valuation approach, the contribution of improved longevity would be slightly less than that shown in table 1.2.

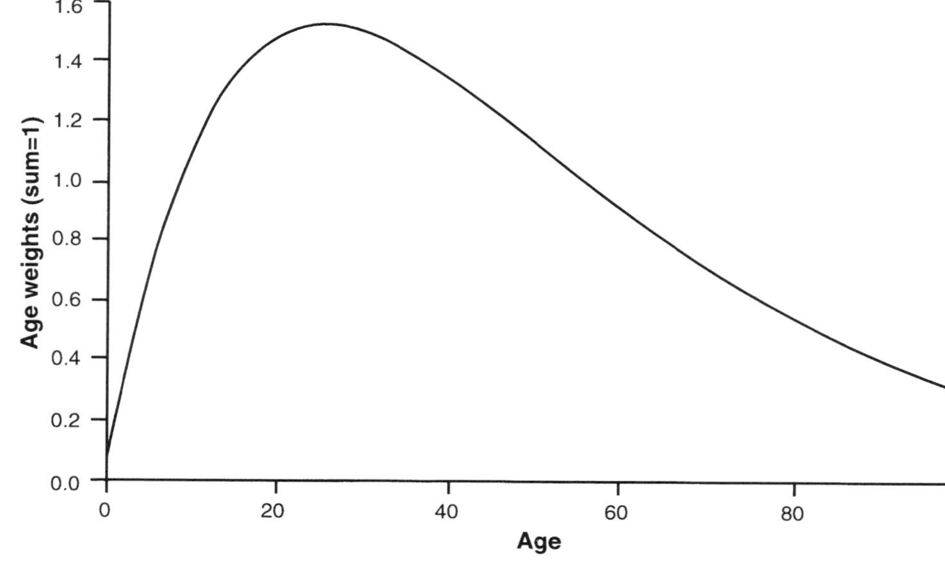

FIGURE 1.7: Alternative value of life-year by age

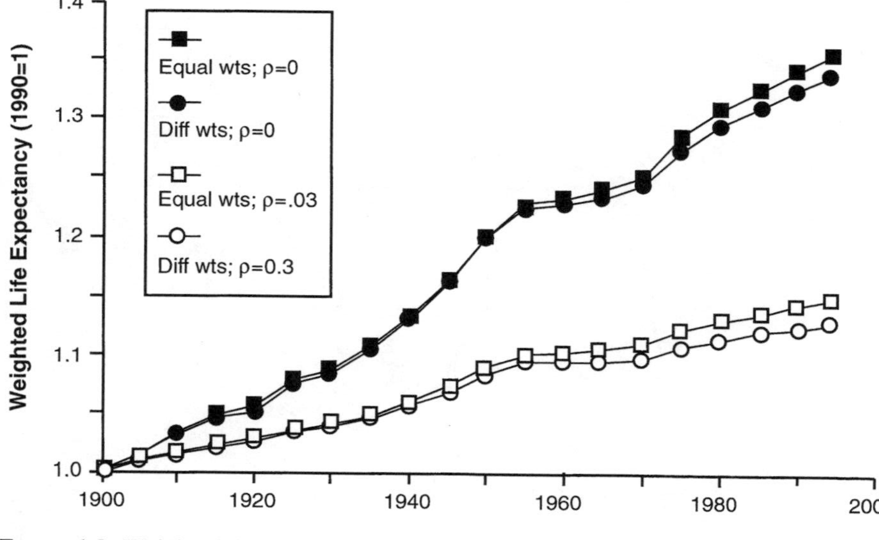

FIGURE 1.8: Weighted life expectancy for different discount rates and weighting factors

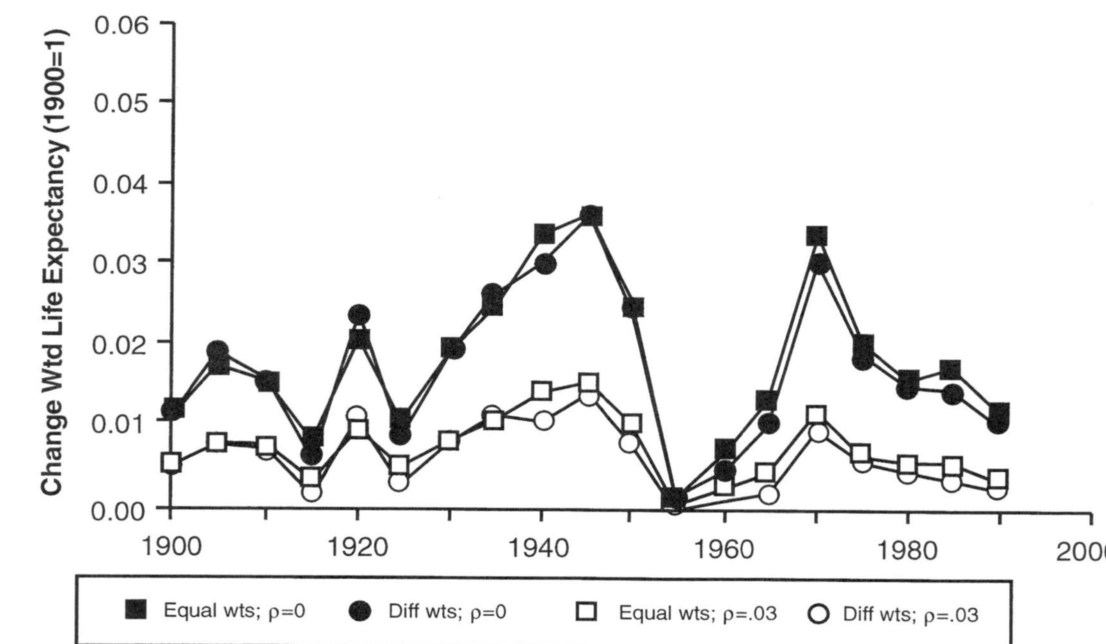

FIGURE 1.9: Change in weighted life expectancy for different discount rates and weighting factors

Another major omission from this study is the value of reduced morbidity. The data on morbidity is both more difficult to obtain and more difficult to value. One recent study indicates that including morbidity might add another 5 percent or so to the value of health improvements estimated here, but methodological issues of implementation raise questions about whether this number is too low.[15]

V. Discussion and Conclusion

This chapter contributes to a new view of the economics of health in which improvements in health status have been a major contributor to economic welfare over the twentieth century. To a first approximation, the economic value of increases in longevity in the last hundred years is about as large as the value of measured growth in nonhealth goods and services. A closer look shows that "health income" probably contributed somewhat more than nonhealth goods and services in the first half of the twentieth century and marginally less than nonhealth goods and services since 1950. The medical revolution over the last century appears to qualify, at least from an economic point of view, for Samuel Johnson's accolade as "the greatest benefit to mankind."

The first question one should ask is whether this finding is plausible. One way of considering the question is to consider the health equivalent of the Sears-catalogue question:

> Consider the improvements to both health and nonhealth technologies over the last half century (say from 1948 to 1998). Health technologies include a variety of changes such as the Salk polio vaccine, new pharmaceuticals, joint replacement, improved sanitation, improved automobile safety, smoke-free workplaces, and so on. Over this period, life expectancy at birth increased from a little above 68 years to a little less than 76 years. Nonhealth technologies were also wide ranging and include the jet plane, television, superhighways, VCRs, and computers (although the economic benefits of these are probably understated in measured consumption growth).
>
> Now consider the following choice. You must forgo either the health improvements over the last half century or the nonhealth improvements. That is, you must choose either (*a*) 1948 health conditions and 1998 nonhealth living standards or (*b*) 1998 health conditions and 1948 nonhealth living standards. Which would you choose?

If you would either choose (*b*) or find it a difficult choice, then you would basically agree with the results of this chapter. An informal poll finds that

TABLE 1.4 Comparison of This Study with Cutler-Richardson
(Increase in health income per person, 1970–90; 1990 prices and incomes)

	Discount rate	
	0%/yr.	3%/yr.
This study		
Health value: Life-Years approach	6,166	5,769
Health value: Mortality approach	7,701	7,701
Cutler-Richardson		
Years of life		
Age 0	5,514	2,526
Age 65	15,000	12,289
Quality-adjusted life-years		
Age 0	5,230	3,117
Age 65	15,438	13,062

SOURCE: This study from table 1. Cutler and Richardson (1997) is from their table 11. The estimates have been annuitized over the life expectancy at the given age and at the given discount rate.
NOTE: "Health income" is defined as the annuitized value of the increase in health capital for Cutler-Richardson study and as the increase in the value of population-weighted mortality or life expectancy in this study.

most people either choose (*b*) or have great difficulty choosing, with older people almost always opting for (*b*).

The findings of a recent study by Cutler and Richardson (1997), which examines the improvements in "health capital" in the United States, are consistent with the new view put forth above. Health capital is the present value of the utility of health status. Cutler and Richardson use both a years of life (YOL) approach and a quality-adjusted life years (QALY) approach. Their estimates are only for the years 1970, 1980, and 1990, and they present results only for persons of age 0 and 65. We can make a crude conversion of the Cutler-Richardson estimates to conform to our income estimates by annuitizing their health capital over the expected lifetimes and then taking the changes in the income from health capital as the increase in health income. Table 1.4 shows the comparison. Two points should be drawn from this table. First, the overall estimates are reasonably comparable. The estimates from Cutler and Richardson bracket the estimates from the present study. One of the most surprising results of Cutler-Richardson, not explained in the paper, is that moving from life-years to QALYs does not change the results significantly. One possible reason for this result is that improvements in the quality of life from lower morbidity are offset by a higher average age (and therefore higher average morbidity) of the population.

There are many questions left open by the present findings. One important point is that we cannot at this stage attribute the growth in health income to particular investments or expenditures. Such a task, which would apply the techniques of growth accounting to health improvements, is especially challenging.[16] It is also necessary if we are to understand not only the historical sources of improved health but also those investments that may best contribute to future improvements.

Another particularly important question is the extent to which improvements arise from improved basic knowledge (such as the germ theory of disease, the discovery of antibiotics, or the DNA revolution) or investments in improved health capital and infrastructure (such as larger investments in health education or improvements in emergency response services). A second issue, particularly relevant for the contribution of basic knowledge, is the extent to which improvements in knowledge were domestically generated or imported. It seems likely, for example, that most of the major medical discoveries in the first part of the period covered here arose in Europe, while the United States was increasingly the source of advances in medical knowledge in the last few decades.[17] To the extent that improvements in health income are due to imported technologies, this emphasizes one of the gains from trade that is largely overlooked in traditional measures of the economic impacts of international trade.

The new view of health economics should shape the way we think about health policy. In the early 1990s, the general hysteria about rising health costs led many to believe that the health care system was wasteful and out of control, and should be reined in. This view was particularly prevalent in the business community, which saw rising health costs as a threat to national competitiveness. The general atmosphere was colored by the substantial rise in (measured) relative medical care prices. Over the period from 1975 to 1995, the CPI for medical care rose 64 percent faster than the CPI for all goods and services. In the face of rising prices and growing budgets, a natural response was to try to control spending and limit services.

If the results of this and other related papers are confirmed, then the role of the health care system should be rethought. Over the last half century, health care expenditures appear to have contributed as much to overall economic welfare as the rest of consumption expenditures. It is an intriguing thought to contemplate that the social productivity of health care spending might be many times that of other spending. If this is anywhere near the case, it would suggest that the image of a stupendously wasteful health care system is far off the mark.

Of course, as table 1.3 suggests, health is more than doctors and hospitals. It encompasses other parts of national output, such as pollution control and highway safety spending, and reflects individual lifestyles, such as decisions about smoking, drinking, driving, drugs, and exercise. Moreover, medical knowledge is a global public good which is increased by efforts in many countries. Because we cannot tally the totality of costs on health care, we cannot say for sure whether we are getting 2 or 4 or 10 times the return on health dollars that we are on nonhealth dollars. And it is surely the case that health care expenditures are often misallocated and wasteful. However, notwithstanding the complexity and bureaucracy, improvements in health status in the United States have yielded prodigious increases in economic welfare. It is sobering to reflect that, were the author of this chapter to have experienced the 1900 life table, the odds are long that it would need to have been written from beyond the grave.

Notes

1. See Eisner (1989). A recent review of environmental and other aspects of nonmarket accounting is contained in National Research Council (1999).

2. See Advisory Commission (1996) and Murray and Lopez (1996).

3. This discussion ignores the subtlety of Hicks's discussion of price changes, interest rate effects, the difference between ex ante and ex post capital, and a number of other factors.

4. This approach is used in an analogous manner in the theory of measuring the cost of living.

5. See Nordhaus (1994, 1995) for a discussion.

6. See Nordhaus (1994).

7. An early treatment of this issue is contained in Shepard and Zeckhauser (1984). A detailed treatment of the value of life with extensions is contained in Rosen in Tolley et al. (1994).

8. See Viscusi (1993) for a comprehensive review of the economics literature. The monumental study edited by Murray and Lopez (1996) is a particularly useful analysis of the issue in the context of health care.

9. This was based on the survey by Unsworth, Neumann, and Browne (1992).

10. Irving Fisher's discussion dates from 1910–14 and is contained in Fisher (1997). Paul Samuelson's approach is contained in Samuelson (1961).

11. See UNDP (1997) for a discussion and the numbers.

12. A useful review of the economic-history literature is contained in Costa and Steckel (1995).

13. Because there is no natural denominator for measuring improvements in health care, we use the same denominator for calculating growth as we do for consumption. That is, the growth in the value of health is calculated as $\Delta Y_t^H/c_{t-1,}$ whereas the growth in consumption is calculated as $\Delta c_t/c_{t-1}$, where ΔY_t^H is the change in the per-capita value of health income and *ct* is the flow of consumption of goods and services during the previous period. This allows us to compare the relative importance of consumption and improvements in health status, whereas there is no obvious way to measure the value of the level of health status (Y_t^H).

14. A particularly interesting discussion is contained in Murray and Lopez (1996).

15. See Cutler and Richardson (1997), discussed below.
16. One of the most comprehensive studies of growth accounting is Denison (1961).
17. A nontechnical history is contained in Porter (1997).

References

Advisory Commission. 1996. "Toward a More Accurate Measure of the Cost of Living: The Final Report of the Advisory Commission to Study the Consumer Price Index," by Michael Boskin and others. 4 December (updated version).Costa, Dora L., and Richard H. Steckel. 1995. "Long-Term Health Trends in Health, Welfare, and Economic Growth in the United States." NBER Historical Working Paper no. 76, Cambridge, Mass.: National Bureau of Economic Research.

Cutler, David, and Elizabeth Richardson. 1997. "Measuring the Health of the U.S. Population." In *Brookings Papers on Economic Activity: Microeconomics,* 217–71.

Cutler, David, Mark B. McClellan, Joseph Newhouse, and Dahlia Remler. 1996. "Are Medical Care Prices Declining?" NBER Working Paper no. 5750. Cambridge, Mass.: National Bureau of Economic Research, September.

Denison, Edward. 1961. *The Sources of Economic Growth in the United States.* New York: Committee for Economic Development.

Eisner, Robert. 1989. *The Total Incomes System of Accounts*. Chicago: University of Chicago Press.

Fisher, Irving. 1997. *The Works of Irving Fisher,* edited by William J. Barber. London: Pickering and Chatto.

Hicks, J. R. 1939. *Value and Capital,* 2d ed. Oxford: Clarendon Press.

Murray, Christopher J., L. Murray, and Alan D. Lopez, eds. 1996. *The Global Burden of Disease*. Cambridge, Mass.: Harvard School of Public Health, distributed by Harvard University Press.

National Research Council. 1999. *Nature's Numbers : Expanding the National Economic Accounts to Include the Environment,* edited by William D. Nordhaus and Edward Kokkelenberg. Washington, D.C.: National Academy Press.

Nordhaus, William D. 1994. "Reflections on the Concept of Sustainable Economic Growth." In *Economic Growth and the Structure of Long-Term Development,* edited by Luigi L. Pasinetti and Robert M. Solow, 309–25. New York: St. Martin's Press in association with the International Economic Association.

———. 1995. "How Can We Measure Sustainable Income?" Cowles Foundation Discussion Paper, May.

Porter, Roy. 1997. *The Greatest Benefit to Mankind: A Medical History of Humanity.* New York: W. W. Norton.

Robinson, John P., and Geoffrey Godbey. 1997. *Time for Life: The Surprising Ways Americans Use Their Time,* Pennsylvania State University Press, University Park, Pennsylvania.

Rosen, Sherwin. 1994. "Modeling of Choices with Uncertain Preferences." In *Valuing Health for Policy: An Economic Approach,* edited by George S. Tolley, Donald Scott Kenkel, and Robert Fabian. Chicago: University of Chicago Press.

Samuelson, Paul A. 1961. "The Evaluation of 'Social Income.'" In *The Theory of Capital,* edited by F. A. Lutz and D. C. Haig. London: Macmillan.

Shapiro, Irving, Matthew Shapiro, and David Wilcox. 1998. "Measuring the Value of Cataract Surgery." In *Medical Care, Output, and Productivity,* edited by E. Berndt and D. Cutler. Chicago: University of Chicago Press, 2001.

Shapiro, Matthew, and David Wilcox (1997). "Mismeasurement in Consumer Price Index: An Evaluation." *Macroeconomics Annual* 11:93–142.

Shepard, Donald S., and Richard J. Zeckhauser. 1984. "Survival versus Consumption." *Management Science* 30, no. 4 (April): 423–39.

Tolley, George S., Donald Scott Kenkel, and Robert Fabian, eds. 1994. *Valuing Health for Policy.* Chicago: University of Chicago Press.

United Nations Development Programme (UNDP). 1997. *Human Development Report, 1997.* New York: Oxford University Press.

Unsworth, Robert, James Neumann, and W. Eric Browne. 1992. "Review of Existing Value of Life Estimates: Valuation Document." Background document prepared for Section 812 Analysis, Industrial Economics Incorporated, Cambridge, Mass., 6 November.

Usher, Dan. 1973. "An Imputation to the Measurement of Economic Growth for Changes in Life Expectancy." In *The Measurement of Economic and Social Performance,* edited by Milton Moss, 193–226. New York: Columbia University Press.

———. 1980. *The Measurement of Economic Growth.* New York: Columbia University Press.

Viscusi, W. Kip. 1993. "The Value of Risks to Health and Life." *Journal of Economic Literature* 31:1912–46.

CHAPTER TWO

The Economic Value of Medical Research

Kevin M. Murphy and Robert H. Topel

In 1995, the United States invested almost $36 billion in medical research. Of this total, $13.4 billion was funded by the federal government, about $18.6 billion by private industry, and about $4 billion by other private and public sources. Funding for medical research accounted for about 21 percent of the overall federal budget for research and development (R&D) in 1995. Spending on health-related research has also increased significantly over time. The $13.4 billion federal dollars allocated for health-related research in 1995 represents a real dollar increase of 23 percent over 1990 and a real dollar increase of 61 percent over the $7.1 billion (in 1995 dollars) allocated to medical research in 1980. Over roughly the same period, real per-capita spending on health care roughly doubled, from $1,969 per person in 1980 to $4,105 in 1998. Health care spending also increased as a share of total spending, accounting for about 19.6 percent of personal consumption expenditures in 1998 versus 13.9 percent in 1980 and only 11.3 percent in 1970. Clearly, the United States has invested heavily in the health of its population in terms of both health care expenditures and in terms of the R&D necessary to support medical advances.

Kevin M. Murphy is the George J. Stigler Professor of Economics in the Graduate School of Business and the Department of Economics at the University of Chicago and a research associate of the National Bureau of Economic Research. Robert H. Topel is the Isidore Brown and Gladys J. Brown Professor in Urban and Labor Economics in the Graduate School of Business at the University of Chicago and a research associate of the National Bureau of Economic Research.

We acknowledge support from the Lasker Charitable Trust, the Milken Foundation, and the Bradley Foundation through the George Stigler Center at the University of Chicago. An earlier version was presented as the Thompson Lecture to the Midwest Economic Association, and in workshops at the World Bank, the University of Chicago, Boston University, Texas A&M University, Clemson, the NBER, the Milken Institute, and the Milken Global Conference.

Our analysis in this chapter is intended to make some progress toward answering the question, What do we get in return for our expenditures on health-related research? We begin by asking a broader question, How do we value improvements in health and life expectancy? Armed with an economic framework for addressing such issues, we are able to estimate the economic value of the changes in life expectancy observed over the past several decades. Our results imply that the economic value of these gains has been enormous. We estimate that improvements in life expectancy alone added approximately $2.6 trillion per year (in constant 1996 dollars) to national wealth over the 1970–98 period. For comparison purposes it is useful to note that the average level of real gross domestic product (GDP) for the 1970–98 period was about $5.5 trillion. While some of the growth in life expectancy stems from factors other than improvements in health care, the overall gains are so large that it would seem hard to believe that the gains from improved health care have not been enormous as well. This view is bolstered by the fact that about $1.1 trillion of the overall $2.6 trillion annual increase is due solely to the reduction in mortality from heart disease, where medical advances have clearly been significant (see Cutler and Richardson [1997]).

Our analysis suggests that the potential gains from further improvements in health care are also extremely large. We estimate that reducing deaths from heart disease by 10 percent would generate approximately $5.1 trillion in economic value, while reducing cancer death rates would be worth roughly $4.4 trillion. Our analysis also suggests that the economic gains from any given increase in life expectancy are growing over time. The economic return to improvements in health is greater the larger the population, the higher the average lifetime incomes, the greater the existing level of health, and the closer the ages of the population to the age of onset of disease. All these factors point to a rising valuation of health improvements over the past several decades and into the future. As the U.S. population grows, as lifetime incomes grow, as health levels improve, and as the baby-boom generation ages toward the primary ages of disease-related death, the economic reward to improvements in health will continue to increase. We find that the growth and aging of the population alone will raise the economic return to improvements in the treatments of many diseases by almost 50 percent between 1990 and 2030. Projected increases in real incomes and life expectancy will add at least that much again over the same period.

Our analysis also highlights some of the interesting economic issues surrounding the valuation of improvements in health, health research, and the growth in health expenditures. Many of these issues have significant policy implications. For example, the annuitization of many public and private retirement benefits (Social Security, private pensions, Medicare, and private medical coverage) and the prevalence of third-party payers increase the incentive to spend on medical care and indirectly skew investments in research toward cost-increasing as opposed to cost-decreasing improvements in technology. These distortions also have important implications for the measurement of the returns to medical research specifically and health care generally. In the presence of such distortions, we must take account of the induced effect research has on expenditures when evaluating the social returns to improvements in technology. Our analysis takes a first step in this direction by comparing the gains from longevity with growth in expenditures required to support the higher level of care. Our analysis also points out that improvements in health are complementary with one another; improvements in life expectancy (from any source) increase the economic reward to further improvements by raising the remaining value of life. Hence, conquering or making significant progress against one disease raises the economic reward to progress on other diseases. This is of significant empirical relevance, as the historical progress against heart disease has increased the economic rewards to progress against cancer and many other diseases.

While our analysis of the benefits of improvements in health illustrates the enormous potential gains to medical research, it stops short of determining the precise value of these returns. Such a link is important and indeed feasible, but it is beyond the scope of our preliminary work. Instead, our analysis at this point is only suggestive, although our results indicate that the return to such research may be quite high, particularly if we make reasonable efforts to control the costs of care.

The chapter is organized as follows. Section I outlines our economic model for valuing improvements in health and life expectancy and relating these values to the economic literature on the value of life. We illustrate how the valuations of life obtained in the economic literature can be interpreted and applied to the problem at hand. Section II outlines our methodology for relating the increase in life expectancy to the improvements in medical technology and identifies the key determinants of the economic return to improved health. Section III begins the empirical section of the chapter with an analysis of the economic gains associated with the improvements in life expectancy from 1970 to 1998 and the potential gains to future progress against several major categories of disease. Section IV provides a preliminary evaluation and analysis of the returns to medical research. Section V presents suggested directions for future research.

I. A Framework for Valuing Improvements to Health and Longevity

Improvements in health and medical knowledge affect the quality of life and the risks of mortality at various stage of the life cycle. How much are people willing to pay for these improvements? According to standard economic principles, the willingness to pay for gains in health and longevity is determined by how such changes affect the discounted present value of lifetime utility. We present a theory based on a natural extension of the life cycle consumption model. In particular we use an expected utility formulation in which utility while alive depends on health and the consumption of goods and nonmarket time. The utility of death is normalized to be 0. We measure the quality of life by a single measure "health," $H(t)$, and measure longevity by the survivor function, $S(t)$, which gives the probability that the individual survives from birth to age t. We consider a world populated by identical individuals that discount the future at a constant rate, ρ, and competitive capital and insurance markets. Given the life cycle pattern of health, $H(t)$, and the survivor function $S(t)$, expected lifetime utility for a representative individual is then

$$(1)\quad V = \int_{0}^{\infty} e^{-\rho t} H(t)u(c(t), l(t))S(t)dt$$

where $c(t)$ is the individual's consumption of goods at date t and $l(t)$ is nonmarket time. Here we have a very particular specification for health in that we assume improvements in health generate a proportional increase in utility. This implies that increases in health raise the level of utility and the marginal utilities of both consumption and nonmarket time by the same proportion (see Murphy and Topel [2002] for more on this point). To focus on key ideas we assume that income and consumption are equal in each period in equilibrium (i.e. there is no aggregate savings) and that people choose hours of work in each period to equate the marginal values of market and nonmarket time (see Murphy and Topel [2002] for a description of a more general life-cycle problem when consumption differs from income). We assume that equilibrium capital prices (i.e. interest rates) adjust so that the consumption path is an optimal solution to the representative individual's life cycle allocation of consumption.

Our goal is to determine how our representative individual will value changes in health and longevity, which we model as exogenous changes in the health and survival profiles, $H(t)$ and $S(t)$. As with all goods, the value, in terms of willingness to pay, of an improvement in health and longevity will be given by the (marginal) change in utility generated by those improvements divided by the marginal utility of consumption. In this case, the change in utility from a differential change in the survivor function, $\Delta S(t)$, and health, $\Delta H(t)$, is

$$(2)\quad dV = \int_0^\infty e^{-pt}[H(t)u(c(t),l(t))\Delta S(t) + u(c(t),l(t))S(t)\Delta H(t)]dt.$$

The marginal utility of consumption at date t is $H(t)u_c(c(t),l(t))S(t)$. The willingness to pay for this change in health and longevity (as of date 0) will be

$$(3)\quad \frac{dV}{\mu} = \frac{\int_0^\infty e^{-pt}[H(t)u(c(t),l(t))\Delta S(t) + u(c(t),l(t))S(t)\Delta H(t)]dt}{H(0)u_c(c(0),l(0))}$$

where μ is the marginal utility of consumption at date 0. With competitive capital and insurance markets, interest rates will adjust, so that the market discount factor will be equal to the ratio of marginal utilities over time, or

$$(4)\quad e^{-\int_0^t r(t)dt} = \frac{e^{-pt}H(t)u_c(c(t),l(t))}{H(0)u_c(c(0),l(0))}.$$

To save on notation we will assume that interest rates are constant, so that the left-hand side of (4) simplifies to e^{-rt}. Substituting (4) into equation (3) and rearranging terms yields our basic valuation equation

$$(5)\quad \frac{dV}{\mu} = \int_0^\infty e^{-rt}\frac{u(c(t),l(t))}{u_c(c(t),l(t))}\Delta S(t)dt + \int_0^\infty e^{-rt}\frac{u(c(t),l(t))}{u_c(c(t),l(t))}S(t)\frac{\Delta H(t)}{H(t)}dt.$$

The term $u(c(t),l(t))/u_c(c(t),l(t))$ has a straightforward interpretation. First, define full consumption (as in Becker [1971]) as the market value of consumption and leisure, or $C_F(t) = c(t) + w(t)l(t)$. Using this definition, we have

$$(6)\quad \frac{u(c(t),l(t))}{u_c(c(t),l(t))} = \left[\frac{u(t)}{u_c\, c(t) + u_l\, l(t)}\right]C_F(t).$$

The term in brackets is the ratio of utility at date t to the marginal value (in utility terms) of the inputs used to produce utility, $c(t)$ and $l(t)$. When this ratio is greater than 1 the individual earns a "surplus" on the resources devoted to consumption in that period over what they would be worth if consumed elsewhere over the life cycle. Equation (6) has several important implications for the value individuals place on life. First, the value will typically exceed the value of income or consumption (which is assumed to be equal in our analysis), since we must include the value of nonmarket time (which is very important for older individuals) as well as the surplus individuals get on their consumption (i.e. the excess of the utility received per dollar over what those dollars are worth on the margin).

To keep things simple, we assume that the ratio of utility to the marginal utility value of full consumption is constant so that consumers receive a constant level of surplus per dollar of full consumption over their lifetime. We denote this constant ratio by θ. With this assumption, we can then rewrite equation (5) as

$$(7)\quad \frac{dV}{\mu} = \int_0^\infty e^{-rt}\theta C_F(t)\Delta S(t)\,dt + \int_0^\infty e^{-rt} S(t)\theta C_F(t)\frac{\Delta H(t)}{H(t)}dt.$$

Equation (7) is the basic building block for thinking about factors such as medical knowledge that provide value by extending lives or improving health. The first term on the right-hand side of (7) is the dollar value of the gain in lifetime expected utility from changes in longevity, which we measure by changes in the survivor function, $\Delta S(t)$. The equation weights changes in the probability of survival by dollar value (including any surplus) of full consumption in each period. The second term represents the value of changes in health (in percentage terms) weighted by the probabilities of survival and the dollar value utility, $\theta C_F(t)$.

Equation (7) measures changes in the "value of life" induced by changes in health and longevity. It is the foundation for our efforts to value the past and prospective contributions of medical research to aggregate welfare. First, we simplify the analysis by focusing on changes in mortality alone. In this case, equation (7) simplifies to

$$(8)\quad \frac{dV}{\mu} = \int_0^\infty e^{-rt}\theta C_F(t)\Delta S(t)\,dt.$$

Often we are interested in valuing changes in death rates at a particular age (holding death rates at other ages fixed). In our framework this corresponds to a change in the survivor function such that $\Delta S(t) = 0$ for $t < a$ and $\Delta S(t) = \lambda\, S(t)$ for $t > a$, where λ measures the magnitude of the reduction in the death rate. If we measure willingness to pay as of age a (as opposed to age 0, as we did in equation [8]), then equation (8) reduces to

$$(9)\quad \frac{dV(a)}{\mu(a)} = \lambda \int_a^\infty e^{-r(t-a)}\theta C_F(t)\frac{S(t)}{S(a)}dt = \lambda W(a).$$

$W(a)$ is often referred to as the "value of a statistical life," since it measures how much an individual demands per unit change in the probability of death (i.e. $\lambda = 1$). Things are simpler to think about if we focus on smaller changes in death probabilities similar to those we might actually observe. For example, if we set $\lambda = 1/10{,}000$ in equation (9), then $dV(a)/\mu(a)$ will measure the individual's willingness to pay to reduce the contemporaneous annual probability of death by 1/10,000 at a given age. The key advantage of the framework laid out here is that it is relatively easy to implement. To empirically implement either equation (8) or equation (9) for a given change in survivor probabilities, we need to measure the life cycle path of full consumption, $C_F(t) = c(t) + w(t)l(t)$, the market rate of interest, r, and the value of the "surplus" parameter θ. In principle, the parameter θ could be estimated from any empirical tradeoff between longevity and goods. Potential candidates are the decision to smoke, tradeoffs between time and safety for modes of travel, tradeoffs between costs and safety for consumer products (e.g. cars), the choice of medical treatment options, or the choice among potentially risky jobs. Of these examples, the choice among jobs is probably the most widely studied. Viscusi (1993) estimates that prime age males are willing to pay somewhere between \$300 and \$700 to reduce their annual probability of death by 1/10,000. We use a value of \$500 for our base year of 1996, a figure somewhat below the midpoint of Viscusi's range, given the growth in nominal income and consumption between Viscusi's study and our reference year of 1996. We use a real interest rate of 3.5 percent and calibrate the model so as to make the average male indifferent to a uniform 1/10,000 increase in the probability of death on the job (from age 20 to age 65) when compensated by an increase in earnings of \$500 per year. We perform this equalizing difference calculation as of age 20, since this is roughly the age at which people choose among careers. We obtain an estimate of $\theta \approx 2.9$. Figure 2.1 gives the resulting life cycle profile for the willingness to pay for a 1/10,000 reduction in the contemporaneous probability of death for men and women.[1]

From an empirical standpoint, the willingness-to-pay function shown in figure 2.1 is the major reason for developing our theoretical model. The data on occupational choice provide an estimate of the willingness to pay to reduce death risks for prime aged males. However, most of the increase in longevity in recent decades has come at much older ages. In order to estimate the value of this growth in life expectancy we need a means to evaluate the willingness to pay to reduce death risks at older ages. The model we develop above can be viewed as a theoretically grounded means of extrapolating evidence on the willingness to pay at prime ages to the

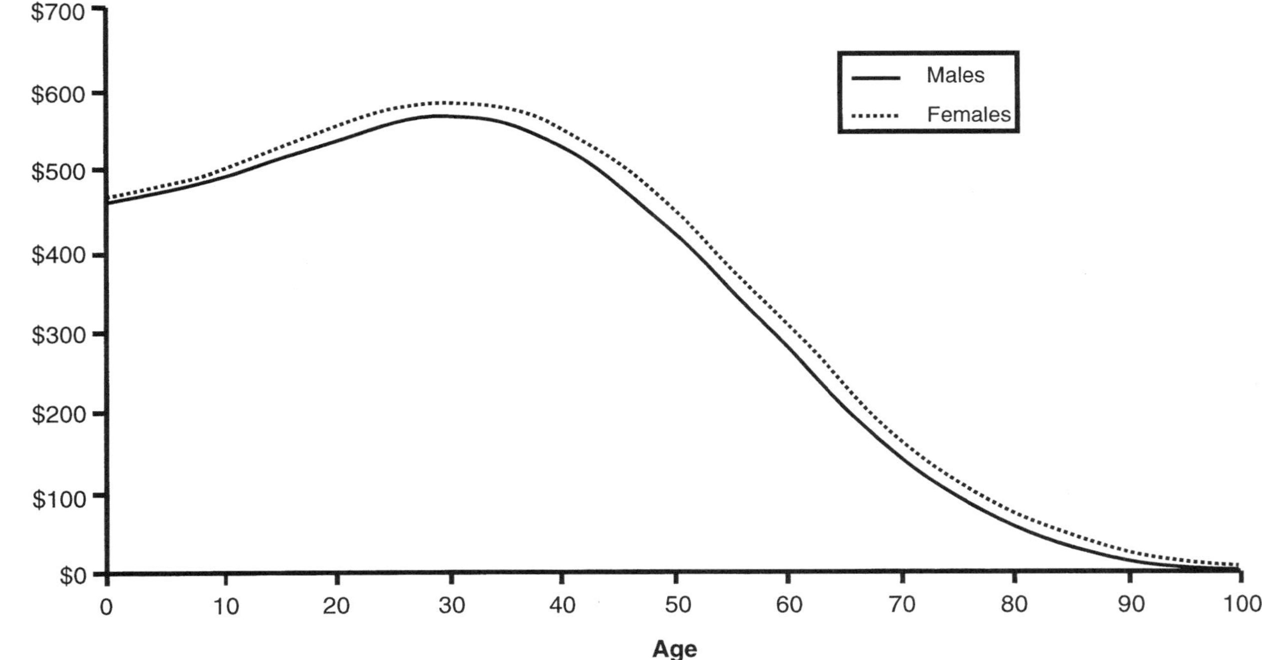

FIGURE 2.1: Value of a 1/10,000 reduction in death rates by age ($1996)

rest of the life cycle (see Murphy and Topel [2002] for a more extensive discussion).

II. Evaluating the Gains from Improvements in Health

The framework laid out in the previous section allows us to determine an individual's valuation of any given improvement in life expectancy and/or health. For our current purposes we will focus solely on the improvements in life expectancy and leave the valuation of improved health for future work. In order to link the improvements in life expectancy to medical research we adopt a simple framework in which death rates are determined by age, real expenditures on health care, and the level of medical knowledge. In our model, medical research increases the stock of medical knowledge—which in turn leads to a reduction in death rates. In this framework, medical knowledge acts like technological progress in that it improves health outcomes for a given amount of health inputs (or equivalently increases the value of health outputs more than it increases the cost of health inputs). Such a formulation translates the problem at hand into one of measuring the contribution of technological progress to the growth in health outputs.

In this framework, the probability of surviving from age a to age t will be a function of the level of medical knowledge, R, and the level of health care expenditures, which we denote by Z. We let $\lambda(a, R, Z)$ be the death rate at age a as a function of medical knowledge, R and health expenditures, Z. Under these conditions, the probability of surviving from age a to age t is given by the survivor function:

$$(10)\quad S(a,t,R,Z) = e^{-\int_a^t \lambda(x,R,Z)dx} = \frac{S(0,t,R,Z)}{S(0,a,R,Z)}.$$

Based on our results from the previous section, the gain to an individual who has survived to age a from an increase in medical knowledge will be given by

$$(11)\quad V_R(a,R) = \int_a^\infty e^{-r(t-a)} S_R(a,t,R,Z)\theta C F(t)dt$$

which can be rewritten in terms of hazard rates as

$$(12)\quad V_R(a,R) = -\int_a^\infty e^{-r(s-a)} S(a,s,R,Z)\lambda_R(s,R,Z)W(s)ds$$

where $W(s)$ is the willingness-to-pay function defined in equation (9) above and illustrated in figure 1.[2] Equation (12) has a simple interpretation: the value to an individual of age a from the increase in medical knowledge,

R, is given by the change in future death rates at each future age times the willingness to pay for a reduction in death rates at that age, $W(s)$, discounted at the market rate of interest and the baseline probability of survival. Empirically, we can measure the value of an improvement in life expectancy due to an increase in medical knowledge (or some other source of technical progress) by applying the resulting decrease in death rates over the remainder of that individual's life weighted by the discounted value (accounting for both time interest rates and survival probabilities) of the willingness-to-pay function given in figure 2.1.

Since equation (11) is linear in the change in survivor function, $\Delta S(t)$, it has a natural extension to discrete changes. The discrete version, which will prove useful empirically, can be used to calculate the value of switching between two survivor functions, $S_1(t)$ and $S_2(t)$, as

$$(13)\quad V_2 - V_1 = -\int_a^\infty e^{-r(t-a)}[S_2(t) - S_1(t)]\theta C_F(t)\,dt.$$

To implement equation 13 empirically we simply need an estimate of θ (which we obtained as roughly 2.9 from our calibration exercise above), a reference consumption profile (such as that we used to calculate figure 2.1), and the two survivor functions we wish to compare, $S_1(t)$ and $S_2(t)$. For all calculations we use 1996 as our "base year," fix the consumption profile (as described in footnote 1), fix the value of θ at 2.9 (which corresponds to a willingness to pay to avoid job-related death risks of \$500 per 1/10,000 increase in the annual risk of death), and use a real interest rate of 3.5%.

Our theoretical framework has several important implications that follow directly from equation (12):

- First, due to the effect of discounting (via both the rate of time preference and the intervening probability of death), the value of improvements in survival probabilities over a given age range is greatest at ages immediately preceding those ages.
- Second, increases in survival probabilities increase the value of further improvements in life expectancy (by reducing the discounting on future ages).
- Third, the values of increases in life expectancy are proportional to the level of consumption.

These results have important implications for the valuation of both historical and prospective future improvements in life expectancy. Figures 2.2 and 2.3, which look at the historical reductions in heart disease between 1970 and 1998, help illustrate these implications. Figure 2.2 shows the

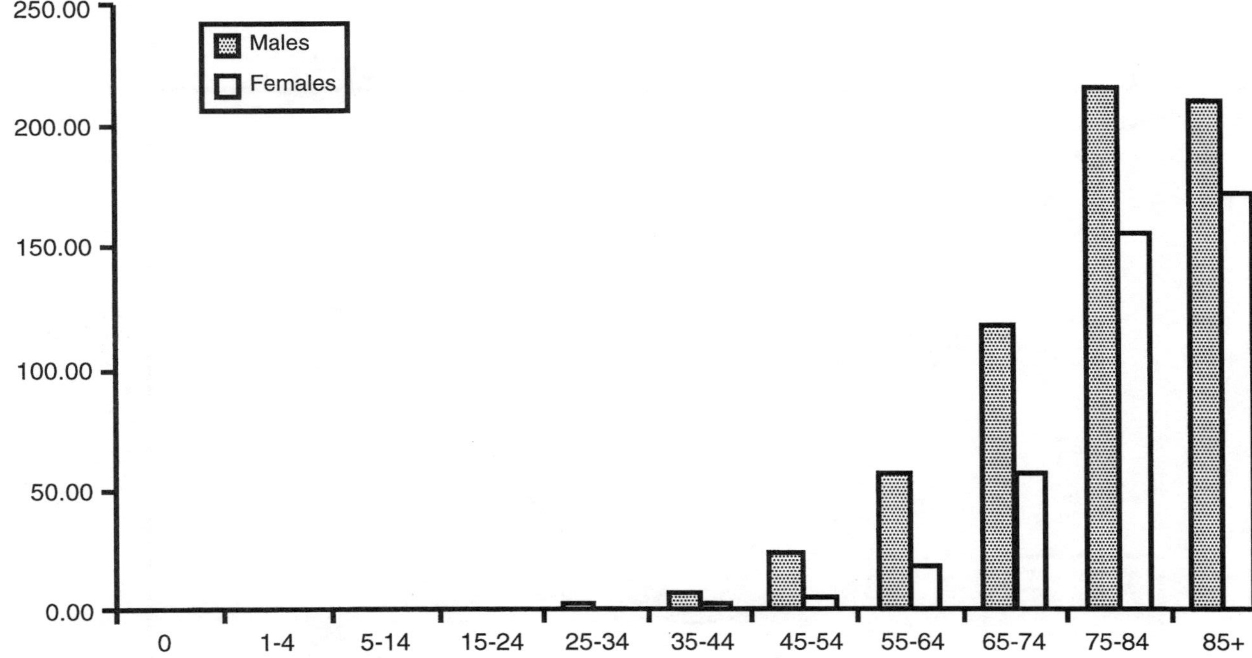

FIGURE 2.2: Reductions in death rates from heart disease, 1970–98

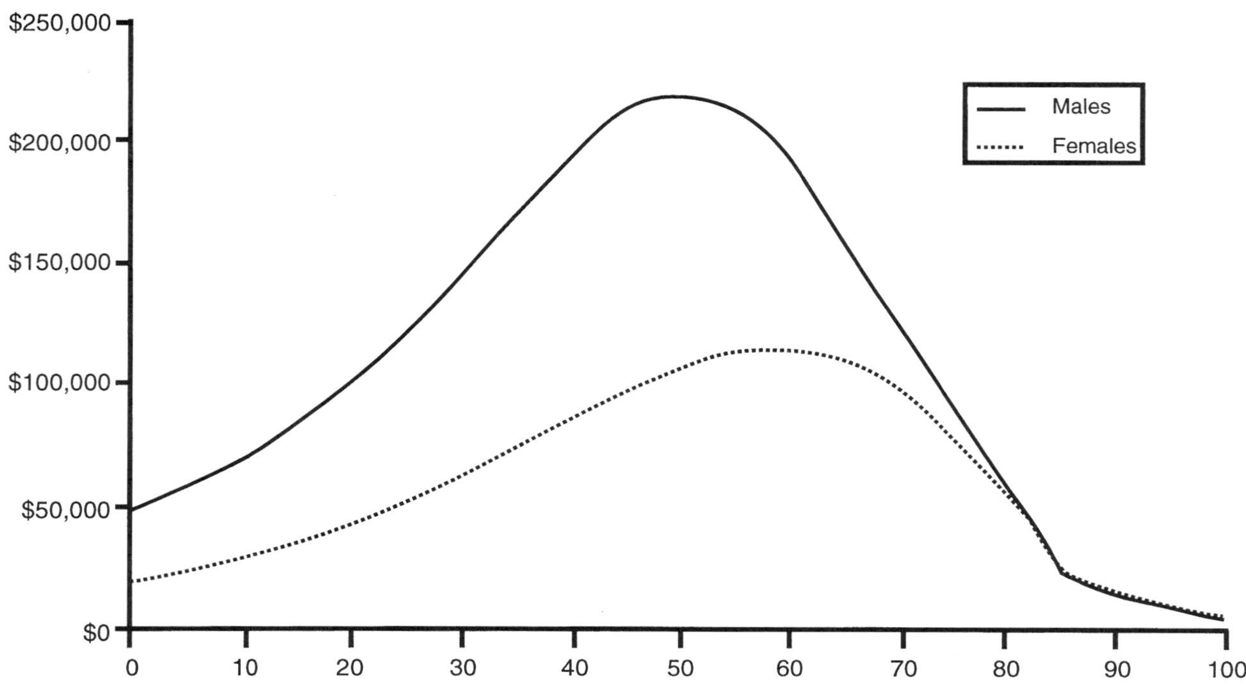

FIGURE 2.3: Gains from reductions in heart disease, 1970–98

reduction in death rates from heart disease for men and women by age category between 1970 and 1998 (measured by the change in annual deaths per 100,000 individuals in the population group). Figure 2.3 shows the gains to individual men and women as a function of age that we calculate using equation (13) based on the change in death rates from figure 2.2, holding the death rates from all other causes fixed at their 1996 level.

The effects of discounting are clearly illustrated by these figures. Figure 2.2 shows that the reduction in death rates is concentrated at ages 55+ for men and 65+ for women. Figure 2.3 uses the framework laid out above to calculate the gains to men and women that result from the decline in death rates shown in figure 2.2. As the figure illustrates, the value of the reduction in heart disease death rates peaks for men at about age 50 (just prior to the major reduction in death rates for men) and for women at about age 60 (just prior to the major reduction in death rates for women). The peak at older ages for both sexes reflects the fact that heart disease deaths are concentrated at older ages. The difference in timing between men and women reflects the fact that deaths from heart disease typically occurred at somewhat younger ages for men than for women. The higher value of the reductions in heart disease for men reflects the greater absolute reduction in death rates from heart disease that occurred for men over the 1970–98 period and the higher value of the willingness-to-pay function at younger ages.

Our second result, that increases in life expectancy are worth more when survival rates are higher, is in many ways the most interesting result and has many implications. In particular, it accounts for the relatively low value placed on even large reductions in death rates at very old ages. At these ages the expected remaining length of life is so low that marginal increases in life have relatively low value. This can be seen by comparing figures 2.2 and 2.3; the greatest reduction in death rates occurs in the two oldest age groups, while the greatest increase in value of life occurs at significantly younger ages. This result also implies that improvements in life expectancy are complementary; progress against one disease raises life expectancy and therefore increases the value of further improvements in survival rates. For example, the reduction in death rates from heart disease shown in figure 2.2 has served to increase the return to reducing death rates from cancer and other diseases prevalent late in life.

The final result regarding the effect of income implies that optimal expenditures on increasing life expectancy will increase with the level of wealth. This may account for at least part of the rapid increase in real per-capita health expenditures seen in most industrialized countries over time.

So far we have addressed the value of increased life expectancy at the individual level only. In order to calculate the aggregate value of any improvements in medical knowledge, we must accumulate the gains for individuals from equation (12) or (13) over the current and future population. Doing so implies that the marginal social value of a permanent increase in medical knowledge that takes place at time t will be

$$(14)\quad V_R(t) = \sum_{a=0}^{T} N(a, t)V_R(a, R) + N^*(t)V_R(0, R).$$

Here $N(a, t)$ is the number of individuals of age a at date t, and $N^*(t)$ is the present value of the number of individuals that will be born in future years. Equation (14) has several important implications:

- First, the social value of an increase in medical knowledge is proportional to the size of the population.
- Second, the social value of an increase in life expectancy is greater when the age distribution of the population is concentrated around (but before) the ages where the largest reductions in death rates occur.

These results, together with the three results on individual values described above, have important implications for the value of medical research today and in future years. Over time the U.S. population is aging, survival rates are continuing to improve, the population is growing, and income levels are increasing. All these effects imply that the economic value of a given improvement in health is higher today than in the past and is likely to grow even more over the next several decades. Hence, it would seem that all else being equal, optimal expenditures on health-related research are likely to be increasing over time.

III. Estimating the Social Value of Actual and Potential Improvements in Health

We begin our empirical analysis of the economic value of medical research by addressing a somewhat broader question: What is the economic value of the observed improvements in life expectancy over the 1970–98 period without regard to the source of these improvements? To make these computations we use Vital Statistics data on death rates from all causes by age and sex for 1970, 1980, 1990, and 1998, together with our reference profile for the willingness to pay by age and sex shown in figure 2.1 above.

We divide the 1970–98 period into three subperiods: 1970–80, 1980–90, and 1990–98. We compute the change in values by age and sex using equation (13). Figures 2.4 and 2.5 calculate the value of moving in succession

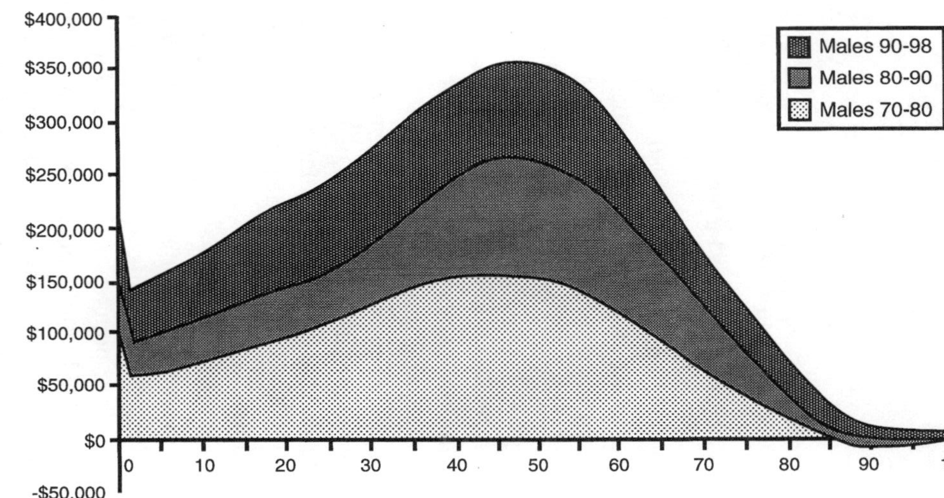

FIGURE 2.4: Gains from increased longevity for males, 1970–98

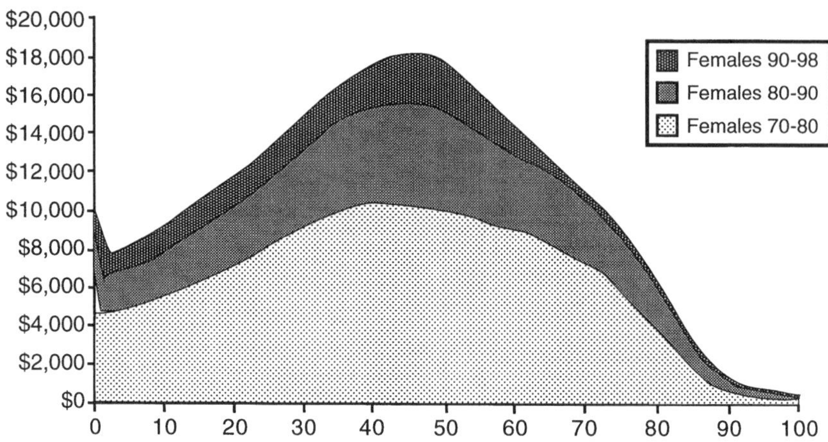

FIGURE 2.5: Gains from increased longevity for females, 1970–98

between the survivor functions from 1970, 1980, 1990, and 1998. Figure 2.4 gives the results for males and figure 2.5 shows the results for females. The graphs cumulate the changes over time with the gain over each subperiod, 1970–80, 1980–90, and 1990–98, shown with a different shade. The total height of the graph at any age measures the cumulative gain over the 1970–98 period. As figures 2.4 and 2.5 illustrate, the gains at the individual level are substantial. Improvements in life expectancy over the period as a whole peak at about $350,000 for men around age 50 and about $180,000 for women around age 45. The discretely larger increase in the value of life at age 0 for both sexes reflects the value of the reduction in infant mortality. The figures also break down the gains by the three subperiods: 1970–80, 1980–90, and 1990–98. In general, the largest gains are for 1970–80 (particularly for women).

Table 2.1 aggregates the individual values in figures 2.4 and 2.5 to determine the aggregate value of the improvements in life expectancy that occurred between 1970 and 1998 (using equation [14]). The first column of table 2.1 gives the base-year population distributions for 1996 (including an estimate of the discounted future population based on Census interpolations of U.S. Census projections). The next four columns give the average gain per capita by age category for each of the three subperiods and the period as a whole. The top panel refers to males, the middle panel refers to females, and the bottom panel provides aggregates over age within sex and over age and sex. The gains by age and sex quantify the results shown in figures 2.4 and 2.5. The bottom panel shows what could not be seen in the figures, namely the aggregate gains for the U.S. population. These values

Table 2.1 Economic Gains from Reductions in Mortality by Age and Overall

	Population	Gains per Capita ($1996)			
Males, yrs		1970–80	1980–90	1990–98	1970–98
Birth	72,134	100,421	48,703	56,688	205,811
1 to 4	7,938	62,655	35,232	48,165	146,052
5 to 14	19,681	75,005	40,599	58,342	173,946
15 to 24	18,618	96,330	48,510	74,322	219,162
25 to 34	20,191	126,548	61,130	81,909	269,588
35 to 44	21,569	151,490	91,878	83,374	326,741
45 to 54	15,836	152,233	113,392	86,992	352,617
55 to 64	10,166	125,013	95,018	79,301	299,333
65 to 74	8,325	70,799	63,151	51,239	185,188
75 to 84	4,486	25,668	29,195	31,818	86,681
85+	1,070	−4,508	8,626	13,930	18,048
Females, yrs					
Birth	68,773	76,514	33,338	19,220	129,073
1 to 4	7,578	46,921	21,162	11,488	79,572
5 to 14	18,741	55,323	23,953	12,555	91,832
15 to 24	17,604	72,452	29,745	15,058	117,255
25 to 34	20,177	92,521	38,186	17,566	148,273
35 to 44	21,824	103,833	48,041	22,582	174,456
45 to 54	16,533	100,971	47,912	27,829	176,712
55 to 64	11,195	91,210	37,851	18,178	147,240
65 to 74	10,345	74,698	33,440	4,013	112,151
75 to 84	6,944	44,147	22,169	499	66,815
85+	2,692	11,488	6,771	−1,446	16,812
		Aggregate Gains (millions of $1996)			
		1970–80	1980–90	1990–98	1970–98
Males		21,215	12,139	13,223	46,577
Females		15,863	6,979	3,461	26,303
Total		37,078	19,117	16,685	72,880

are truly enormous: over $37 trillion for the change from 1970 to 1980, $19 trillion from 1980 to 1990, and almost $17 trillion for the eight-year span from 1990 to 1998. The total gain of approximately $72 trillion translates into a gain of about $2.6 trillion per year. By comparison, real GDP over this period averaged about $5.7 trillion. If we were to include the increased value of life generated by increases in longevity between 1970 and 1998 in our measures of national output, it would increase real output over this period by roughly 50%.

The individual gains shown in figures 2.4 and 2.5 and the aggregate gains shown in table 2.1 measure the gain associated with changing from the cross-sectional survivor function from one year to another. For example, the individual gains in figures 2.4 and 2.5 or in the last column of table 2.1 measure our estimate of what males and females would be willing to pay at each age to have the 1998 survivor function for the rest of their lives rather than the 1970 survivor function. Similarly, the aggregate values shown in the bottom panel of table 2.1 represent our estimate of what the 1996 population and all future cohorts would be willing to pay (in present value) to shift permanently from the cross-sectional survivor function for 1970 to the 1998 survivor function.

The improvements in health shown in figures 2.4 and 2.5 and table 2.1 come from many sources in addition to improvements in medical knowledge. Improvements in public health, changes in lifestyles (some of which may themselves be related to increases in medical knowledge), and increased access to health care are just three examples. As such, these gains do not isolate the contribution of medical research and the knowledge gained from that research from the contribution of these or other factors. They also do not deduct the economic cost of either the underlying medical research or the expansion of per-capita medical expenditures over this same period. Tables 2.2, 2.4, and 2.5 attempt to address each of these two shortcomings. Table 2.2 calculates the economic value of the reduction in the risk of death from heart disease over the 1970–98 period, assuming that death rates from other diseases remained fixed (as we did in figures 2.2 and 2.3). The final column and row in the table give the percentage of the overall gains from longevity that is due to the reduction in heart disease mortality. As can be seen by comparing table 2.2 and table 2.1 or examining the percentage figures in the final column, the gains against heart disease account for roughly half of the overall gain and significantly more than half of the gains at older ages. Gains from the reduction in heart disease are about twice as large for men as they are for women in absolute terms but only slightly larger when measured as a share of the overall gain.

It is also possible to deal explicitly with the increase in medical expenditures over time. Allowing for increases in expenditures seems important from both a theoretical and an empirical perspective. From a theoretical perspective, identifying the marginal effect of knowledge requires us to control for changes in other inputs. This seems particularly important, since many of the technological advances that extend life also increase optimal expenditures. Second, from an empirical perspective we know that medical expenditures expanded enormously from 1970 to 1998, so it is necessary to control for expenditure growth whether or not these increases are causally related to the growth in knowledge. By allowing expenditures to change

TABLE 2.2 Economic Gains from Reductions in Heart Disease Mortality

	Population	Gains per Capita ($1996)				
Males, yrs		1970–80	1980–90	1990–98	1970–98	% of Total
Birth	72,134	18,786	20,534	10,443	49,763	24.2
1 to 4	7,938	21,601	22,410	11,113	55,124	37.7
5 to 14	19,681	27,768	28,495	14,141	70,403	40.5
15 to 24	18,618	39,618	40,306	20,125	100,049	45.7
25 to 34	20,191	56,475	57,777	29,064	143,316	53.2
35 to 44	21,569	71,969	77,371	40,287	189,627	58.0
45 to 54	15,836	77,722	87,515	50,995	216,232	61.3
55 to 64	10,166	66,544	77,221	50,971	194,736	65.1
65 to 74	8,325	39,672	54,378	37,157	131,207	70.9
75 to 84	4,486	14,858	29,368	24,063	68,288	78.8
85+	1,070	−3,164	12,189	11,160	20,185	111.8
Females, yrs						
Birth	68,773	9,457	8,998	3,807	22,261	17.2
1 to 4	7,578	11,056	9,769	4,001	24,826	31.2
5 to 14	18,741	14,270	12,369	5,000	31,639	34.5
15 to 24	17,604	20,208	17,388	7,105	44,701	38.1
25 to 34	20,177	28,238	24,662	10,477	63,377	42.7
35 to 44	21,824	36,527	33,123	15,665	85,315	48.9
45 to 54	16,533	43,837	40,489	21,697	106,023	60.0
55 to 64	11,195	46,958	44,596	23,450	115,003	78.1
65 to 74	10,345	38,591	41,465	20,043	100,098	89.3
75 to 84	6,944	19,982	27,022	14,453	61,457	92.0
85+	2,692	2,615	9,925	6,227	18,766	111.6
		Aggregate Gains (billions of $1996)				
		1970–80	1980–90	1990–98	1970–98	% of Total
Males		7,804	8,574	4,705	21,083	45.3
Females		4,520	4,263	2,010	10,793	41.0
Total		12,324	12,837	6,715	31,876	43.7
		33.2%	67.2%	40.2%	43.7%	

over time we can calculate a "net" number that subtracts the growth in health expenditures from the gross gains in longevity.[3]

The growth in health expenditures is easily added to our model. If we denote the increase in real expenditures at age a by $\Delta X(a)$ and the net gain at age a by $\Delta V^N(a)$, then our formula for comparing two points in time for an individual of age a becomes

$$(15)\quad \Delta V^N(a) = \int_a^\infty e^{-r(s-a)}[S_2(s) - S_1(s)]\theta C_F(t)ds - \int_a^\infty e^{-r(s-a)}S^*(s)\Delta X(s)ds.$$

The first term represents the total increase in the future value of life generated by both the increase in knowledge and the increase in expenditures. The second term represents the change in the discounted value of future health expenditures measured against a fixed survival profile.

Equation (15) implies that we can measure technical improvement (including the impact of changes in medical knowledge) as a sort of production residual equal to the increase in the discounted value of the increase in longevity less the corresponding increase in expenditures. In fact, if health expenditures are chosen efficiently, then this expression will reduce to equation (12), since the net return to the marginal increase in Z will be 0. However, equation (15) will measure the net contribution of health knowledge regardless of the source of the growth in health expenditures as long as health expenditures are chosen efficiently on the margin. We discuss the case where health expenditure choices are distorted in section IV below.

Since we use 1996 as our base year, we fix the survival profile at its 1996 value when calculating the growth in lifetime expenditures. There are several important caveats to this analysis. First, to the extent that health expenditures accomplish goals other than life extension (such as improvements in the quality of life), subtracting the growth in overall health expenditures represents too large of a correction. In addition, it is difficult to know how to allocate expenditures precisely across ages in terms of their effect on longevity (i.e. expenditures at one age affect longevity at all futures ages). Nevertheless, it is possible to perform some simple aggregate calculations that give a general idea of the importance of the growth in expenditures.

We begin our analysis with aggregate expenditures on health care for 1970, 1980, 1990, and 1998 as given in the top row of table 2.3. Next we translate these to 1996 dollars and correct for the differences between the actual population in each of the years and our 1996 base-year population.[4]

TABLE 2.3 U.S. Health Expenditures, 1970–98

	1998	1990	1980	1970
Nominal expenditures ($billions)	1,146	696	246	73
% of total consumption expenditures	19.6	18.2	13.9	11.3
Real expenditures ($billions)				
Current-year population	1,109	812	445	261
Fixed 1996 population	1,080	883	548	369
Per-capita expenditures ($)				
Current-year population	4,105	3,271	1,969	1,286
Fixed 1996 population	3,994	3,554	2,423	1,816
Present value of total expenditures ($trillions)	40,249	32,904	20,419	13,556

The table also provides estimates of per-capita expenditures to help illustrate the growth in expenditures over time. The final row of the table, labeled "Present Value of Total Expenditures," calculates the present value of expenditures for our 1996 population (including expenditures for future cohorts) if we fixed expenditures by age at their level from each of the indicated years. As can be seen from the table, real expenditures have increased enormously over time even for our fixed 1996 population. In particular, the present discounted value of expenditures is about \$27 trillion higher using the 1998 level of expenditures by age than it would be with the 1970 level of expenditures. The largest growth in expenditures occurs over the 1980–90 period, when the discounted value increases by about \$12.5 trillion. While these numbers are much smaller than the corresponding gains from increased longevity, they are nevertheless very large (particularly over the last two time periods).

Since the improvements in health that we measured in tables 2.1 and 2.2 include increases in life expectancy from all sources (including health expenditures), equation (15) implies that we can control for the effects of increased health expenditures by subtracting the growth in expected future expenditures from the observed increase in the value of life (however, as we noted earlier, this is likely to "overcorrect" when health expenditures generate benefits other than longevity. Table 2.4 uses the results from table 2.3 to deduct the increase in discounted aggregate expenditures from the aggregate results in table 2.1. As the table shows, the growth in the discounted future expenditures has been significantly smaller than our estimate of the economic value of the growth in longevity (on the order of 37 percent for the period as a whole). Moreover, correcting for the increase in health expenditures reduces the growth in the value of life from \$72 trillion to \$46 trillion for the period as a whole and \$36 trillion to \$16 trillion for the period since 1980 (i.e. 1980–98). The results in table 2.4 imply that the gains in longevity have outstripped the gains in expenditures by somewhat more than $2\frac{1}{2}$ to 1 over the period as a whole and roughly 2 to 1 since 1980. In economic terms, these estimates would imply that the health production sector has seen rapid rates of technological improvement

TABLE 2.4 Estimated Gains Net of the Increase in Health Expenditures (\$billions)

	1970–80	1980–90	1990–98	1970–98
Gross gains (from table 2.1)	\$37,078	\$19,117	\$16,685	\$72,880
Increase in expenditures	\$6,863	\$12,485	\$7,345	\$26,693
Gains net of expenditure growth	\$30,215	\$6,632	\$9,340	\$46,187
Expenditure increase as a % of gain	18.5%	65.3%	44.0%	36.6%

TABLE 2.5 Prospective Gains from a Permanent 10% Reduction in Death Rates by Major Cause of Death ($billions)

	Males	Females	Total
ALL CAUSES	10,016	7,147	17,163
MAJOR CARDIOVASCULAR DISEASES	2,994	2,149	5,142
Diseases of heart	2,471	1,614	4,085
Cerebrovascular diseases	356	399	755
MALIGNANT NEOPLASMS	2,258	2,101	4,359
Respiratory and related organs	793	516	1,309
Breast	3	421	424
Genital organs and urinary organs	271	282	553
Digestive organs	538	393	931
INFECTIOUS DISEASES (Including AIDS)	498	146	644
CHRONIC OBSTRUCTIVE PULMONARY DISEASE	309	295	605
PNEUMONIA AND INFLUENZA	192	166	358
DIABETES	222	227	449
CHRONIC LIVER DISEASE AND CIRRHOSIS	212	98	310
ACCIDENTS AND ADVERSE EFFECTS	962	407	1,369
MOTOR VEHICLE ACCIDENTS	514	244	757
HOMICIDE AND LEGAL INTERVENTION	323	90	413
SUICIDE	407	101	508

(particularly if subtracting the total increase in expenditures is a significant overcorrection).

A key remaining question from our perspective is, How much of this technological progress can be attributed to the output of medical research?

To many, the numbers in tables 2.1, 2.2, and 2.4 may seem unbelievably large; however, these amounts really are a direct result of three facts: the willingness to pay $500 for a 1/10,000 reduction in the risk of death, suggested by economic research on individuals' willingness to take on risk; the magnitude of the reduction in death rates over the 1970–98 period; and the sheer size of the U.S. population (calculating gains at the worldwide level would magnify the numbers still further).

The data in table 2.5 address the potential for seeing large economic gains from progress against particular diseases. The table lists the gains to men, women, and the population as a whole from reducing deaths from various causes based on data for 1996 on deaths by primary cause. Figures 2.6 and 2.7 give the corresponding changes in the value of life at individual ages for men and for women for 6 selected causes of death. The numbers are computed using the same 1996 population distribution used in our earlier calculations and estimate the effect of a 10 percent reduction in

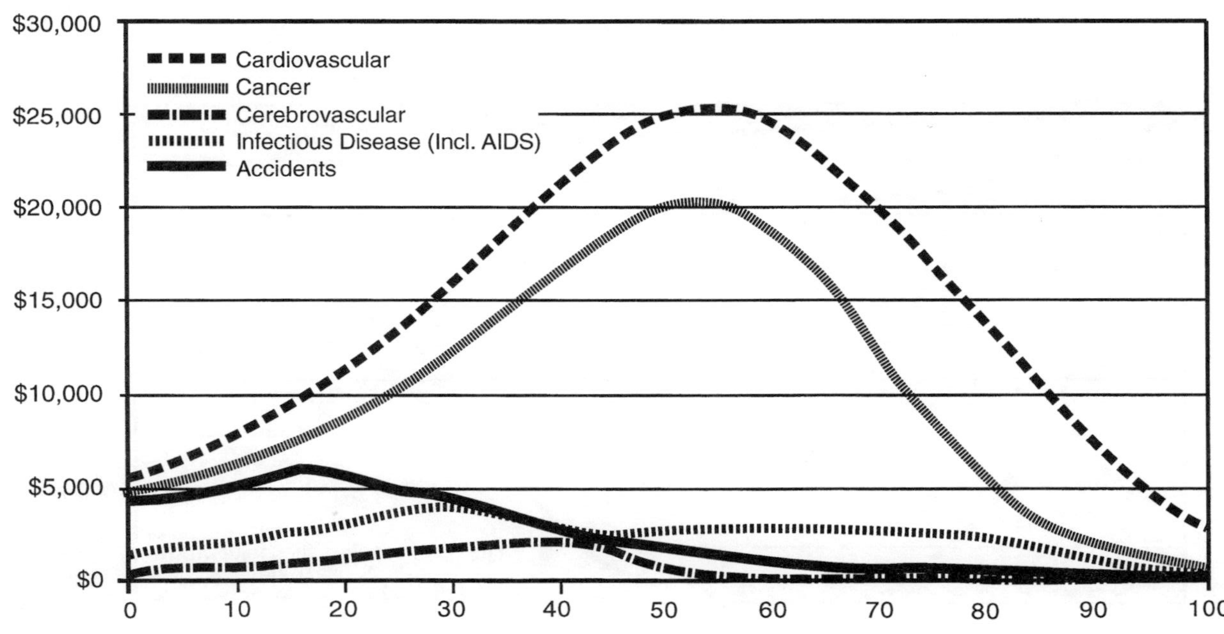

FIGURE 2.6: Value of a 10% reduction in death rates from selected disease by age for males

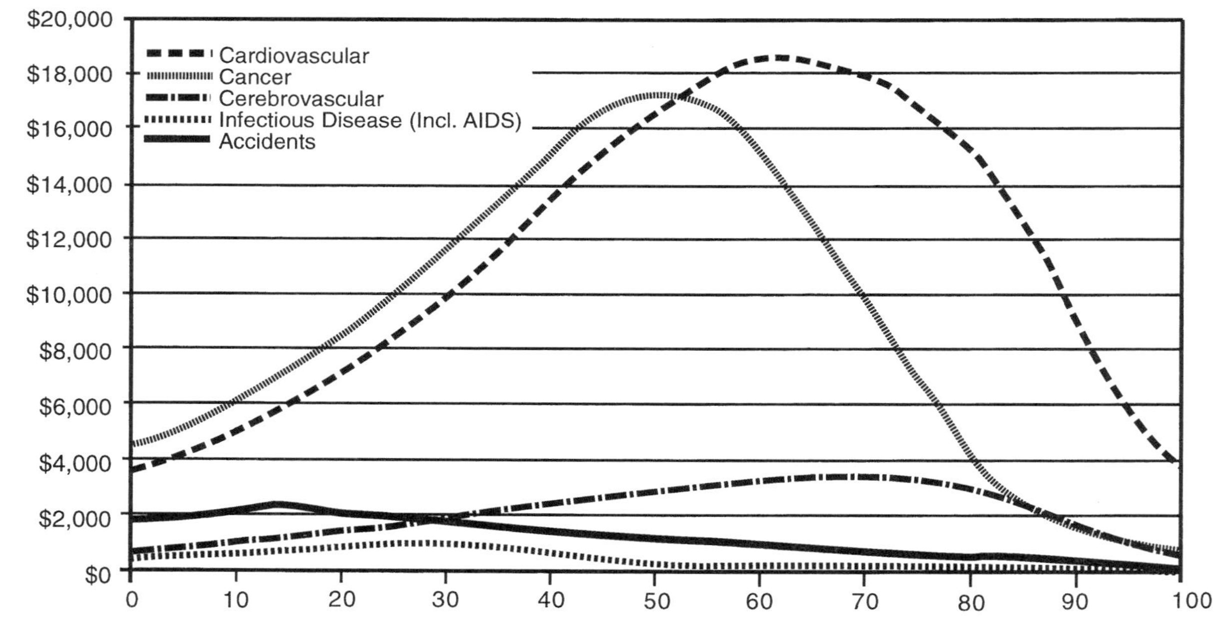

FIGURE 2.7: Value of a 10% reduction in death rates from selected disease by age for females

death rates from each specific cause, holding age-specific death rates (not deaths) from other causes constant. In table 2.5, the $4.4- and $4.1-trillion numbers for cancer and heart disease are staggering. These estimates imply that an innovation that reduced overall cancer death rates by only 1 percent would be worth over $440 billion, or about 5 percent of GDP. Reducing age-specific death rates from a single category of cancer such as breast or genitourinary by 10 percent would have a similar value. Moreover, reducing the age-specific death rate from AIDS (and other infectious diseases) by 10 percent would be worth about $650 billion. To put these numbers in perspective, we should note that total federal support for health-related research in 1997 was about $12 billion, or about $\frac{1}{40}$ of the gain from a 1 percent reduction in the overall death rate from cardiovascular disease. The results in table 2.5 suggest that the potential economic gains to progress against the categories of disease listed therein are very large indeed.

The results in figures 2.6 and 2.7 help illustrate how different age distributions of risk translate into differences in the age patterns of gains. For males, the gains from reducing both cancer and heart disease (the two biggest killers) peak around age 55, an age just before the major risks from these diseases set in. For women the peak in cancer occurs slightly earlier (around age 50), reflecting the wider age span of deaths from breast cancer, while the heart disease peak occurs somewhat later (around age 65), reflecting the later onset of heart disease among women. The curves for accidents and infectious diseases (including AIDS) reflect the greater risks for accidents and AIDS for males and the concentration of these risks at younger ages. The peak for cerebrovascular disease (which includes stroke) occurs late in the life cycle, reflecting the fact that the risks for this category of disease are concentrated at old ages.

IV. Investments in Medical Research

Our discussion so far has focused on the social value of past improvements in health and the potential gains for progress against various categories of disease. We now turn our discussion to funding for medical research. Table 2.6 provides some crude estimates of the investments in medical and aggregate R&D for the United States in 1995 and the growth in R&D over the preceding nine years. Our estimate of spending on medical research is based on federal funding for health-related research, R&D investments in the drug industry, and nongovernment-funded research in biological and medical sciences at U.S. colleges and universities. All values are based on the *Science and Engineering Indicators—1998* published by the National Science Foundation. While this total should capture the vast majority of

TABLE 2.6 Expenditures on R&D–Biomedical and Aggregate by Funding Source and Industry, 1995

Biomedical R&D Funding	Expenditure ($millions)	% of Total	Real % Growth, 1986–95
Total government	15,846	44.2	49.8
Federal government	13,423	37.5	45.8
NIH	10,682	29.8	50.7
Industry (total)	18,645	52.1	125.6
Private nonprofit	1,325	3.7	26.9
Total	35,816	100.0	80.1
Spending on health care	1,021,500		64.7
Health R&D as % of health expenditures	3.5%		9.3
Health R&D as % of GDP	0.5%		46.6
Health R&D as % of Total R&D	19.6%		57.5
Aggregate R&D Funding			
Federal	63,147	34.5	−13.2
Industry	110,998	60.7	36.1
Other	8,868	4.8	52.6
Total R&D funding	183,013	100.0	14.3
GDP	7,253,800		22.9
Total R&D as % of GDP	2.5%		−7.0
R&D as % of Sales (Selected Industries)			
Drugs and medicines	10.4%		
Office and computing equipment	8.1%		
Communications equipment	8.0%		
Electronic components	8.0%		
Optical, surgical, & photographic equipment	8.0%		
Scientific instruments	6.6%		
Industrial chemicals	4.7%		
Motor vehicles	3.0%		
Nonelectrical machinery	2.4%		

SOURCES: NIH Extramural Data (1996), NSF Science and Engineering Indicators (1998).

medical research funding, it ignores some internal and outside funding in research centers and health-related research in other industries (such as instruments). As table 2.6 makes clear, the investment in medical R&D by the United States is substantial, about $35.8 billion in 1995. Moreover, the level of funding for health research grew 80.1 percent in real terms between 1986 and 1995. In 1995 spending on health-related research was equal to 3.5 percent of total health care spending, a percentage only modestly larger than the 2.5 percent of GDP accounted for by spending on aggregate R&D.

The growth in funding for medical research of 80.1 percent from 1986 to 1995 modestly outpaced the 64.7 percent growth in health care spending over the same period and significantly outpaced the growth in overall GDP of 22.9 percent. The growth in medical research also outpaced the growth in overall R&D (80.1 percent versus 14.3 percent). The biggest contrast is for federally funded research, where federal funding for health-related research increased by 45.8 percent in real terms, while aggregate federal funding for R&D actually declined by 13.2 percent. In terms of private-sector funding, real aggregate R&D funding by industry grew by an amazing 125.6 percent. It would appear based on the numbers in table 2.6 that health-related research funding is about in line with funding in the economy as a whole on a percent of output basis and growth in this funding has roughly kept pace with the rapid growth in health care expenditures. Moreover, while the federal government's real-dollar commitment to R&D in the economy as a whole has declined, its commitment to health-related research has increased faster than GDP and almost as rapidly as health care expenditures.

Is the $35.8 billion spent on health-related R&D in 1995 too high or too low from a social standpoint? While a precise answer to this question is beyond the scope of our analysis here, we can put some perspective on the issue. First, the amount spent on medical research is very small relative to the growth in the overall value-of-life figures shown in tables 2.1, 2.2, and 2.4. In fact, if we take the (conservative) net annual figure from table 2.4 of $1.6 trillion per year for the 1970 to 1998 period as a starting point and assume that only 10 percent of this increase is due to increases in medical knowledge, then we would be left with roughly a $160-billion annual gain compared with the $21-billion annual expenditure on medical research for 1995. The numbers on the value of progress against specific disease categories from table 2.5 tell a similar story. Reducing the death rate from heart disease or cancer by 0.1% (e.g. reducing the death rate per 100,000 from 1,000 to 999) would be worth about $50 billion, or about twice our annual expenditures on health research.

The lower panel in table 2.6 also provides some perspective on the current level of funding for health-related research. The panel lists R&D expenditures as a percent of net sales for some of the most research-intensive industries. As can be seen from the table, the 10.4 percent figure for the drug industry is the highest of any industry. However, the 3.5 percent figure for the health care sector as a whole ranks significantly behind the 8 percent ratios for the office and computing equipment, communications equipment, electronic components, and specialized instruments sectors. The actual differences may in fact be somewhat larger, since the R&D numbers for these industries are understated due to the fact that the figures represent only industry-based research and do not include academic research in related underlying disciplines. In contrast, the 3.5 percent ratio for medical care is more similar to the 3.0 percent ratio for motor vehicles or the 2.4 percent ratio for nonelectrical machinery than it is to the high-technology sectors. The identity of the sectors with the highest ratios of R&D to sales listed in table 2.6 provides no real surprises, as the heavy R&D sectors are those closely linked to basic technologies: electronics, optics, and biotechnology.

The R&D-to-sales figures in table 2.6 suggest two types of comparisons. First, we can compare the 3.5 percent figure for the health care sector as a whole to the figures for the other industries listed in the table and the 2.5 percent figure for the economy as a whole. As we noted above, the sectors with high R&D ratios are those where the links to underlying technological advances (e.g. microelectronics) are highest. The question then would be, Should we expect the R&D ratio for health care to be closer to that for high-technology sectors, or closer to the ratio for technologically mature sectors such as motor vehicles (3.0 percent) or the economy as a whole (2.5 percent)? Our basic reaction is that medicine would seem to be an area closely tied to basic research and that the 3.5 percent figure seems surprisingly close to the 2.5 percent aggregate figure.

One of the potential reasons for the relatively low ratio of R&D to sales for health care (and the high dependence on government-supported research) compared to high-technology areas is that in a service-based industry it may be difficult for private investors to capture the economic gains on their investments. For service-based industries, many of the advances may come in the form of procedures or techniques that cannot be patented or copyrighted and hence do not lend themselves to providing returns to the original investor. The embodiment of ideas into physical goods creates an indirect way for innovators to collect on their investments in ideas. The view that the inability to reap the rewards of innovation limits private-sector investments in medical knowledge is bolstered by the difference between the 3.5 percent R&D-to-sales ratio for medical care as a whole and the 10.4 percent ratio for the drug sector. Since drugs are patentable, they are not subject to many of the limitations characteristic of other advances in health knowledge. The reliance on federal funding also mirrors this idea: funding for drug-related research is largely industry based, while funding for other areas of medical research is dominated by federal support. While not conclusive, the analysis of industry R&D-to-sales ratios would suggest that spending on medical research is not high by economywide standards. In fact, it may be low relative to what we spend in other sectors, with strong links to basic technological advances (particularly if we were to take the drug industry numbers out of the health care figures). The overall figure is also low relative to what is spent in the drug component of medical care sector itself.

The issue of the divergence between the social return to investments in medical knowledge and the incentives for private investors is endemic to discussions of R&D generally. As we stated above, this divergence may be particularly severe for innovations that cannot be embodied in physical goods (which can be patented and sold). We believe that such distortions are important for understanding the current configuration of research funding and for guiding policy to funding medical research. The medical sector is also subject to several other distortions that are important for our purposes. The first and most widely recognized factor is the prevalence of third-party payers. As a result of the prevalence of this payment system, medical spending decisions are made by individuals who bear only a small share of the economic costs of those decisions. While the growth in managed care has altered this situation to some extent, it seems clear that third-party payers will remain a key part of the medical care sector for the foreseeable future.

The key implication of the prevalence of third-party payers is that medical spending will tend to be higher than under a system where individuals bear all or most of the economic costs of their decisions. From the perspective of medical research this has two implications. First, when we evaluate the gains to society from medical research, we must take account of the effect of increased knowledge on medical spending. Essentially, since individuals do not bear the costs of the increased expenditures, it is possible that the induced increase in health expenditures could greatly offset or even exceed the direct gains from the medical knowledge. The most practical solution to this potential problem from an empirical standpoint is to calculate the increased value of improved health net of the increase in medical spending (as we attempted to do in table 2.4). This eliminates the need to separate the contributions to health of increases in medical knowledge and the associated increases in medical spending (which may be difficult, both theoretically and empirically). Second, if increases in medical knowledge increase (or decrease) medical spending, any divergence between the cost and value of these expenditures will be accounted for in the calculations. Thus it would appear that while important, the impact of third-party payers for evaluating the returns to medical research is something that can be dealt with.

The effect of third-party payers also skews the pattern of research. Ideally, the search for medical advances would be driven by the potential net gains, the gains in terms of increased health and life expectancy net of the economic costs of the treatments and facilities needed to implement these advances. In the presence of third-party payers, the weight placed on the economic costs of treatments will be reduced relative to the weight placed on the increased value of life, thereby skewing innovations toward cost-increasing as opposed to cost-decreasing innovations. This is aggravated by the fact that cost-increasing innovations often involve new equipment or drugs which allow at least limited ability to collect some portion of the economic gains produced. Thus it would appear that funding for medical research ought to account for this fact and lean at least somewhat toward funding research directed at cost-reducing rather than cost-increasing innovations, since these are the most likely to be underfunded.

Another potential issue is the annuitization of benefits for older individuals. Private pensions, Social Security, private medical plans, and Medicare all provide annuitized benefits for retired workers. Under such systems, program benefits show up at the individual decision-making level as income at older ages (since they will not be received if the individual dies), yet from a social perspective they are really transfers and should not be part of the value of life extension calculus. As Becker and Mulligan (1997) have pointed out, this generates an excess incentive for individuals to invest in life-preserving activities relative to the social optimum. Empirically, this issue can be handled within our framework by reducing the estimated gains to life extension for each specific age by the value of annuitized payments received at those ages. From a policy standpoint the prevalence of annuitized payments is one force leading toward an incentive to overinvest in both treatments and research to increase life expectancy (but not quality of life) at these ages.

While our analysis in this section is far too crude to support any definite conclusions, it appears based on our preliminary numbers that current expenditures on medical research are extremely small relative to both the economic value of the historical improvements in health and the potential gains from even small progress against many major categories of disease. Second, the level of R&D relative to sales for the health care sector is surprisingly close to the overall economy average and much smaller than for many of the "high-technology" sectors. The R&D intensity for the medical sector as a whole is also small relative to the level of R&D intensity for the drug industry. This discrepancy may be related to the basic nature of much medical research and the inability for individuals to capture a substantial fraction of the social gains for many types of medical research.

We also find that there are several other distortions in the medical marketplace, in particular the prevalence of third-party insurance and the annuitization of old-age benefits. Both factors distort incentives to expend resources on health care and thus indirectly distort research incentives (toward cost-increasing life extension). The remaining question is whether medical research is able to capitalize on the enormous potential for social gain identified in our analysis. Based on our calculations, even limited progress would easily justify current expenditures and most likely expenditures above current levels. Even within the context of a fixed level of expenditures, our type of analysis can be very useful in that it provides a road map as to the potential gains from progress on alternative research fronts and outlines the areas where the system is most likely to over- or underinvest.

Finally, a simple comparison of the data presented in tables 2.4 and 2.6 provides an important message. The gains from the historical increases in life expectancy and the historical growth in the costs of health care each measure in the trillions of dollars, while annual research expenditures in 1995 are on the order of $35 billion. In particular, our estimates from table 2.4 imply an annual aggregate gain of $2.6 trillion from increases in longevity offset by an annual growth in the present value of health expenditures of just under $1.0 trillion per year for a net gain of about $1.6 trillion per year. By comparison, annual expenditures on research were only about 2 percent of this net gain and less than 4 percent of the growth in the present value of health expenditures. The relative magnitude of the research and health care cost numbers implies that the calculus of research funding should focus far more on how research will affect expenditures than on the direct cost of the research itself. For example, a $100 billion investment that reduced deaths from cancer by 2 percent would generate about $870 billion in gains (given our results in table 2.5) but would have a negative return if it increased per-capita expenditures on health care by as little as 2.5 percent (about $100). The basic message from a policy perspective is that research funding and cost control are complements. Expenditures on research that prolong life without increasing expenditures are almost sure to be worthwhile (in our cancer example, the $100-billion investment would need to reduce the death rate from cancer by only 0.23 percent if it did not increase the costs of care), but expenditures that significantly increase costs could easily generate more expenditures than gains given the distortions in the care market (the prevalence of third-party payers and the annuitization of benefits).

V. Further Research

Our analysis so far has been very preliminary. While we have identified the enormous magnitude of the historical and potential future gains to increasing life extension, our analysis has also left much out. First, we have explicitly ignored the role of advances in medical knowledge for improving the quality (and not just the length) of life. Second, we have made no attempt to isolate the impact on life expectancy of advances in medical knowledge specifically or the output of the health care system as a whole from the influence of other factors. Finally, the theoretical and analytical framework we have outlined here can be expanded along several dimensions, including dealing with changes in health (as opposed to simply dealing with longevity) and allowing for lags in the impacts of medical knowledge and expenditures on health.

As part of implementing the work described above, we will need to extend the analytical framework outlined in this work to account for several factors, including the cumulative nature of the effects of health knowledge and health expenditures on health and life expectancy. Essentially, this amounts to thinking of health as a stock variable that is accumulated by investments where the efficiency of these investments is determined by health care and other consumption expenditures and the level of health knowledge. This adds a dynamic element above and beyond that built into the model above. Exactly how much can be done on this margin from an empirical perspective remains to be seen, but it seems like a direction of research worth pursuing. Dealing with a correlated structure of disease incidence will also require an expanded analytical framework. Finally, a more thorough theoretical and empirical analysis of the impact of third-party payers, the annuitization of retirement benefits, and variation across treatments in the ability to collect returns on research breakthroughs are all potential policy offshoots of the analysis outlined in this chapter.

Clearly, much remains to be done.

Notes

1. The life cycle profile of "full income" plus the risk premium on "full consumption" is assumed to be proportional to a representative earnings profile for men aged 20 to 65 years. We use the value of the profile at age 20 for all years from birth to age 20 and assume that the value of a life year declines at a rate of 5 percent per year after age 65. While somewhat ad-hoc, this profile should be sufficient to provide some general feel for the value of changes in life expectancy.

2. Technically, $W(s)$ would be the willingness to pay per unit change in the probability of death (rather than per 1/10,000 risk), what is commonly referred to as the "value of life." Of course, this would just change the scale of the figure without changing its shape.

3. If all health care inputs produce only gains in longevity and the value marginal products of health inputs are equal to their marginal cost, this will allow us to isolate the gains from knowledge (and any other omitted factors) from the contribution of health care inputs.

4. To correct for changes in the age distribution of the population we use estimates of expenditures on health care by age and sex from the National Health Expenditure Surveys for various years (1967, 1977, 1987, and 1997) and adjust the levels to match the overall level of expenditures. The figures also correct for changes in the age distribution and the size of the population based on published population data from the U.S. Census.

References

Becker, Gary S. 1971. *Economic Theory.* New York: Alfred A. Knopf.

Becker, Gary S., and Casey B. Mulligan. 1997. "The Endogenous Determination of Time Preference." *Quarterly Journal of Economics* 112, no 3: 729–58.

Cutler, David, and Elizabeth Richardson. 1997. "Measuring the Health of the U.S. Population." *Brookings Papers: Microeconomics 1997,* 217–71.

Murphy, Kevin M., and Robert H. Topel. "The Economic Value of Health and Longevity." Working Paper (2002).

National Medical Expenditure Survey. Various years.

National Science Foundation. 1998. *Science and Engineering Indicators.* <http://www.nsf.gov/sbe/srs/seind98/start.htm>.

Viscusi, W. Kip. 1993. "The Value of Risks to Life and Health." *Journal of Economic Literature* 31:1912–46.

CHAPTER THREE

Pharmaceutical Innovation, Mortality Reduction, and Economic Growth

Frank R. Lichtenberg

I. Introduction

The explanation of long-run growth in the value of per-capita output is a central issue in economics. In recent years, economists have increasingly recognized that traditional, official measures of growth in real per-capita output significantly understate true economic growth. One reason for this shortcoming is that the price indexes that are used to deflate nominal output tend to overestimate inflation, by approximately 1–1.5 percentage points per year (Advisory Commission to Study the Consumer Price Index, 1996).

A second reason is that gross domestic product (GDP) does not fully account for several important, highly valued "commodities," such as leisure, health, and longevity. The average person born in 1995 expects to live 22 years (41 percent) longer than the average person born in 1920. Although the rate of increase of longevity appears to be declining, as table 3.1 indicates, between 1970 and 1991 mean age at death still increased 5.4 years. In a recent paper, Nordhaus (this volume) argues that the underestimation of economic growth resulting from failure to account for increased longevity is substantial: he estimates that, "to a first approximation, the economic value of increases in longevity over the twentieth century is about as large as the value of measured growth in non-health goods and services" (p. 17). In other words, economic growth adjusted for longevity increase is twice as large as unadjusted economic growth.

Frank R. Lichtenberg is the Courtney C. Brown Professor of Business at Columbia University and a research associate of the National Bureau of Economic Research.

I am grateful to Judith Jones, Richard Levy, Richard Manning, and Gary Persinger for helpful comments and discussions, and to conference and seminar participants at Columbia University, NBER, NYU, the University of Chicago, Ohio State University, Purdue University, Georgia State University, and the International Schumpeter Society for their comments. I am responsible for any errors.

TABLE 3.1 Mean Life Expectancy and Statistics of Age Distribution of Deaths, 1970, 1980, and 1991

	1970	1980	1991
Life expectancy at birth (years)[a]	70.8	73.7	75.5
Age at death (years)[b]			
Mean	64.6	67.7	70.0
Standard deviation	21.8	20.4	19.8
Coefficient of variation	.337	.302	.283
Median	70	72	74
25%	57	60	63
10%	35	41	43
5%	10	22	28

[a]SOURCE: Health, United States, 1994, table 30.
[b]SOURCE: Author's calculations based on 1970, 1980, and 1991 Vital Statistics—Mortality Detail files.

The Solow model, which is perhaps the most widely accepted theory of economic growth, implies that technological progress is the fundamental source of growth in per-capita income. While early models of growth treated the rate of technological progress as an exogenous variable, more recent ("endogenous growth") models recognize that technological progress depends on investment in research and development (R&D) and on the creation of new products and processes. There is abundant empirical evidence supporting the hypothesis that the growth in conventionally defined per-capita output (or total-factor productivity) is positively related to previous investments in research and development. Griliches and Lichtenberg (1984), for example, found that the most R&D intensive manufacturing industries tend to have the highest rates of growth of output per worker.

In this chapter, we investigate econometrically whether the "other" (unmeasured) half of economic growth—the increase in longevity—can also be explained by a certain kind of technological progress: the development and diffusion of new drugs. Since Nordhaus argues that increased longevity accounts for half the total U.S. economic progress, and Bresnahan and Gordon claim that, in general, "new goods are at the heart of economic progress" (1997: 1), the hypothesis that new drugs deserve a substantial amount of credit for increased longevity seems quite plausible.

Econometric investigations of the impact of technological change are usually hampered by lack of reliable data. In the case of pharmaceuticals, however, it is possible to identify, date, and classify every major and minor innovation since 1939 (because the industry has been strictly regulated by the FDA since then), and to measure the consumption (utilization) of

TABLE 3.2 Number of New Molecular Entities Approved by FDA

Period	Frequency	Percentage	Cumulative Frequency	Cumulative Percentage
1940–44	2	0.2	2	0.2
1945–49	11	1.1	13	1.3
1950–54	116	11.2	129	12.5
1955–59	142	13.7	271	26.2
1960–64	100	9.7	371	35.8
1965–69	53	5.1	424	41.0
1970–74	81	7.8	505	48.8
1975–79	92	8.9	597	57.7
1980–84	98	9.5	695	67.1
1985–89	106	10.2	801	77.4
1990–94	114	11.0	915	88.4
1995–97	120	11.6	1035	100.0

SOURCE: Author's calculations based on unpublished FDA data.
NOTE: Year of approval unknown for 15 NMEs.

about 900 distinct drugs (molecules) since 1980. We obtained from the Food and Drug Administration (by submitting a Freedom of Information Act request) a computerized list of all New Drug Approvals (NDAs) and Abbreviated New Drug Approvals (ANDAs) since 1939. The list includes the NDA or ANDA number, the approval date, the generic and trade names of the drug, the dosage form, route of administration, strength, applicant name, "therapeutic potential" (priority or standard), and "chemical type" (new molecular entity, new formulation, new manufacturer, etc.). This enables us to reconstruct the precise history of pharmaceutical innovation during the last almost 60 years.

We obtain data on the utilization (market shares) of various drugs from the 1980 and 1991 National Ambulatory Medical Care Surveys (NAMCS), which survey doctor-office visits, and the 1993 National Hospital Ambulatory Medical Care Survey (NHAMCS), which surveys visits to hospital outpatient departments and emergency departments.[1] These surveys enable us to estimate the number of drug "mentions" (prescriptions), by molecule, in 1980 and subsequent years.

Time-series data on the number of new molecular entities (NMEs) approved by the FDA are shown in table 3.2. More than half of the 1,035 NMEs that the FDA has approved since its inception were approved after 1974. It is therefore not surprising that, as table 3.2 shows, the distribution of drugs prescribed by physicians changed considerably between 1980 and 1994. Ten of the drugs that were among the top 20 prescribed in 1980 lost that standing by 1994 (see table 3.3). Similarly, ten of the top 20 drugs in 1994 were not in the top 20 in 1980. Some of them, such as albuterol (for which

Table 3.3 Top 20 Drugs Prescribed in Doctor-Office Visits in 1980 and 1994

Rank in 1980	Percentage of 1980 Prescriptions	Percentage of 1994 Prescriptions	Drug	Class
1	2.9	1.4	Hydrochlorothiazide	Diuretics
2	2.3	1.5	Aspirin	General analgesics
3	1.9	x	Penicillin	Penicillins
4	1.8	1.0	Phenylpropanolamine	Nasal decongestants
5	1.8	x	Alcohol	Antitussives, expectorants, mucolytics
6	1.7	1.2	Erythromycin	Erythromycins and lincosamides
7	1.7	1.0	Phenylephrine	Nasal decongestants
8	1.7	3.0	Acetaminophen	General analgesics
9	1.5	0.9	Codeine	Antitussives, expectorants, mucolytics
10	1.4	x	Tetracycline	Tetracyclines
11	1.4	x	Pseudoephedrine	Nasal decongestants
12	1.3	x	Riboflavin	Vitamins, minerals
13	1.3	1.1	Digoxin	Cardiac glycosides
14	1.3	x	Chlorpheniramine	Nasal decongestants
15	1.3	x	Ampicillin	Penicillins
16	1.2	3.8	Amoxicillin	Penicillins
17	1.2	x	Propranolol	Antihypertensive agents
18	1.1	1.2	Furosemide	Diuretics
19	1.1	x	Ergocalciferol	Vitamins, minerals
20	1.1	x	Neomycin	Ocular anti-infective and anti-inflammatory agents
	31		SUM OF TOP 20 DRUGS	

continued

TABLE 3.3 *continued*

Rank in 1994	Percentage of 1994 Prescriptions	Percentage of 1980 Prescriptions	Drug	Class
1	3.8	1.2	Amoxicillin	Penicillins
2	3.0	1.7	Acetaminophen	General analgesics
3	1.6	x	Albuterol	Bronchodilators, antiasthmatics
4	1.5	2.3	Aspirin	General analgesics
5	1.4	x	Ibuprofen	Antiarthritics
6	1.4	2.9	Hydrochlorothiazide	Diuretics
7	1.3	x	Multivitamins General	Vitamins, minerals
8	1.2	1.1	Furosemide	Diuretics
9	1.2	1.7	Erythromycin	Erythromycins and lincosamides
10	1.2	x	Guaifenesin	Antitussives, expectorants, mucolytics
11	1.1	x	Estrogens	Estrogens and progestins
12	1.1	1.3	Digoxin	Cardiac glycosides
13	1.1	x	Prednisone	Adrenal corticosteroids
14	1.0	x	Diltiazem	Antianginal agents
15	1.0	x	Beclomethasone	Unclassified
16	1.0	1.7	Phenylephrine	Nasal decongestants
17	1.0	1.8	Phenylpropanolamine	Nasal decongestants
18	0.9	x	Triamcinolone	Adrenal corticosteroids
19	0.9	1.5	Codeine	Antitussives, expectorants, mucolytics
20	0.9	x	Levothyroxine	Agents used to treat thyroid disease
	27.6		SUM OF TOP 20 DRUGS	

NOTE: x denotes not in top 20 in that year. Total estimated number of prescriptions was 899 million in 1980 and 921 million in 1994.

Schering received FDA approval in 1981), had not yet been approved by the FDA in 1980.

We analyze the relationship *across diseases* between the long-term reduction in life-years lost before age 75 and the relative utilization of new pharmaceutical products. In other words, we investigate whether there were *above-average* reductions in mortality from diseases for which there were above-average utilization rates of new drugs. By combining the FDA and NAMCS data, we can calculate (subject to some measurement problems) *disease-specific* measures of pharmaceutical innovation—that is, quantify the amount of innovation relevant to each disease, since NAMCS reveals the relative frequency with which each drug is used for each disease.

This methodology controls for the effects of any general economic and social trends (such as changes in wealth, nutrition, smoking, or sanitation) that affect *average* mortality. The analysis of mortality change in a cross section of diseases seems quite analogous to the analysis of output or productivity growth in a cross section of industries. Industries produce goods; diseases may be considered "bads," or negative goods. The extent of innovation varies across both industries and diseases, due, in part, to variation in the extent of "technological opportunity."

We estimate this relationship for the entire period 1970–91 and for two subperiods (1970–80 and 1980–91), and for different categories of disease (based on the average age at which people die from the disease). We also distinguish between "drugs that appear (to the Food and Drug Administration) to represent an advance over available therapy" ("priority drugs") and "drugs that appear to have therapeutic qualities similar to those of already marketed drugs" ("standard drugs"). The data we analyze cover all diseases and all (outpatient) drugs, thus allowing us (assuming that our model is correctly specified) to draw general conclusions about the impact of new drugs on longevity, something that cannot be accomplished using existing studies, which are about specific diseases and/or drugs.

In the next section we briefly review some of the previous evidence on the impact of drugs on life expectancy, including anecdotal evidence, a case study of a specific disease (heart attacks), and data from a few clinical studies of specific drugs. In section III we present a simple econometric model for estimating this impact, describe our procedures for constructing the variables included in this model, and discuss issues pertaining to estimation and interpretation of parameter estimates. Estimates of the model and their economic implications are discussed in section IV. The effects of controlling for physician counseling, vaccine availability, and surgical innovation are presented in section V. An estimate of the social rate of return to pharmaceutical innovation is derived in section VI. The final section contains a summary and conclusions.

II. Previous Evidence

Pharmaceutical Research and Manufacturers of America (2001) provides an informal, anecdotal account of the contribution of drug innovation to medical progress in this century. We simply quote their account here:

> Antibiotics and vaccines played a major role in the near eradication of major diseases of the 1920s, including syphilis, diphtheria, whooping cough, measles, and polio. Since 1920, the combined death rate from influenza and pneumonia has been reduced by 85 percent. Despite a recent resurgence of tuberculosis (TB) among the homeless and immuno-suppressed populations, antibiotics have reduced the number of TB deaths to one tenth the levels experienced in the 1960s. Before antibiotics, the typical TB patient was forced to spend three to four years in a sanitarium and faced a 30 to 50 percent chance of death. Today most patients can recover in 6 to 12 months given the full and proper course of antibiotics.
>
> Pharmaceutical discoveries since the 1950s have revolutionized therapy for chronic as well as acute conditions. From 1965 to 1995 cardiovascular drugs such as antihypertensives, diuretics, beta-blockers, and ACE inhibitors drastically reduced deaths from hypertension, hypertensive heart disease, and ischemic heart disease.[2]
>
> Similarly, H2 blockers, proton pump inhibitors and combination therapies cut deaths from ulcers by more than 60 percent. Anti-inflammatory therapies and bronchodilators reduced deaths from emphysema by 31 percent and provided relief for those with asthma. Had no progress been made against disease between 1960 and 1990, roughly 335,000 more people would have died in 1990 alone.
>
> Since 1960, vaccines have greatly reduced the incidence of childhood diseases—many of which once killed or disabled thousands of American children. Likewise, vaccines for Hepatitis B introduced during the 1980s now protect a new generation of American children from a leading cause of liver disease. (chap. 1, pp. 2–4)

Brand-new evidence indicates that new drug therapies have sharply reduced fatalities from AIDS:

> AIDS deaths in New York City plummeted by 48 percent last year, accelerating earlier gains attributed to improved drug therapies. . . . [T]he declines crossed sex and racial lines, suggesting that the new therapies were reaching all segments of the AIDS population. National figures for the first six months of 1997 also showed a similar sharp decline, 44 percent, from

> the corresponding period of 1996. . . . Theoretically, the decline in AIDS deaths could have resulted from prevention efforts or some unknown factor. . . . But the likeliest explanation is expanded use of combinations of newer and older drugs that began to be introduced in recent years, New York City and Federal health officials said.[3]

The anecdotal evidence about the impact of new drugs on mortality is in stark contrast to econometric evidence presented by Skinner and Wennberg (2000) about the relationship between total medical expenditure in the last six months of life and outcomes.[4] They analyzed this relationship using both a 20 percent sample of all Medicare enrollees and a 5 percent sample of very ill Medicare patients hospitalized with heart attack (acute myocardial infarction, or AMI), stroke, gastrointestinal bleeding, and lung cancer. Per-capita medical expenditures vary considerably across regions. For example, average Medicare expenditures on elderly patients in the last six months of life are twice as high in Miami as they are in Minneapolis, and the average number of visits to specialists is five times as high. However, intensive econometric analysis provided "no evidence that higher levels of spending translates into extended survival" (p. 188).[5]

Cutler, McClellan, and Newhouse (1998) performed a case study of a single but important disease—heart attacks—by compiling results about the effect of various treatments on mortality from the universe of clinical studies published in the medical literature. They found that changes in the medical treatments used in the acute management of AMI account for approximately 55 percent of the reduction in mortality that has occurred in AMI cases between 1975 and 1995, with the bulk of this improvement (50 percent) coming from pharmaceuticals. Three drug therapies—aspirin, thrombolytics, and beta-blockers—resulted in the largest improvements in heart attack mortality. They also noted that "the long-term improvement in mortality may be even more substantial than the acute improvements" (p. 17). Many innovations have occurred in the treatment of patients whose heart sustained substantial damage from the attack, including drug therapies such as ACE inhibitors and anticoagulation therapy, but limited quantitative evidence makes it difficult to quantify these important effects. Cutler, McClellan, and Newhouse's findings are extremely interesting; as they observe, "the important question is whether [their] results generalize to other types of medical care" (p. 34).

Frech and Miller (1999) examined the relationship between pharmaceutical expenditures per capita (in 1990 U.S. dollars) and life expectancy at different ages (birth, 40 years, and 60 years), controlling for a number of other variables and using longitudinal country-level data for 21 Organisation for Economic Co-Operation and Development (OECD) countries. They found a significant positive relationship between pharmaceutical expenditure and life expectancy at age 40, and a stronger one at age 60. But because older people tend to consume more drugs, this correlation may reflect the effect of life expectancy on pharmaceutical expenditure as well as the effect of pharmaceutical expenditure on life expectancy. The following table shows the mean number of medications ordered by physicians in office visits, by patient age:[6]

Patient Age	Mean Number of Medications Ordered
0–17 years	0.986
18–44	0.948
45–64	1.332
65+	1.652

45- to 64-year-old patients receive 37 percent more medications per visit, and patients over the age of 65 receive 70 percent more, than patients under age 45. (Moreover, older patients probably visit doctors more frequently.) Hence, the coefficient on pharmaceutical expenditure in Frech and Miller's life expectancy equation overstates the effect of the former on life expectancy.[7]

Clinical trials, of which there have undoubtedly been thousands, have provided a great deal of evidence about the impact on mortality of new drugs. One such study was the West of Scotland Coronary Prevention Study of 6,595 ostensibly healthy men aged 45 through 64 years. The results of the study indicated that

> [the cholesterol-lowering drug] pravastatin reduces the risk of heart attack and death in a broad range of people, not just those with established heart disease, but also among those who are at risk for their first heart attack.... Over five years, those [healthy individuals] treated with ... pravastatin suffered 31 percent fewer nonfatal heart attacks and at least 28 percent fewer deaths from heart disease than a comparable group of men who received a placebo.... In previous studies, pravastatin had been shown to reduce the risk of heart attack by 62 percent in patients with high cholesterol who already had heart disease.[8]

Evidence from clinical trials is extremely useful and of great scientific value, but some public health experts argue that clinical-trial results cannot simply be extrapolated to real-world experience. Also, there does not appear to be any way to summarize or combine all the clinical-trial evidence to shed light on the average or aggregate contribution of pharmaceutical innovation to mortality reduction and economic growth, which is our goal.

III. Model Specification and Estimation

To assess the contribution of pharmaceutical innovation to the reduction in ("premature") mortality of Americans, I will perform several different analyses of the relationship, across diseases, between the relative utilization of new drugs and the reduction in life-years lost, including estimation of models of the form

$$(1)\quad \ln\,(\mathrm{LYL}_{t-k}/\mathrm{LYL}_t) = \alpha + \beta(\mathrm{DRUGS}_{t-k,t}/\mathrm{DRUGS}_{.t}) + \varepsilon$$

using data on a cross-section of diseases, where LYL_t = aggregate life-years lost before age 75 divided by population in year t (defined below); $\mathrm{DRUGS}_{t-k,t}$ = the number of drugs prescribed in year t that received FDA approval in year $t-k$ or later; and $\mathrm{DRUGS}_{.t} = \Sigma_k \mathrm{DRUGS}_{t-k,t}$ = the total number of drugs prescribed in year t. For example, if $t = 1991$ and $k = 21$, the equation becomes

$$\ln\,(\mathrm{LYL}_{1970}/\mathrm{LYL}_{1991}) = \alpha + \beta(\mathrm{DRUGS}_{1970,1991}/\mathrm{DRUGS}_{.1991}) + \varepsilon.$$

The dependent variable is the percentage reduction in life-years lost between 1970 and 1991. As Murray and Lopez (1996: 6–7) observe, "since the late 1940s, researchers have generally agreed that . . . time (in years) lost through premature death" is the appropriate way to measure the burden of premature mortality. However, "in order to measure burden, a society has to decide what the ideal or reference status should be. This involves [deciding], how long 'should' people live? If health researchers are to estimate how many years of life are lost through death at any given age, they must decide on the number of years for which a person at that age should expect to survive in the ideal, or reference, population. That could be, for example, 60, 80, or 90 years from birth." The "reference age" used by the National Center for Health Statistics and the World Health Organization is 65 years. For making international comparisons, Murray and Lopez use reference ages of 82.5 years for women and 80 years for men—life expectancy in the world's longest-surviving population, the Japanese.[9] I will use an intermediate value of the reference age: 75 years. (Our main findings are essentially unchanged when a reference age of 65 years is used instead.) The mortality measure that we will analyze is life-years lost before age 75 per population (LYL). This measure is defined as follows:

$$\mathrm{LYL} = \left\{\sum_i \max(0, 75 - \mathrm{age\_death}_i)\right\}/\mathrm{POP},$$

where age_death_i is the age of death of the ith decedent, and POP is the population. For example, in a population of 1,000, if in a given year 2 people die at age 60, 3 people die at age 70, and 5 people die at age 75 or later, $LYL = [2(75 - 50) + 3(75 - 60) + 5(0)]/1000 = 95/1000 = .095$. This measure gives a great deal of weight to deaths that occur at early ages (especially infant mortality), and no weight at all to deaths beyond age 75.

Data on LYL, by disease, were computed from the 1970, 1980, and 1991 Vital Statistics-Mortality Detail Files. Each record in the file includes a single *International Classification of Diseases, Ninth Revision (ICD-9)* code to indicate the cause of death.[10] We used this code to calculate the various mortality statistics by *ICD-9* disease, by year.[11]

The independent variable in equation (1) is the fraction of drugs prescribed in 1991 that were approved in 1970 or later. We hypothesize that the greater the percentage of drugs prescribed in 1991 that were not yet available in the "baseline" year (1970), the greater the reduction in mortality since the baseline year.[12] We recognize that, due to a heterogeneous rate of obsolescence of drugs across diseases, a given value of the new-drug share may reflect varying degrees of drug improvement. Suppose that for disease *A*, there is only one drug approved after 1970, and this has a 50 percent market share in 1991. For disease *B*, one new drug is approved in 1975, and it captures 50 percent of the market; another drug is approved in 1985, and all patients on the first drug (and only those patients) switch to the second drug. Disease *B* has the same new-drug share in 1991 as disease *A*, even though it has benefited from two waves of innovation rather than one. Although diseases with a given new-drug share may have different rates of drug improvement, we postulate that, on average, diseases having higher new-drug shares have higher rates of drug improvement.

This specification is very consistent with the most widely accepted theory of economic growth, the Solow model. As Mankiw (1992: 102) observes, the Solow model implies that "once the economy is in a steady state, the rate of growth of output per worker depends only on the rate of technological progress." We argued above that mortality reduction may be interpreted as a component or form of per-capita income (or output) growth. As Bresnahan and Gordon (1997: 1) observe, "new goods are at the heart of economic progress," so the fraction of all goods (drugs) consumed that are new appears to be a very appropriate measure of the rate of technological progress.

Although there is only one variable on the right-hand side of equation (1), the validity of our analysis is *not* based on the assumption that pharmaceutical innovation is the *only* source of mortality reduction. Changes in mortality are likely to depend upon a number of factors, such as changes in wealth, changes in environmental quality, and changes in the prevalence of smoking. If the changes in these other factors were "across the board" changes—they did not vary across diseases—then their effect would be captured by the intercept term (α), which reflects the mean reduction in mortality not explained by pharmaceutical innovation (α = mean (Y) – β mean(X)).[13] Our estimates of, and hypothesis tests about, the effect of pharmaceutical innovation on mortality reduction (β) depend entirely on diseases' *deviations from sample means* and not at all on the mean values of Y and X.

It is likely, of course, that changes in these other factors vary to some extent across diseases. If determinants of mortality change other than pharmaceutical innovation are uncorrelated across diseases with pharmaceutical innovation, then equation (1) still yields unbiased estimates of β.[14] There does not appear to be good reason to expect changes in most determinants of mortality other than drug innovation to be correlated across diseases with drug innovation. It is not obvious, for example, why diseases for which many new drugs were developed should be the ones whose sufferers reduced smoking the most or whose wealth increased the most.[15] Ideally, one might estimate an expanded version of equation (1) that includes a large number of other potential determinants of mortality change. Many of these are difficult or impossible to measure at the disease level. But there are several potentially relevant covariates that we can measure, and will include in a more elaborate model of mortality reduction (presented in section V), to check the robustness of our estimates. These are (1) the probability that the physician provides nonmedication therapy—primarily counseling and education—to the patient; (2) a dummy variable indicating whether a vaccine is available for a disease; and (3) the rate of introduction of new surgical procedures.

The *ICD-9* classification includes three kinds of codes: disease (or natural causes of death) codes (000–799), nature of injury codes (800–999), and external causes of death codes (E800–E999).[16] In the mortality files, only the first and last sets of codes are used, whereas in the ambulatory care surveys, only the first and second sets of codes are used. We therefore confine our analysis to diseases (natural causes of death).

Equation (1) can be estimated using data at different levels of aggregation, such as either *ICD-9* two-digit- or three-digit-level disease data (at which there are approximately 80 and 1,000 diseases, respectively). There is no theoretical reason to believe that the parameter estimates should depend in any particular way on the level of aggregation. As a practical matter, greater disaggregation has both advantages and disadvantages.[17] The advantages are that the number of observations (and statistical degrees of freedom) increases, and that each observation is less heterogeneous (covers a less diverse group of diseases). The disadvantages are that both measurement or classification error (in the dependent variable) and sampling error (in the independent variable) are amplified. Murray and Lopez (1996: 16) note that "miscoding of deaths—that is, assigning the death to the 'wrong' cause in *ICD-9,* occurs regularly in all countries with registration systems. For example, the choice of codes for cardiovascular diseases is notoriously variable between industrialized countries, with a significant proportion of ischaemic heart disease deaths being attributed to ill-defined codes such as heart failure." Since we are analyzing *changes* in mortality, by disease, our estimates would not be affected by systematic (permanent) miscoding of deaths, for example if ischaemic heart disease deaths were always underestimated by 25 percent. But the miscoding of cause of death is likely to have a random component as well, and the probability that a three-digit diagnosis is wrong is undoubtedly much greater than the probability that a two-digit diagnosis is wrong. The greater the extent of miscoding, the lower the precision of our parameter estimates. As we will describe below, the data we use on the new-drug share are *estimates* based on random 1 in 10,000 or 1 in 16,000 samples of doctor-office visits. The greater the extent of disaggregation by disease, the smaller the number of visits in each disease category, and the larger the sampling error associated with each observation. Amplification of sampling error biases the coefficient on the new-drug share toward 0; it increases the probability of finding no relationship between pharmaceutical innovation and mortality reduction when there really is a relationship. Since the statistically optimal level of disease aggregation is not obvious a priori, we tried performing the analysis at both the two-digit and the three-digit level. The two-digit-level estimates were more significant and robust, so these are the ones that we will present.

Estimates of $\text{DRUGS}_{t-k,t}$—the number of drugs prescribed in year t that received FDA approval in year $t - k$ or later—were obtained by combining data from several sources. The first data source was the NAMCS, which contains records of 46,081 doctor-office visits in 1980 and of 33,795 visits in 1991. Each record lists the drugs (if any) prescribed by the physician. Up to five drugs may be coded. If a drug is a combination drug, its ingredients (up to five) are coded, so that as many as 25 ingredients (molecular entities) could be coded in a single record. The record also lists up to three diagnoses (*ICD-9* codes) along with a "drug weight," which is used to compute population-level estimates of drug utilization from the sample data. Because multiple diagnoses may be cited in a given record, we sometimes confront the problem of "allocating" the mention of a drug across diagnoses. We adopted the simple, feasible approach of *equal* allocation of the drug mention across the several diagnoses. For example, if two diagnoses were cited and the drug weight was 10,000, we replaced the mention of that drug by two mentions of the same drug, one for each diagnosis, each with a drug weight of 5,000; this procedure does not change the population estimates of drug mentions by molecule. We then calculated estimates of the aggregate number of prescriptions by molecule and patient diagnosis.

To calculate the fraction of drugs that were approved by the FDA after a certain date, we linked these data to a list of all New Drug Applications since 1939 provided by the administration. Both files included the scientific name of the drug, and the FDA file included the date the drug was first approved as a new molecular entity (NME).[18]

Figure 3.1 shows the distribution of drugs prescribed in 1994 by year of FDA approval. Almost half the drugs prescribed in 1994 were approved after 1979; about a quarter were approved after 1984.

Only patient visits to doctors' offices are covered by NAMCS. In 1992 the National Center for Health Statistics began conducting a similar survey (NHAMCS) of visits to hospital outpatient departments and emergency rooms, the number of which is believed to have grown much more rapidly during the last 10 to 15 years than the number of doctor-office visits. Doctor-office visits still accounted for more than 80 percent of total visits in the 1990s,[19] but we sought to improve the precision of our estimates of the new-drug proportion by combining information from the NAMCS and NHAMCS surveys. We calculated the share of new drugs in total drugs prescribed in the consolidated sample as well as separately for each of the three outpatient "sectors."[20]

In the course of the approval process, the FDA classifies drugs into two categories: "priority review drugs"—drugs that appear to represent an advance over available therapy—and "standard review drugs"—drugs that appear to have therapeutic qualities similar to those of already marketed drugs.[21] One might reasonably hypothesize that new priority drugs have a larger impact on mortality than new standard drugs. Indeed, whether a new drug is expected to reduce mortality may be one of the FDA's classification criteria.[22] We will test this hypothesis by estimating versions of equation (1) in which the new-drug share is disaggregated into two components: the shares of new priority drugs and new standard drugs in total drugs prescribed at the end of the period.

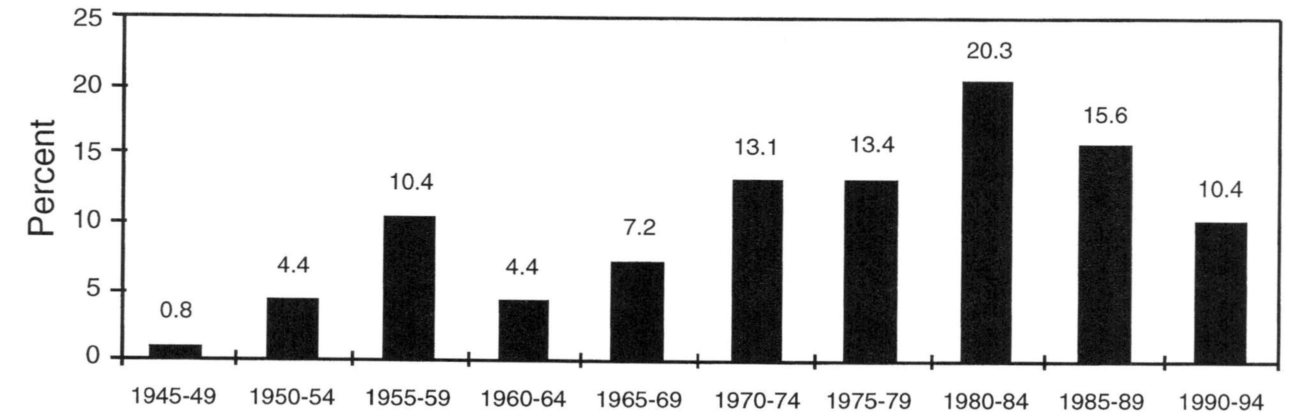

FIGURE 3.1: Distribution of drugs prescribed in 1994, by year of FDA approval

We have mortality data for 1970, 1980, and 1991, and data on the vintage distribution of drugs prescribed in both 1980 and 1991, so we can estimate equation (1) for the entire 21-year period 1970–91 and for the two subperiods, 1970–80 and 1980–91. Since some drugs may have to be consumed for a sustained period of time for their full health benefits to be realized, it would not be surprising if the longer-term estimated relationship were stronger than either of the two shorter-term relationships.[23] Moreover, the data indicate that the important (in terms of market demand) new drugs introduced in the 1970s and the 1980s were targeted at different diseases and patient populations. The top panel of table 3.4 shows the percentage distribution by drug class of drugs prescribed in 1980 that were less than 10 years old. The top three classes of new drugs were pain relievers, antimicrobial agents, and respiratory tract medications; together these accounted for about half of new drug prescriptions. The lower panel of the table shows the percentage distribution by drug class of drugs prescribed in 1991 that were less than 11 years old. Cardiovascular-renal drugs accounted for over a third of the new drugs prescribed in 1991, more than four times their share of new drugs in 1980; the new-drug share of hormones also increased sharply. As table 3.5 indicates, the average age of patients receiving drugs varies significantly across drug classes. The average age of patients receiving drugs used for relief of pain—the largest new drug class in 1980—is 48, while the average age of patients receiving cardiovascular-renal drugs—the largest new drug class in 1991—is 66. Further calculations show that, consistent with this finding, the average age of patients receiving any new drug in 1980 was 44, whereas the average age of patients receiving any new drug in 1991 was 52. Since the clientele for drugs introduced in the 1980s tended to be older than the clientele for drugs introduced in the 1970s, one would expect the mortality reductions in the 1980s to be more concentrated among older patients. We will test this prediction by estimating equation (1) for different categories of diseases, classified by the mean age at which people die from the disease.

The dependent variable in equation (1) is the log-change (growth rate) of per-capita life-years lost, ln $(\text{LYL}_{t-k}/\text{LYL}_t)$. The variance of the dependent variable is strongly inversely related to the average size or burden of the disease, $(\text{LYL}_{t-k} + \text{LYL}_t)/2$. The growth rates of diseases affecting a relatively small number of people are likely to be much farther away (in both directions) from the mean than those of major diseases.[24] To correct for heteroskedasticity, the equation is estimated via weighted least squares, where the weight is $(\text{LYL}_{t-k} + \text{LYL}_t)/2$. Diseases that are responsible for larger average numbers of life-years lost are given more weight.

TABLE 3.4 Percentage Distribution of Drugs Prescribed in 1980 That Were less than 10 Years Old, by Drug Class

Drugs used for relief of pain	19.7
Antimicrobial agents	17.1
Respiratory tract drugs	11.2
Psychopharmacologic drugs	9.5
Skin/mucous membrane	8.7
Cardiovascular-renal drugs	8.6
Metabolic and nutrient agents	8.0
Gastrointestinal agents	6.7
Ophthalmic drugs	4.0
Anesthetic drugs	2.3
Neurologic drugs	1.7
Unclassified/miscellaneous	1.2
Oncolytics	0.7
Antidotes	0.2
Hormones and agents affecting hormonal mechanisms	0.2
Antiparasitic agents	0.1

Percentage Distribution of Drugs Prescribed in 1991 That Were less than 11 Years Old, by Drug Class

Cardiovascular-renal drugs	36.5
Respiratory tract drugs	12.6
Hormones and agents affecting hormonal mechanisms	10.8
Psychopharmacologic drugs	9.9
Antimicrobial agents	7.3
Drugs used for relief of pain	5.9
Gastrointestinal agents	5.1
Skin/mucous membrane	4.7
Metabolic and nutrient agents	4.5
Ophthalmic drugs	2.5
Oncolytics	0.2
Neurologic drugs	0.0
Otologic drugs	0.0

There are a number of reasons why estimates of the parameters of equation (1) might be biased. Several considerations imply that estimates of β will be biased toward 0, and therefore that our hypothesis tests will be strong tests. Measurement error in the new-drug proportion is perhaps the main reason to suspect downward bias.[25] The variable we calculate ($\text{DRUGS}_{t-k,t}/\text{DRUGS}_{.t}$) may be a noisy measure of the true share of new drugs for a number of reasons.

- Sampling error: the NAMCS survey is a random 1 in 10,000 or 1 in 16,000 sample of doctor-office visits;

TABLE 3.5 Average Age (in 1991) of Patients Receiving Drugs, by Drug Class

Cardiovascular-renal drugs	66.4
Ophthalmic drugs	60.9
Hematologic agents	57.6
Oncolytics	57.0
Gastrointestinal agents	53.3
Anesthetic drugs	52.2
Psychopharmacologic drugs	50.9
Hormones and agents affecting hormonal mechanisms	49.5
Antiparasitic agents	48.3
Drugs used for relief of pain	48.2
Neurologic drugs	46.4
Unclassified/miscellaneous	43.6
Otologic drugs	40.7
Metabolic and nutrient agents	39.1
Antidotes	36.8
Skin/mucous membrane	36.2
Respiratory tract drugs	32.0
Antimicrobial agents	29.6
Radiopharmaceutical/contrast media	20.4
Immunologic agent	12.4

SOURCE: Author's calculations based on 1991 NAMCS file.

- Coverage: our drug data refer only to doctor-office visits in 1980, and to outpatient visits in 1991 (no inpatient data), and primarily refer to prescription rather than over-the-counter drugs;[26]
- Misallocation: drugs assigned to the wrong diseases because of errors in allocation procedure described above (when there are multiple diagnoses); and
- Noncompliance: Our data refer to drugs prescribed by physicians, not drugs consumed by patients. It is estimated that only about half the medicine prescribed is taken correctly. The National Council on Patient Information & Education divides the problem of noncompliance into two categories: acts of omission and acts of commission. Acts of omission include never filling a prescription; taking less than the prescribed dosage; taking the drug less frequently than prescribed; taking medicine "holidays"; and stopping the regime too soon. Acts of commission include overuse, sharing medicines, and consuming food, drink, or other medicines that can interact with the prescribed drug.[27]

It is plausible that reverse causality (endogenous innovation), as well as measurement error in the independent variable, could bias estimates of

β toward 0. Suppose that there is a significant anticipated increase in fatalities from a certain disease (such as AIDS), and that this prospect stimulates a high rate of development and diffusion of new drugs targeted at that disease. Behavior of this sort would reduce the probability of observing a positive relationship across diseases between mortality reduction and new drug utilization.

We can also think of one possible reason for the least-squares estimate of β to be biased upward, in other words, to overestimate the average contribution of pharmaceutical innovation to medical progress. Suppose that the rate of progress (P) against a disease is a deterministic, concave function of research expenditure on the disease (X) and research productivity (π): $P_i = \pi_i X_i^{\theta}$, where i denotes disease i and $0 < \theta < 1$. Taking logarithms of the progress function, $\ln P_i = \ln \pi_i + \theta \ln X_i$. Suppose that disease-specific research productivity (π_i) is unobservable. If π_i were uncorrelated with research expenditure X_i, the least-squares estimate of the elasticity of progress with respect to spending θ would be unbiased. However, as argued in Lichtenberg (2001a), if decision makers are efficiently allocating the research budget across diseases (i.e. to maximize the total number of people cured of all diseases), they should devote more research funds to diseases where research productivity is high. Therefore π_i and X_i are likely to be positively correlated, and the slope coefficient from the simple regression of $\ln P_i$ on $\ln X_i$ would overestimate θ. More progress tends to be made on diseases with high research funding in part because those are the diseases where research productivity is highest. We are examining the relationship between progress and the new drug proportion, not research expenditure, but the latter two variables are likely to be positively correlated.[28]

IV. Empirical Results

Descriptive statistics for the dependent and independent variables for two-digit *ICD-9* diseases over the 1970–91 period and the two subperiods are shown in table 3.6.

The weighted-average decline in per-capita LYL during the period 1970–91 was 42.9 percent [$= 1 - \exp(-.561)$]; 5 percent of diseases exhibited a decline of more than 85 percent; however, 5 percent of diseases exhibited an increase of at least 117.3 percent.

As table 3.7 indicates, the mean shares of drugs prescribed in 1991 that were approved after 1970 and 1980, computed from NAMCS data, are quite close to the shares of drugs approved by the beginning of 1991 that were approved after 1970 and 1980, computed from FDA data.

TABLE 3.6

Variable	N	Mean (wtd)	5%	25%	Median	75%	95%
ln (LYL_{1970}/LYL_{1991})	75	.561	−.776	.101	.563	1.267	1.955
ln (LYL_{1970}/LYL_{1980})	75	.339	−.704	−.026	.432	.979	1.970
ln (LYL_{1980}/LYL_{1991})	78	.204	−.357	.025	.185	.419	.786
$(DRUGS_{1970,1991}/DRUGS_{.1991})$	75	.627	.337	.490	.584	.693	.904
$(DRUGS_{1970,1980}/DRUGS_{.1980})$	75	.225	.046	.106	.190	.284	.564
$(DRUGS_{1980,1991}/DRUGS_{.1991})$	78	.365	.084	.241	.317	.441	.637

TABLE 3.7

Period	% of Drugs Prescribed at the End of the Period That Were Approved since the Beginning of the Period	% of Drugs Approved by the End of the Period That Were Approved since the Beginning of the Period
1970–91	62.7	65.7
1970–80	22.5	43.0
1980–91	36.5	39.7

While these shares need not be close to one another, their proximity is reassuring. However, the mean share of drugs prescribed in 1980 that were approved after 1970 is much smaller than (about half) the share of drugs approved by the beginning of 1980 that were approved after 1970. This suggests that (for unknown reasons) the new-drug share data may be understated, by a factor of about 2, for the 1970–80 period. If this were the case, it would not affect the level of significance of our test of the null hypothesis of no relationship between the new-drug share and mortality reduction.[29] However, it would cause the point estimate of β to be twice as large as it would be in the absence of understatement. Since the 1970–91 and 1980–91 new-drug share data do not appear to be understated, the *ratio* of the estimate of β for 1970–80 to the estimate in 1980–91 (or 1970–91) would be overstated by a factor of 2.

Table 3.8 presents illustrative data for two diseases—*ICD-9* codes 20 (malignant neoplasm of lymphatic and hematopoietic tissue) and 48 (pneumonia and influenza)—which exhibited very different patterns of mortality reduction and new drug utilization during the period 1970–91. The table shows the five drugs most frequently prescribed in 1991 to patients diagnosed as having each of the diseases.[30] Only one of the top five drugs prescribed in 1991 for *ICD-9* code 20 was approved after 1970, and the decline in per-capita life-years lost (28 percent) was below the average for all diseases (43 percent).[31] In contrast, *all* of the top five drugs prescribed to patients diagnosed as having pneumonia and influenza were new drugs,

Table 3.8 Five Drugs Most Frequently Prescribed in 1991 to Patients with Two Different Diagnoses

Percentage of Total Prescriptions in 1991	Drug	Drug Class	1 = Post-1970 Approval 0 = 1970 or Earlier Approval	FDA Approval Date	P = Priority Status Drug S = Standard Drug
Diagnosis = Pneumonia and influenza (ICD-9 code 48) (74% reduction in per-capita life-years lost, 1970–91)					
13.34	Amoxicillin	Antibacterial	1	01/18/74	P
10.35	Albuterol	Bronchodilator	1	05/01/81	P
6.75	Ibuprofen	Anti-inflammatory	1	09/19/74	P
6.13	Cefaclor	Antibacterial	1	04/04/79	S
5.34	Ceftriaxone	Antibacterial	1	12/21/84	P
Diagnosis = Malignant neoplasm of lymphatic and hematopoietic tissue (ICD-9 code 20) (28% reduction in per-capita life-years lost, 1970–91)					
8.16	Cyclophosphamide	Antineoplastic	0	11/16/59	P
7.66	Prednisone	Glutocorticoid	0	09/15/55	P
5.65	Vincristine	Antineoplastic	1	03/07/84	P
5.13	Digoxin	Cardiotonic	0	11/16/54	P
4.70	Allopurinol	Xanthine Oxidase Inhibitor	0	08/19/66	P

and the decline in per-capita life-years lost (74 percent) was well above average. The data for these two diseases are consistent with the hypothesis that utilization of new drugs reduces mortality, but we need to analyze data on the full cross section of diseases in order to have meaningful, general tests of this hypothesis.

Key econometric results are summarized in table 3.9. The first part of the table reports estimates of our basic model (equation [1]) by period. The second part reports estimates of models in which we allow priority and standard drugs to have different effects on mortality. The third part reports the results of estimating the basic model separately for three different groups of diseases, classified by the mean age at which people die from the disease.

Part I of the table indicates a highly significant positive relationship between the new-drug share and mortality reduction in all three periods. The magnitude and significance of the effect of the new-drug share on mortality reduction is much higher in 1970–80 than it is in 1980–91. As noted above, the ratio of the 1970–80 point estimate of β to the 1980–91 estimate may be overstated by a factor of about 2 due to apparent systematic underestimation of the new-drug share in the first period. But even in the second

TABLE 3.9 Estimates of the Relationship across Diseases between Relative Utilization of New Drugs and Reduction in Life-Years Lost, by Period

Period:	1970–80	1980–91	1970–91
		I. Basic Model	
β	2.069	0.378	2.866
	(3.85)	(2.34)	(7.06)
Weighted R^2	.1687	.0670	.4058
		II. Priority vs. Standard Drugs	
Priority	3.306	0.429	2.840
	(5.81)	(1.88)	(7.13)
Standard	−0.245	0.351	1.965
	(0.33)	(1.53)	(2.72)
Prob>F:	0.0001	0.8082	0.1287
		III. Estimates by Disease Group, Classified by Mean Age at which People Die from the Disease	
Low age	6.577	−0.077	2.796
	(7.89)	(0.33)	(5.66)
Middle age	2.920	0.573	1.451
	(2.86)	(1.08)	(1.09)
High age	−0.436	1.024	2.910
	(0.79)	(3.49)	(2.85)

NOTE: *t*-statistics are in parentheses.

period, we can reject the null hypothesis of no relationship between these two variables at about the 2 percent level. The magnitude and significance of β is larger over the entire 21-year period than it is in either of the two subperiods. This is consistent with the view that the long-run effects of new drugs on mortality are larger than the short-run effects. Over 40 percent of the variation across diseases in the 1970–91 reduction in mortality is explained by the new-drug share.

We wanted to ensure that our estimates were not unduly affected by a small number of highly influential observations. Following Belsley, Kuh, and Welsch (1980), we used the studentized residual with the current observation deleted (RSTUDENT) as the measure of that observation's influence. This statistic is approximately distributed as standard normal,[32] so that if RSTUDENT is greater than 2, "the particular observation may deserve scrutiny as perhaps not conforming to the model" (Greene, 1997: 445). Estimating the 1970–91 model excluding 7 observations for which the absolute value of RSTUDENT exceeds 2[33] reduces β, but not dramatically—by about 25 percent, from 2.87 to 2.14. The coefficient remains highly

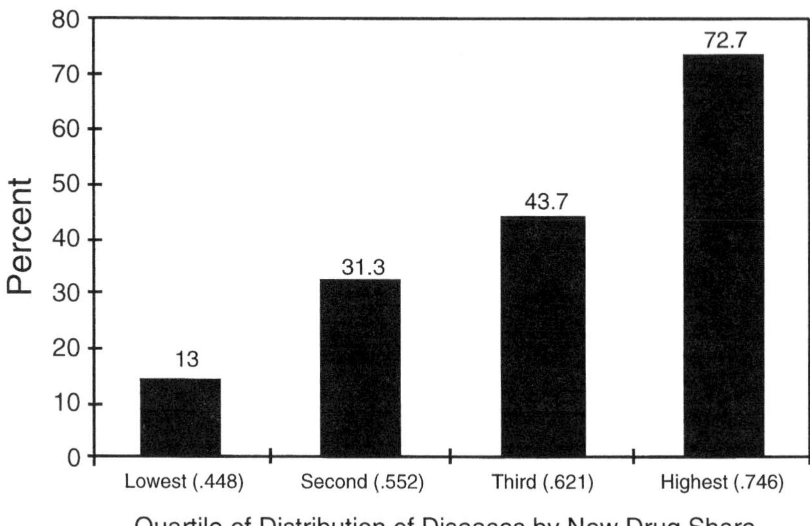

FIGURE 3.2: Mean 1970–91 reduction in life-years lost, by diseases grouped by new drug share

significant ($t = 4.26$). Moreover, Greene (p. 411) states that there is a "general principle that allowing the data and the values of sample test statistics to dictate the form of the model can lead to estimators with demonstrably poor statistical properties," and that "there is a certain danger in singling out particular observations for scrutiny or even elimination from the sample on the basis of statistical results that are based on those data. At the extreme, this may invalidate the usual inference procedures" (p. 415).

An alternative way of analyzing this relationship is to group diseases into a number of categories on the basis of the new-drug share, and to calculate the mean reduction in mortality for each group of diseases. The results from performing this procedure on the 1970–91 data with the number of groups equal to 4 are summarized in figure 3.2. The mean percentage reduction in life-years lost for the 19 diseases with the highest relative utilization of new drugs (whose mean new-drug share was 74.6 percent) was over five times as great—72.7 percent versus 13.0 percent—as the mean percentage reduction in life-years lost for the 19 diseases with the lowest relative utilization of new drugs (whose mean new-drug share was 44.8 percent).

The estimates in part II of table 3.9 indicate that in the 1970–80 period, only priority drugs had a statistically significant effect on mortality reduction. In the 1980–91 period, the coefficient on priority drugs is larger than the coefficient on standard drugs, but we cannot reject the hypothesis that the effects of the two types of drugs are the same. The same is true for the 1970–91 period as a whole, so the data provide only weak support for the view that new priority drugs reduce mortality more than new standard drugs.

The estimates in part III of the table indicate that in the 1970–80 period, new drugs reduced mortality in the lowest and middle thirds of the age distribution of diseases—especially in the former—but not in the highest third of the distribution. In contrast, in the 1980–91 period, new drugs had a significant positive effect on mortality reduction only in the highest third of the age distribution. Hence, new drugs appear to have reduced mortality in all three age categories in one of the two periods. In tables 3.4 and 3.5 we showed that the drugs introduced in the 1980s tended to be targeted at older patients than the drugs introduced in the 1970s, so the "vintage-age interaction" evident in table 3.9 is not at all surprising.

V. The Effects of Controlling for Physician Counseling, Vaccine Availability, and Surgical Innovation

As discussed earlier, the (simple regression) coefficients on pharmaceutical innovation presented in table 3.9 could be biased due to failure to control for other determinants of mortality reduction. Improved patient knowledge about the impact of behavior on health is a potentially important source of mortality reduction. Although this knowledge can be acquired in a number of ways (e.g. via the mass media), counseling by physicians is likely to be a major means of its acquisition. According to 1991 NAMCS data, physicians provide therapeutic services other than medication in about one-third of office visits (they prescribe medications in about two-thirds of visits). Most of these nonmedication therapeutic services are in the form of counseling and education; the kinds of counseling and education offered are as follows:

Type of Counseling/Education	Percentage of Office Visits in which Provided
Diet	11.4%
Exercise	8.2
Cholesterol reduction	3.1
Weight reduction	3.8
Drug abuse	0.2
Alcohol abuse	0.5
Smoking cessation	1.9
Family/Social	1.9
Growth/Development	3.1
Family planning	0.8
Other counseling	8.3

The probability that nonmedication therapeutic services are offered varies according to patient diagnosis. For example, some kind of nonmedication therapy is provided to almost half of patients with hypertension, but to only 10 percent of patients with upper respiratory tract diseases. We will attempt to control for the effect of improved patient knowledge by including as a covariate the fraction of 1991 patients receiving nonmedication therapeutic services (denoted NON_MED%).

There is good reason to believe that the development and diffusion of *vaccines,* as well as drugs, contributes to mortality reduction. The NAMCS file includes data on vaccine utilization; the vaccines cited in the 1991 file are as follows:

Vaccine	Estimated Number of Vaccinations in 1991
Influenza virus	2,725,489
Diph Pertussis Tetanus	943,313
Polio	683,140
Haemophilus B	525,842
Pneumococcal	214,401
Measles Virus	48,484
Mumps Virus	34,335
Rabies	22,252
Bcg	14,966

Unlike a drug, it would not make sense to link a vaccine with the patient's *current* diagnosis, since a vaccine is administered to *prevent* the person from receiving that diagnosis. Vaccines are therefore excluded from the pharmaceutical variable ($\text{DRUGS}_{t-k,t}/\text{DRUGS}_{.t}$) in equation (1). In order to control (admittedly imperfectly) for the effect of vaccine availability on mortality reduction, we included a dummy variable (denoted VACCINE) equal to 1 for diseases for which a vaccine was available in 1991, and equal to 0 for other diseases.[34]

The third potential nonpharmaceutical source of mortality reduction we can account for is the rate of introduction of new surgical procedures. Using data from the 1980 and 1991 National Hospital Discharge Surveys, we construct an index (denoted NEWSURG), by disease, of the rate at which new surgical procedures were introduced during the period 1980–91.[35] Let N_{ijt} represent the number of times surgical procedure i was performed on patients with two-digit diagnosis j in year t ($t = 1980, 1991$). Then $N_{.jt} = \Sigma_i N_{ijt}$ denotes the total number of surgical procedures performed on patients with diagnosis j in year t, and $n_{ijt} = N_{ijt}/N_{.jt}$ denotes

TABLE 3.10 Effect of Controlling for Counseling /Education and Vaccine Availability in 1991 on 1970–91 Mortality Reduction

Column:	(1)	(2)	(3)	(4)
$(DRUGS_{1970,1991}/DRUGS_{.1991})$	2.87			2.43
	(7.06)			(5.21)
NON_MED%		1.85		0.95
		(3.41)		(1.81)
VACCINE			0.52	0.37
			(1.39)	(1.13)
Weighted R^2	.4058	.1393	.0261	.4343

NOTE: *t*-statistics are in parentheses. NON_MED% denotes the fraction of 1991 patients receiving non-medication therapeutic services. VACCINE equals 1 for diseases for which a vaccine was available in 1991, and 0 for other diseases.

procedure i's share in total procedures performed on patients with diagnosis j in year t. We computed NEWSURG as follows:

$$NEWSURG_j = 1 - \frac{\sum_i n_{ij,80}\, n_{ij,91}}{[(\sum_i n_{ij,80}{}^2)(\sum_i n_{ij,91}{}^2)]^{1/2}}$$

This index measures the degree of similarity (or dissimilarity) of disease j's 1980 and 1991 percentage distributions of surgical procedures.[36] It is bounded between 0 and 1; a value of 0 indicates no novelty, that is, perfect similarity of the two distributions; and a value of 1 indicates complete novelty, or zero similarity.

Table 3.10 presents 1970–91 mortality-reduction regressions that include the counseling and vaccine variables, NON_MED% and VACCINE. Because the surgical innovation variable NEWSURG pertains to the 1980–91 period, we will analyze the effect of that variable separately below. Column 2 of table 3.10 indicates that diseases for which there was a higher probability of physician counseling in 1991 had greater declines in life-years lost between 1970 and 1991; this is consistent with the hypothesis that improved patient knowledge reduces mortality. Column 3 reveals that diseases for which a vaccine was available in 1991 exhibited greater reductions in mortality than nonvaccine diseases. The relationship is not very significant (p-value = .17), however, perhaps due to the crudeness of this measure. When both of these variables and the new drug variable are included in the model (column 4), the coefficient on the latter is reduced by only 15 percent, and it remains highly significant. Neither of the other two coefficients is significant at the 5 percent level. This suggests that failure to account for counseling/education and vaccine availability produces little, if any, upward bias in our estimate of the impact of pharmaceutical innovation on mortality reduction.[37]

When NEWSURG is included in the 1980–91 mortality reduction model, the results are as follows (t-statistics in parentheses):

$$\ln (LYL_{1980}/LYL_{1991}) = \underset{(0.89)}{.080} + \underset{(2.21)}{.359} \ (DRUGS_{1970,1980}/DRUGS_{.1980}) + \underset{(1.31)}{.158} \ NEWSURG$$

$N = 78$; weighted $R^2 = .0880$

As might be expected, the coefficient on NEWSURG is positive—consistent with the view that surgical innovation as well as pharmaceutical innovation contribute to mortality reduction—but it is only significant at the 20 percent level. Moreover, both the point estimate of the drug coefficient and its t-statistic are virtually identical to their values when NEWSURG is excluded from the model.[38] Controlling for a potentially important other form of medical innovation has no effect on the estimate of the impact of pharmaceutical innovation.

VI. Estimation of the Social Rate of Return

Our data can be used to obtain approximate measures of the economic benefits (in terms of reduced mortality) of, and social rate of return to, pharmaceutical innovation. Estimates of equation (1) provide one possible way to do this. Note that the intercept of this equation, α, is the expected or predicted value of mortality reduction under no innovation, in other words, $E[\ln (LYL_{1970}/LYL_{1991})|(DRUGS_{1970,1991}/DRUGS_{.1991}) = 0] = \alpha$. The total benefit of innovation could be measured by the difference between actual mortality reduction and predicted mortality reduction under no innovation. The problem with this approach is that, because there are very few diseases with low values of NEWDRUG%—there is only 1 disease for which NEWDRUG% = 0, and 2 for which NEWDRUG% < 1/3—predicting mortality reduction under no innovation requires extrapolating far from the sample mean and is therefore subject to high forecast error variance.

A second approach, and the one we will adopt because it does not entail extrapolation far from the sample mean, is based on a slightly different functional form of the relationship between the new-drug share and mortality reduction. Suppose that there is a log-linear relationship between the ratio of beginning-of-period to end-of-period LYL and the number of drugs approved during the period (APPS):

(2) $\ln (LYL_{1970}/LYL_{1991}) = \alpha + \beta \ln (APPS_{1970,1991}) + \varepsilon.$

If $0 < \beta < 1$, there are positive but diminishing marginal benefits to approvals. $-\beta$ is the elasticity of LYL_{1991} to $APPS_{1970,1991}$, conditional on LYL_{1970}:

$$-\beta = \frac{d \ln (LYL_{1991})}{d \ln (APPS_{1970,1991})} = \frac{d (LYL_{1991})}{d (APPS_{1970,1991})} \frac{(APPS_{1970,1991})}{(LYL_{1991})}$$

The marginal effect of the number of drugs approved on LYL_{1991} is

$$\frac{d (LYL_{1991})}{d (APPS_{1970,1991})} = -\beta \frac{LYL_{1991}}{APPS_{1970,1991}}$$

At the beginning of 1970, 424 drugs had already been approved by the FDA. Hence the percentage of drugs approved by the beginning of 1991 that were approved after 1970 (%APP7091) is

$$\%APP7091 = APPS_{1970,1991}/(424 + APPS_{1970,1991}).$$

Solving this expression for $APPS_{1970,1991}$,

$$APPS_{1970,1991} = 424\,[\%APP7091/(1 - \%APP7091)]$$

and

$$\ln APPS_{1970,1991} = \ln 424 + \ln [\%APP7091/(1 - \%APP7091)].$$

Substituting this expression into equation (2),

$$(3)\quad \ln (LYL_{1970}/LYL_{1991}) = \alpha' + \beta \ln [\%APP7091/(1 - \%APP7091)] + \varepsilon,$$

where $\alpha' = \alpha + \beta \ln (424)$. Thus, one can estimate the parameter β by regressing $\ln (LYL_{1970}/LYL_{1991})$ on $\ln [\%APP7091/(1 - \%APP7091)]$, where %APP7091 is the percentage of drugs *approved by the beginning of 1991* that were approved after 1970. The latter variable cannot be measured on a disease-by-disease basis. However, a closely related variable, the percentage of drugs *prescribed in 1991* that were approved after 1970, whose average value is fairly similar to that of %APP7091,[39] *can* be measured on a disease-by-disease basis. We therefore estimated the following equation (t-statistics in parentheses):

$$\ln (LYL_{1970}/LYL_{1991}) = \underset{(4.329)}{0.304} + \underset{(7.652)}{0.507} \ln [(DRUGS_{1970,1991}/DRUGS_{.1991})/(1 - (DRUGS_{1970,1991}/DRUGS_{.1991}))]$$

$N = 73$, weighted $R^2 = .4519$.

The estimated elasticity of mortality with respect to the number of new drug approvals is about one-half: a 10 percent increase in new drug approvals is estimated to reduce mortality by 5 percent. This functional form fits the data slightly better than equation (1) does; the weighted R^2 has increased from .4058 to .4519.

We can use this estimate of β and sample aggregate values of LYL_{1991} and $APPS_{1970,1991}$ to calculate the number of life-years *saved* by the average new drug approval:

$$\frac{-d\,(LYL_{1991})}{d\,(APPS_{1970,1991})} = \beta\frac{LYL_{1991}}{APPS_{1970,1991}} = \frac{0.507\ (14.8\text{ million})}{399} = .0188\text{ million} = 18{,}800.$$

On average, each new drug approved during the period 1970–91 saved 18,800 life-years in 1991 (and presumably will do so in all future years). This is the "marginal physical product" of new drug approvals. By attaching "prices" to new drug approvals and to life-years, we can calculate the social rate of return to investment in pharmaceutical innovation. Myers and Howe (1997) estimate the cost of a new drug approval to be \$697 million with program costs allocated and \$429 without program costs. Cutler et al. (1996), citing Viscusi (1993), use a "benchmark estimate" of the value of a life-year of \$25,000, and upper and lower bounds of \$50,000 and \$10,000. The aggregate value of 18,800 life-years, each valued at \$25,000, is \$470 million. If the cost of a new drug approval is \$697 million, the social rate of return to pharmaceutical innovation is (\$470 m./\$697 m.) = 67.5 percent.[40]

This should be regarded as a very rough estimate; for a number of reasons it may be either too high or too low. Industry R&D expenditure may understate the true social cost of drug development. Toole (1998) presents evidence consistent with the view that the number of new molecular entities approved in a given year is positively related to *government*-funded biomedical research expenditure many (e.g. 25) years earlier, as well as to industry-funded R&D. It may therefore be appropriate to include some government-funded R&D in our cost estimate.[41] On the other hand, pharmaceutical innovation probably confers benefits other than reduced mortality, such as reduced hospitalization and surgical expenditures (see Lichtenberg 1996, 2001b), reduced workdays and schooldays lost, and improved quality of life; the above calculation does not account for these.

A rate of return of 68 percent is very high. However, many previous econometric and case studies (see Griliches [1998]) have indicated that the rate of return to R&D investment in general is high—much higher than the rate of return to ordinary investment. Moreover, Cutler, McClellan, and Newhouse (1998: 34) argue that "medical care is a more productive investment than the average use of our funds outside the medical sector," and Nordhaus (this volume) concluded that "the social productivity of health care spending might be many times that of other spending."

VII. Summary and Conclusions

We have analyzed the relationship *across diseases* between the long-term reduction in life-years lost before age 75 and the relative utilization of new pharmaceutical products. This methodology controls for the effects of any general economic and social trends (such as changes in wealth, nutrition, or sanitation) that affect *average* mortality. The data we analyzed cover all diseases and all (outpatient) drugs, thus allowing us (assuming that our model is correctly specified) to draw general conclusions about the impact of new drugs on longevity—a conclusion that cannot be drawn from existing studies, which are about specific diseases and/or drugs.

Previous investigators have argued that increased longevity should be considered an important part of economic growth, and the model we estimated is very consistent with the most widely accepted theory of growth, which implies that the rate of growth of per-capita output depends only on the rate of technological progress. The fraction of drugs prescribed by physicians that are new is, we believe, an excellent indicator of the rate of technical progress in the health care sector of the economy.

We found a highly significant positive relationship between the new-drug share and mortality reduction in all three periods we analyzed. Over 45 percent of the variation across diseases in the 1970–91 reduction in mortality is explained by the new-drug share. The mean percentage reduction in life-years lost for the 19 diseases with the highest relative utilization of new drugs (whose mean new-drug share was 74.6 percent) was over five times as great—72.7 percent vs. 13.0 percent—as the mean percentage reduction in life-years lost for the 19 diseases with the lowest relative utilization of new drugs (whose mean new-drug share was 44.8 percent).

Cutler, McClellan, and Newhouse (1998) found that drug therapies resulted in substantial improvements in heart attack mortality during the period 1975–95, and wondered whether their results "generalize to other types of medical care"(p. 34). Our econometric results strongly suggest that they *do* generalize.

The effect of the new-drug share on mortality reduction appears to have been much higher in 1970–80 than it was in 1980–91. Also, the magnitude and significance of this effect is larger over the entire 21-year period than it is in either of the two subperiods, which is consistent with the view that the long-run effects of new drugs on mortality are larger than the short-run effects. The data provide only weak support for the view that new priority drugs reduce mortality more than new standard drugs.

New drugs appear to have reduced mortality among all broad age groups in one of the two periods. In the 1970–80 period, new drugs reduced mortality only in the lowest and middle thirds of the age distribution of diseases—especially in the former—while in the 1980–91 period, new drugs had a significant positive effect on mortality reduction only in the highest third of the age distribution. Since the drugs introduced in the 1980s tended to be targeted at older patients than the drugs introduced in the 1970s, this "vintage-age interaction" is not surprising.

Pharmaceutical innovation, like most other economic activities, appears to be subject to the law of diminishing marginal productivity: the estimated elasticity of mortality with respect to the number of new drug approvals is about one-half (e.g., a 10 percent increase in new drug approvals is estimated to reduce mortality by 5 percent).

In principle, our initial estimates of the effect of pharmaceutical innovation on mortality reduction could be biased due to failure to control for other determinants of mortality reduction. But further investigation indicated that controlling for counseling/education and vaccine availability has only a small effect on our estimate of the impact of pharmaceutical innovation on mortality reduction. Controlling for the rate of introduction of new surgical procedures had no effect.

We used the data to obtain approximate measures of the economic benefits (in terms of reduced mortality) of, and social rate of return to, pharmaceutical innovation. On average, each new drug approved during the period 1970–91 is estimated to have saved 18,800 life-years in 1991 (and presumably continued to do so in subsequent years). If, as previous researchers have argued, the value of a life-year is about $25,000, and the average cost of a new drug approval is $697 million, then to a first approximation, the social rate of return to pharmaceutical innovation is about 68 percent. This is a very high rate of return, but previous studies have also found high social returns to innovation, and have suggested that "the social productivity of health care spending might be many times that of other spending." This estimate only accounts for the mortality-reduction benefits of new drugs; it does not account for possible morbidity reduction or quality-of-life enhancement. We plan to assess these in future research.

Notes

1. The National Center for Health Statistics first administered the NHAMCS in 1992. Unfortunately, there are no publicly-available data on pharmaceutical utilization in an inpatient setting.

2. Dustan et al. (1996: 1926) arrive at a similar conclusion: "In the past 2 decades, deaths from stroke have decreased by 59% and deaths from heart attack by 53%. An important component of this dramatic change has been the increased use of antihypertensive drugs."

3. "AIDS Deaths Drop 48% in New York," *New York Times,* 3 February 1998, p. A1.

4. Pharmaceutical expenditure accounts for about 10 percent of total U.S. health expenditure.

5. Lichtenberg's (2000) analysis of longitudinal quinquennial country-level data for a sample of 17 member countries of the Organisation for Economic Co-Operation and Development during the period 1960–90 also found no significant effect of either inpatient or ambulatory expenditure on mortality. I did, however, find significant effects of pharmaceutical consumption on both life expectancy at age 40 and life-years lost.

6. Source: author's calculations based on 1991 NAMCS file.

7. It might be possible to eliminate or at least reduce this overstatement by using data similar to those shown above to calculate *age-adjusted* pharmaceutical expenditure.

8. "Benefit to Healthy Men Is Seen from Cholesterol-Cutting Drug," *New York Times,* 16 November 1995, p. A1.

9. Of course, these mean life expectancies are affected by premature mortality.

10. As Murray and Lopez (1996: 16) observe, "Under the rules of the International Classification of Diseases, deaths must be assigned to one cause only, and this must be the underlying cause: for example, if someone has a heart attack and later dies of pneumonia in hospital, the cause of death must be recorded as ischaemic heart disease."

11. The calculated distribution of the log change between 1980 and 1991 of life-years lost included two extreme outliers. The mean, median, and highest and lowest five values of this distribution (N = 79) were as follows: mean = .079; median = .093; lowest = (−4.31, −1.21, −1.07, −0.61, −0.50); highest = (0.66, 0.70, 0.81, 0.86, 3.51). The lowest value was for poliomye . . . ; the highest was for Disorder . . . A log change of −4.31 corresponds to a 75-fold increase in life-years lost, and a log change of 3.51 corresponds to a 33-fold decrease. We were suspicious of such extreme magnitudes, and these observations were statistically quite influential, so we excluded them from the sample.

12. This model embodies the assumption of diminishing marginal returns to innovation. Suppose that there were 100 old drugs. If 25 new drugs were introduced, the "new-drug share" (the share of new drugs in total end-of-period drugs) would be 20 percent [$= 25/(100 + 25)$]. If twice as many new drugs (50) were introduced, the new-drug share would be less than twice as high, 33 percent [$= 50/(100 + 50)$]. If mortality reduction is a linear function of the new-drug share (as in equation [1]), the first 25 new drugs reduce mortality more than the second 25 new drugs.

13. Some general societal trends, such as the increase in the fraction of the population that is obese, may be mortality-increasing rather than mortality-reducing.

14. In aggregate time-series analyses of overall trends in mortality (e.g. Frech and Miller [1999]), to obtain unbiased estimates of the impact of drugs, it is crucial to control for trends in nondrug determinants of mortality. In contrast, in our longitudinal, disease-level analysis, it is necessary to control only for those determinants that are correlated across diseases with pharmaceutical innovation.

15. The extent of drug innovation seems more likely to depend on the *level* of average wealth than on its growth rate.

16. There is no direct correspondence between the nature of injury codes and the external cause of death codes, e.g. 821 does not correspond to E821.

17. For a discussion of the statistical tradeoffs associated with aggregation, see Grunfeld and Griliches (1960).

18. The FDA data enable us to identify the dates of "minor" innovations—new formulations of existing molecules—as well as the dates of "major" innovations—new molecules. For example, approval dates of different dosage forms of the molecule aminophylline are as follows:

1940 tablet
1979 tablet, sustained action
1982 solution
1983 suppository
1991 injection

Minor as well as major innovations may confer health benefits. Unfortunately, we are unable to monitor the diffusion of minor innovations, since the drug information provided in NAMCS does not include the dosage form or route of administration of the drug prescribed, only the name of the compound.

19. Estimated annual number of outpatient visits, by venue, are as follows.

Doctors' offices : 670 million
Hospital outpatient departments: 63 million
Emergency rooms: 90 million

20. Unfortunately, there is a slight temporal misalignment between the two surveys: the NAMCS data are for 1991 (the same year as the mortality data), but the NHAMCS data are for 1993.

21. The FDA's stated goal is to review and act on complete applications for "priority" drugs within 6 months of an NDA's submission date, and to review and act on NDAs for "standard" drugs within 12 months. However, until the recent prescription drug fee legislation, few drugs were approved within 6 months. All AIDS drugs are classified as priority drugs.

22. Of course, new drugs may confer health and economic benefits to patients other than mortality reduction. In future research, we plan to investigate the effect of pharmaceutical innovation on morbidity and "quality of life" using data from National Health Interview Surveys. (If, as we argue in this paper, new drugs tend to reduce mortality, one should examine the impact of pharmaceutical innovation on morbidity reduction *controlling for mortality reduction*, since new drugs are likely to keep less healthy people alive.) The introduction of a new, standard drug is likely to make the market for drugs in that class more competitive, and to lower prices to consumers.

23. Many economic relationships are stronger in the long run than they are in the short. For example, as Hall and Taylor (1997: 265–67) observe, the relationship between consumption expenditure and disposable income is stronger in the long run than it is in the short run.

24. To illustrate this, we estimated the unweighted regression of the log change between 1980 and 1991 in LYL on the share of new, priority drugs in 1991, and computed the absolute value of the residuals from this regression. We then divided the diseases into three size categories, based on the average number of LYL in 1980 and 1991. The means of the absolute residuals in each of the three size groups were

smallest: 0.322
middle: 0.288
largest: 0.137.

Also, there is a highly significant (p-value $< .01$) inverse correlation between the absolute residual and the logarithm of mean LYL.

25. The consequences of random measurement error in the independent variable are well known to econometricians. Suppose the true model is $y = \beta x^* + u$, but x^* is not observed; instead we observe $x = x^* + e$, where e is a random error term, with mean 0 and variance σ_e^2.

Then $E(b) = \beta\ (\sigma_*^2/(\sigma_*^2 + \sigma_e^2))$, where b is the OLS slope coefficient, and σ_*^2 is the variance of x^*. The larger the "noise-to-signal ratio" (σ_e^2/σ_*^2), the greater the bias toward 0 of b.

26. 9.8 percent of the medications whose prescription status could be determined in 1991 were nonprescription drugs.

27. Compliance rates vary with the disease and setting of the patient group. According to data reported in the *Journal of Clinical Pharmacy and Therapeutics,* patients in homes for the aged had relatively high rates of compliance, as did patients in the first year of antihypertensive treatment. In contrast, patients taking penicillin for rheumatic fever had relatively low rates of compliance.

28. We attempted to explore the relationship across drug classes between unpublished PhRMA data on R&D intensity (the ratio of R&D expenditure to sales) and our data on the share of new drugs in total prescriptions. Unfortunately, the PhRMA data are available for only eight highly aggregated drug classes (e.g. cardiovascular drugs), and we failed to find a statistically significant relationship based on such a small sample.

29. If the coefficient from the regression of Y on X is b, the coefficient from the regression of Y on $(X/2)$ is $2b$. The t-statistic on b and the R^2 of the two regressions are the same.

30. Since, as noted above, patients may have multiple diagnoses, the drugs are not necessarily prescribed *for* these diseases.

31. Fortunately, however, at the present time many people expect that there will soon be a number of highly effective drugs to fight cancer.

32. In our sample, we can't reject the null hypothesis that the studentized residuals are a random sample from a normal distribution (p-value = .24).

33. The studentized residuals for these observations are −2.89 (Other forms of heart disease [420–29]), −2.56 (Chronic obstructive pulmonary disease and allied conditions), −2.43 (Malignant neoplasm of respiratory and intrathoracic organs), −2.23 (Nonspecific abnormal findings, Ill-defined and unknown causes), 2.21 (Acute rheumatic fever [390–92] and chronic rheumatic heart disease), 2.60 (congenital anomalies), and 2.83 (Other conditions originating in the perinatal period [764–77]).

34. VACCINE = 1 for *ICD-9* codes 03-07 and 48. Unfortunately, we lack data on the date of FDA approval of these vaccines.

35. Unfortunately, it does not appear to be feasible to measure the fraction of surgical procedures performed that are new, analogous to the fraction of drugs prescribed that are new, since comprehensive data on the date of introduction of all surgical procedures are not available. Unlike drugs, the introduction of new surgical procedures is not subject to government regulation.

36. Jaffe (1986) used the cosine of firms' distributions of patents by patent class to measure their technological proximity.

37. Since new vaccines, as well as new drugs, are the fruits of innovative activity, the total effect on mortality of drug-cum-vaccine innovation is the *sum* of the drug and vaccine coefficients.

38. We also estimated the model including an interaction term between the two regressors, to allow for the possibility of complementarity between pharmaceutical and surgical innovation. In this model, the main effect of NEWSURG is positive and significant and the interaction term is negative and significant. However, the marginal effect of surgical novelty, evaluated at the sample mean value of NEWDRUG, is not significantly different from 0 (p-value = .49). The significance of the NEWDRUG effect (evaluated at the sample mean value of NEWSURG), increases slightly (the p-value falls from .022 to .004).

39. FDA data indicate that 46.4% (= 1 − (442/824)) of the drugs approved by the beginning of 1991 were approved after 1970; NAMCS data reveal that 62.7 percent of the drugs prescribed in 1991 were approved after 1970.

40. If life-years are valued at $10,000, the social rate of return is 27 percent.

41. In 1992, about half the total health R&D expenditure in the United States was publicly supported, but during the last few decades, private funding has grown much more rapidly than public funding. In 1980, government R&D accounted for almost 80 percent of U.S. health R&D. Source: National Science Board (1993: 365).

References

Advisory Commission to Study the Consumer Price Index. 1996. "Toward a More Accurate Measure of the Cost of Living." Final report to the Senate Finance Committee, 4 December. <http://www.ssa.gov/history/reports/boskinrpt.html>

Belsley, D. A., E. Kuh, and R. E. Welsch. 1980. *Regression Diagnostics*. New York: John Wiley & Sons.

Bresnahan, Timothy, and Robert J. Gordon. 1997. *The Economics of New Goods.* Chicago: University of Chicago Press.

Cutler, David, Mark McClellan, and Joseph Newhouse. 1998. "The Costs and Benefits of Intensive Treatment for Cardiovascular Disease." National Bureau of Economic Research Working Paper no. 6514, April.

Cutler, David, Mark McClellan, Joseph Newhouse, and Dahlia Remler. 1996. "Are Medical Prices Declining?" NBER Working Paper no. 5750, September.

Dustan, Harriet, et al. 1996. "Controlling Hypertension: A Research Success Story." *Archives of Internal Medicine* 56 (23 September): 1926–35.

Frech, H. E., and Richard D. Miller Jr. 1999. *The Productivity of Health Care and Pharmaceuticals: An International Comparison.* Washington, D.C.: AEI Press.

Greene, William H. 1997. *Econometric Analysis.* Upper Saddle River, N.J.: Prentice Hall.

Griliches, Zvi. 1998. *R&D and Productivity: The Econometric Evidence.* Chicago: University of Chicago Press.

Griliches, Zvi, and Frank Lichtenberg. 1984. "R&D and Productivity at the Industry Level: Is There Still a Relationship?" In *R&D, Patents, and Productivity,* edited by Zvi Griliches. Chicago: University of Chicago Press.

Grunfeld, Yehuda, and Zvi Griliches. 1960. "Is Aggregation Necessarily Bad?" *Review of Economics and Statistics* (February): 1–13.

Hall, Robert, and John Taylor. 1997. *Macroeconomics,* 5th ed. New York: Norton.

Jaffe, Adam B. 1986. "Technological Opportunity and Spillovers of R&D: Evidence from Firms' Patents, Profits and Market Value." *American Economic Review* 76 (December): 984–1001.

Lichtenberg, Frank. 1996. "Do (More and Better) Drugs Keep People Out of Hospitals?" *American Economic Review* 86 (May): 384–88.

———. 2000. Comment on papers by Richard Frank and David Salkever and by Jonathan Skinner and John Wennberg in *The Changing Hospital Industry: Comparing Not-for-Profit and For-Profit Institutions,* edited by David M. Cutler, pp. 221–26. Chicago: University of Chicago Press.

———. 2001a. "The Allocation of Publicly Funded Biomedical Research." In *Medical Care Output and Productivity,* 565–89, edited by Ernst Berndt and David Cutler. Studies in Income and Wealth, vol. 62. Chicago: University of Chicago Press.

———. 2001b. "Are the Benefits of Newer Drugs Worth Their Cost? Evidence from the 1996 MEPS." *Health Affairs* 20, no. 5 (September/October): 241–51.

Mankiw, N. Gregory. 1992. *Macroeconomics.* New York: Worth Publishers.

Myers, Stewart C., and Christopher D. Howe. 1997. "A Life-Cycle Financial Model of Pharmaceutical R&D." MIT Sloan School of Management Program on the Pharmaceutical Industry Working Paper no. 41–97, April.

Murray, Christopher, and Alan Lopez. 1996. *The Global Burden of Disease: Summary* Cambridge, Mass.: Harvard School of Public Health.

National Science Board. 1993. *Science and Engineering Indicators—1993.* Washington, D.C.: GPO.

Pharmaceutical Research and Manufacturers of America (PhRMA). 2001. *Pharmaceutical Industry Profile 2000.* Washington, D.C.

Skinner, J., and J. E. Wennberg. 2000. "How Much Is Enough? Efficiency and Medicare Spending in the Last Six Months of Life." In *The Changing Hospital Industry: Comparing Not-for-Profit and For-Profit Institutions,* 169–93, edited by David Cutler. Chicago: University of Chicago Press.

Toole, Andrew. 1998. "The Impact of Federally Funded Basic Research on Industrial Innovation: Evidence From the Pharmaceutical Industry." Unpublished paper, Laurits R. Christensen Associates, Madison, Wis., 22 February.

Viscusi, W. Kip. 1993. "The Value of Risks to Life and Health." *Journal of Economic Literature* 31: 1912–46.

CHAPTER FOUR

The Return to Biomedical Research: Treatment and Behavioral Effects

David M. Cutler and Srikanth Kadiyala

What is the value of medical research? Medical research clearly leads to improvement in medical practice. As nearly every medical journal—or broadcast of the evening news—attests, advances in medicine can lead to substantial improvements in health. Observers of the medical system frequently cite these advances as confirming the high value of medical research.

But medical research may affect health in other ways as well, by influencing the choices that individuals make. Behavioral factors such as smoking, diet, exercise, and the like have profound influences on health. These behaviors also change markedly over time. Smoking rates have fallen by one-third since 1960, and fat intake has been reduced. These changes have occurred at least partly as a result of research findings relating them to health outcomes.

In this chapter, we study the link between medical research and health, focusing on the dual effects of medical research on medical treatments and behavioral change.[1] Our analysis focuses on cardiovascular disease. The rationale for this choice is shown in figure 4.1, which presents trends in mortality by cause of death. Cardiovascular disease is the leading cause of death in the United States. It also fell by two-thirds between 1950 and 1994, leading to an increase in life expectancy of 4.5 years for the average 45-year-old person in the population. The reduction in cardiovascular disease mortality was far more rapid than the mortality reduction for any other

David M. Cutler is professor of economics at Harvard University and a research associate of the National Bureau of Economic Research. Srikanth Kadiyala is a student in the Graduate School of Art and Sciences at Harvard University.

We are grateful to Angus Deaton, Alan Garber, Nancy Keating, Mark McClellan, Barbara McNeil, Kevin Murphy, Eve Rittenberg, Sherwin Rosen, Bob Topel, and Milt Weinstein for helpful comments, and to the National Institutes on Aging for research support.

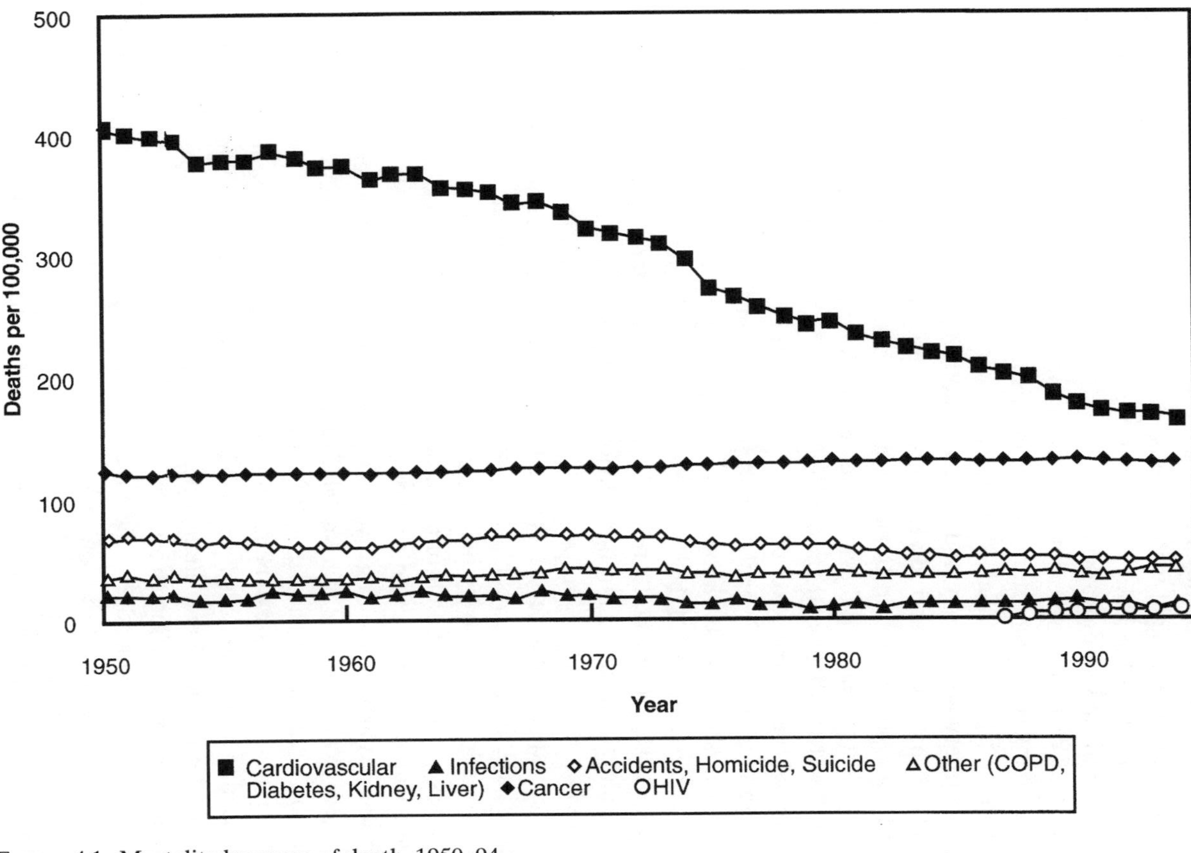

FIGURE 4.1: Mortality by cause of death, 1950–94

SOURCE: National Center for Health Statistics, unpublished data.

condition. For example, mortality figures for cancer, the second leading cause of death, actually rose over this time period. Focusing on cardiovascular disease thus allows us to learn about the value of research in a situation where it might matter a great deal.

Our analysis has three aims. First, we discuss the broad factors leading to reduced cardiovascular disease mortality. Based on our research and that of others, we show that both medical treatments and behavioral changes are important factors in this health improvement. Medical treatments consist of high-tech invasive treatments, such as coronary bypass surgery, angioplasty, and cardiac catheterization for people who have had a heart attack, and lower-tech treatments, such as antihypertensive and antilipidemic medications, for people who have hypertension or hypercholesterolemia. Behavioral changes include reduced rates of smoking, lower-fat diets, and reduced salt intake. While a precise decomposition of the contribution of each of the factors to the improvement in health is difficult, our analysis and past work in the field lead to rough approximations of the importance of the different factors. We estimate that about one-third of the improvement in mortality stems from high-tech invasive treatment, about one-third from low-tech pharmaceutical innovation, and the final third from behavioral changes such as reduced rates of smoking.

Second, we analyze the factors leading to changes in medical treatments and behaviors. As has been well documented, medical treatments are greatly influenced by biomedical research; new surgeries and medications are a direct result of advances in such inquiry. More surprisingly, we document a similar finding about behavioral changes, analyzing in particular changes in smoking, hypercholesterolemia, and hypertension. Our review of medical research knowledge, public opinion surveys, and population estimates of adverse risk factors at different points in time shows that a substantial share of behavioral changes result from medical research indicating how people can become healthier or remain healthy. Knowledge about these behaviors is communicated to the public and is incorporated rapidly into peoples' behavior.

Third, we consider the implication of these findings for medical research. The increasing sophistication of medical treatment has led to substantial cost increases. The average 45-year-old spends about $30,000 more on cardiovascular disease than he or she did in 1950. But the gains from longer life are much greater. Using common values in the literature, we estimate that the improved health resulting from medical treatment changes is approximately $120,000. Therefore, the rate of return to medical technology innovation is about 4 to 1. The return to new knowledge is even greater: we estimate that basic knowledge about disease risk has a return of about 30 to 1. Our unambiguous conclusion is that medical research on cardiovascular disease is clearly worth the cost.

The chapter proceeds as follows: The first section examines the nature of cardiovascular disease. In the second section we examine why cardiovascular disease mortality has fallen over the last half century. Sections III to V focus on changes in knowledge and prevalence of three risk factors: smoking, high cholesterol, and high blood pressure. The final section summarizes and discusses the implications of these changes.

I. The Basics of Cardiovascular Disease

Cardiovascular diseases affect the circulatory system, and more specifically the heart and blood vessels. Heart attacks and strokes are the two most severe manifestations of the disease. Less severe manifestations include angina (stable or unstable), rheumatic heart disease, and arteriosclerosis.

Figure 4.2 shows the epidemiology of cardiovascular disease. Individual risk for cardiovascular disease is based on three factors: demographics (older men are more susceptible), genetics, and behaviors. Relevant behaviors include smoking, diet, exercise, and alcohol intake.

On the basis of these variables, individuals may develop one or more of a series of primary risk factors for cardiovascular disease. Five risk factors are commonly identified: smoking, hypertension (or high blood pressure), hypercholesterolemia (or high cholesterol), obesity, and diabetes. These risk factors are related to one another in many ways; for example, obesity leads to high blood pressure as well as diabetes. But the risk factors are separable in that each has an independent effect on the progression of cardiovascular disease when the others are controlled for. In addition to these factors, several others have been speculated about in the literature. Physical inactivity is associated with increased cardiovascular disease risk, although it is not clear whether this effect happens because physical activity is associated with the other risk factors (for example obesity) or whether the effect is separate. It has also been suggested that postmenopausal women are at higher risk of cardiovascular disease, and clinical trials are now testing whether hormone-replacement therapy reduces their risk. Finally, recent findings have attributed heart disease to excess levels of free radicals, the level of homocysteine in the blood, consumption of omega-3 fatty acids, the level of folic acid, the level of stress, or environmental factors such as the control a person has on their job. The

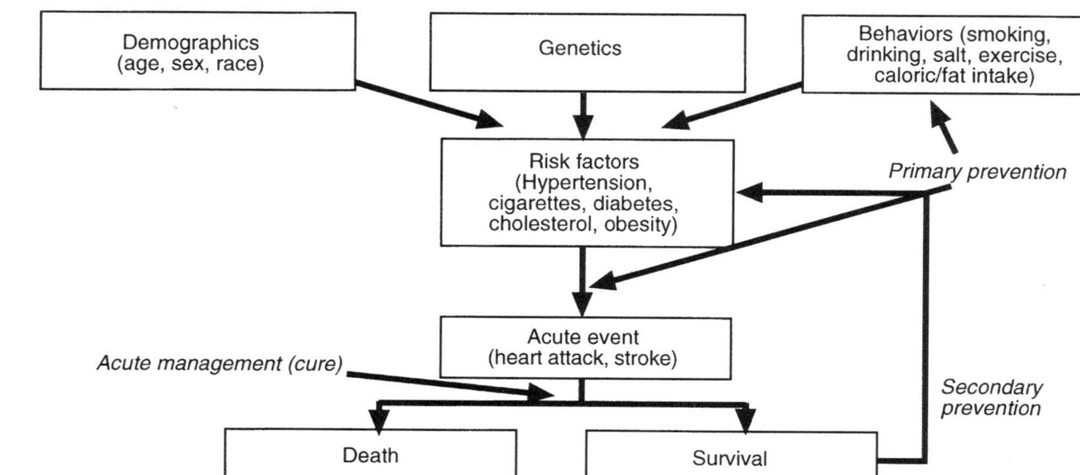

FIGURE 4.2: Cardiovascular disease progression

process of preventing a person from developing one of these risk factors, or preventing those factors from leading to an acute incident, is termed primary prevention.

Those at elevated risk may suffer a severe cardiovascular disease incident, of which two types are particularly severe: acute myocardial infarction (AMI, or heart attack), and cerebrovascular disease (stroke). Hemorrhaging of blood vessels as a result of pressure on vessel walls, or blockages in blood vessels due to the buildup of materials such as cholesterol and fat, leads to a reduction in oxygen supplied to parts of the brain and heart. The lack of oxygen leads to tissue death, which is referred to as a heart attack or a stroke. Both conditions are life threatening and often leave survivors with substantial disability. After a person has an acute incident, there is a period of acute management designed to ensure survival. Acute survival is generally measured within the first 90 days of the incident.

Survival of a serious cardiovascular disease incident is a risk factor for a subsequent incident. Heart muscle that dies, for example, does not recover and leaves people with a permanently impaired heart. *Secondary prevention* is the term given to preventing a recurrence in a person who has had an acute episode. It involves many of the same factors as primary prevention.

II. Explanations for the Decline in Mortality

A variety of hypotheses have been suggested for the decline in cardiovascular disease mortality. We focus here on a number of different explanations for this phenomenon.

Acute Disease Management

Considerable advances have been made in the treatment of acute heart disease in the last half century. Table 4.1 shows the timing of this progress.[2] In 1950, a person who had a heart attack was generally hospitalized for 6 weeks, given painkillers, and placed on bed rest for 6 months in the hope that reduced strain on the heart would improve its functioning. Cardiac catheterization, the first diagnostic procedure to determine the location of the damaged blood vessels, was developed in the late 1950s. Coronary bypass surgery, introduced in 1968, is a very technologically intensive treatment that involves creating new pathways through which the blood can flow through the heart. Cardiac intensive care units, with special monitoring devices and specially-trained personnel, were developed in the 1970s.

TABLE 4.1 Innovation in the Acute Treatment of Heart Disease

Technology	Year of Innovation
Cardiac catheterization	1959
Coronary Bypass	1968
Cardiac ICUs	1970s
Angioplasty	1978
Thrombolytics	1980s
Aspirin	late 1980s

NOTE: based on Cutler, McClellan, and Newhouse (1999)

Angioplasty, developed in 1978, involves the insertion of a tiny balloon into a clogged artery in order to increase blood flow.

New pharmaceuticals have also been important in treating acute incidents. Beta-blockers, developed in the early 1960s, interfere with the neurotransmitter epinephrine and decrease heart rate and blood pressure. More recently there has been a realization that aspirin is effective in treating patients after an attack, because of its anticoagulant properties. The most recent advances in pharmaceuticals for the treatment of heart attacks are thrombolytics. These reduce acute mortality by helping to dissolve clots once they occur.

Many of these technologies have undergone substantial refinement over time. For example, angioplasty is now commonly used in conjunction with stents, which reduce reocclusion of the affected artery. As experience with these procedures has grown and good outcomes have been demonstrated, the technologies have spread widely.

Heidenreich and McClellan (2000) show evidence of the changing use of these technologies over time. All the high-tech treatments have been employed much more frequently since the time of their innovation. For example, the use of cardiac-catheterization procedures within 30 days of an AMI increased from approximately 3 percent in the early 1970s to 42 percent by the mid-1990s. The rate of coronary bypass surgery quintupled from 3 percent to 14 percent over the same period, while the rate of angioplasty more than doubled from 6 percent to 15 percent since its introduction in the mid-1980s.

Similarly, there was a large increase in the use of medications. Beta-blocker usage rose from 21 percent in the early 1970s to 50 percent by the mid-1990s. Aspirin usage was at a relatively low rate of about 15 percent for much of the 1970s and 1980s and then rose dramatically to 75 percent by the mid-1990s. Thrombolytics use rose from 9 percent to 31 percent since their relatively recent introduction in the late 1980s.

Prevention

The developments in medical treatments for cardiovascular disease are well known. What is less familiar is the substantial change in knowledge about the risk factors related to cardiovascular disease and the corresponding changes in behavior.

As we discuss in more detail below, prevention involves two paths. The first path is behavioral change: people who smoke are encouraged to quit; obese people are urged to lose weight; at-risk people are encouraged to cut back on foods containing fat, cholesterol, and sodium; and excessive alcohol intake is discouraged. The second path is pharmaceutical. Particularly in the case of high cholesterol and hypertension, pharmaceutical innovation has created new classes of drugs, which have helped people bring these risk factors under control.

To understand changes in risk factor knowledge, we have conducted reviews of the medical literature at different points in time. We placed particular emphasis on different editions of *Harrison's Principles of Internal Medicine,* perhaps the leading textbook of its kind in the country. *Harrison's* is updated every few years to reflect developments in the field. We also examined consensus panels and conferences, such as those from the Joint National Committee on Prevention, Detection and Evaluation and Treatment of High Blood Pressure (JNC) and the National Cholesterol Education Program (NCEP). These events are generally sponsored by the National Institutes of Health (NIH).

Table 4.2 identifies the year in which different risk factors were identified in Harrison's text. In 1950, hypercholesterolemia and hypertension were seen as the two risk factors for cardiovascular disease, although the former was more widely believed than the latter. Medical textbooks at the time described the relationship between cholesterol and heart disease as strong, but were more speculative in linking hypertension with heart disease. By 1962, tobacco use was also identified as being associated with cardiovascular

Table 4.2 Knowledge of Risk Factors Influencing Cardiovascular Disease

Risk Factor	Year of Mention
Hypertension	1950
High cholesterol	1950
Tobacco	1962
Obesity	1970
Diabetes	1970

Note: based on *Harrison's Principles of Internal Medicine* (various editions)

disease. By 1970, obesity and diabetes had been added to the list of risk factors.

Knowledge of existing risk factors also changed. The levels at which blood pressure and high cholesterol are deemed dangerous were refined and treatment recommendations improved. We discuss these particular changes later in this chapter.

Prevention versus Acute Treatment

A number of epidemiological studies have examined the relative importance of prevention versus acute treatment in explaining the decline in cardiovascular disease mortality. Goldman and Cook (1984) presented the first accounting of reduced mortality, examining the period from 1968 through 1976. Sytkowski (1996) examined this issue using data from the Framingham Heart Study covering the 1950–89 period. Hunink et al.(1997) used a model of cardiovascular disease progression to estimate the factors influencing mortality reductions during the 1980s.

The results of the Goldman and Cook and Hunink studies are summarized in table 4.3. Each reached similar conclusions. Acute management of cardiovascular disease (particularly coronary heart disease) accounts for between 15 percent and 33 percent of reduced mortality. The remaining two-thirds or more of better health results from preventive activities. The primary reason for the studies' differences in estimates is that the time periods they examined are not the same. Studies encompassing the entire time period find a larger role for acute treatments than do studies focusing on the early period. This finding is consistent with an increasing role for medical technology in improving health over time. Our best estimate for the entire time period is that one-third of reduced cardiovascular disease mortality results from improved acute survival.

TABLE 4.3 Prevention versus Acute Treatment in Reduced Cardiovascular Disease Mortality

Factor	Goldman and Cook (1968–76)	Hunink et al. (1980–90)
Acute treatment	21%	15%
Cholesterol	30	33
Smoking	24	6
Hypertension	9	14
Medical treatment of disease	10	29

NOTE: Goldman and Cook study ischemic heart disease. Hunink et al. study coronary heart disease.

Changes in acute survival may result overall from several factors, both medical and nonmedical. Heidenreich and McClellan (2000) have attempted a decomposition of improvements in acute mortality for heart attack patients. Their results show that over 60 percent of this mortality reduction is a result of improved medical treatment, while the remaining 40 percent results from the treatment of less severe AMI patients. If 60 percent of the acute survival results from improved medical care and acute survival contributes to approximately one-third of overall survival, these intensive technologies can explain about 20 percent of overall survival improvements.

In addition, some intensive medical treatments are used in management of less severe cardiovascular disease. For example, bypass surgery and angioplasty may be performed on patients who physicians believe are in danger of having a heart attack, but have not yet had one. We do not have firm estimates of the importance of this factor in leading to health improvements. In recent years, such procedure use has grown rapidly, but was used more sparingly over most of the time period.

As a benchmark, we estimate that one-third of improved survival from cardiovascular disease in the post-1950 time period is a result of intensive medical procedures. This conclusion is necessarily somewhat speculative, but as we discuss below, none of our results are particularly sensitive to the exact share used.

These results imply that prevention, particularly the improved management of risk factors, is the primary source of health improvements. All the studies explicitly evaluate the role of prevention in reduced mortality. Goldman and Cook (1984), Hunink et al. (1997), and Sytkowski et al. (1996) each find large roles for reduced cigarette smoking, cholesterol, and hypertension in lowering risk of cardiovascular disease. Goldman and Cook estimate that 63 percent of the mortality reduction in ischemic heart disease (a subset of coronary heart disease) from 1968 to 1976 is due to prevention. Their analysis indicates that changes in cholesterol contributed to 30 percent of the decline, while smoking and hypertension reduced mortality by 24 percent and 9 percent respectively. Hunink et al. analyze the change in coronary disease mortality from 1980 to 1990 and ascribe 53 percent of the reduction in mortality to prevention: cholesterol declines contributed to 33 percent of the mortality decline; hypertension reductions, 14 percent; and smoking, a considerably smaller role at 6 percent. Sytkowski et al. use the Framingham Data to analyze the changes in cardiovascular disease mortality over the 1950–89 period. Their analysis of risk factors is restricted to coronary heart disease; for this they show that for women more than

TABLE 4.4 Changes in Risk Factors over Time

Measure	1959–62	1971–74	1976–80	1988–94
Elevated blood pressure*	51%	56%	46%	30%
Elevated cholesterol*	51	43	41	30
Smoking	—	34	31	24
Obesity	25	23	24	34
Diabetes	—	7	6	8
Hypertension controlled by medication	2	3	6	10
Hypercholesterolemia controlled by medication	—	—	—	3

*Using current definition of high blood pressure and cholesterol.

SOURCE: National Health and Nutrition Examination Surveys. The sample is African American and Caucasians, aged 45–74 years, who have not had a prior cardiovascular disease incident. Data are adjusted to the age, sex, and racial mix of the population in 1990. See Cutler and Kadiyala (2001) for details.

50 percent of the mortality decline is a result of improvements in risk factors, and for men the percentage lies between thirty-three percent and fifty percent. They do not present results separately for each risk factor.

We have undertaken a similar analysis in our research. Table 4.4, taken from Cutler and Kadiyala (2001), shows changes in rates of elevated blood pressure, high cholesterol, smoking, obesity, and diabetes over time. The sample comprises African Americans and Caucasians aged 45–74 years who have not experienced a prior cardiovascular disease incident. The data are from National Health and Nutrition Examination Surveys (NHANES) conducted in 1959–62, 1971–74, 1976–80, and 1988–94. The numbers, benchmarked to the 1990 age, sex, and race distribution of the population, indicate that rates of elevated blood pressure fell by nearly one-half from the early 1970s until about 1990, and rates of high cholesterol dropped by 30 percent as had the smoking rate.[3] In contrast, obesity and diabetes rates increased. Overall, these changes are consistent with large reductions in disease incidence and reduced recurrence rates.

To understand how medical research is related to these changes in risk factors, we need to consider the behavioral changes in more detail. We do this in the next three sections, examining smoking, hypercholesterolemia, and hypertension in turn. Our conclusion in each case is that medical research is a primary factor in driving these changes. In some cases, medical research leads to new therapies that improve risk factor control. In other cases, the research improves the information that people and physicians have about health practices, and people consequently act on this knowledge. We highlight both of these roles for medical research. Before doing so, though, we consider other possible risk factors for cardiovascular disease.

Other Explanations

Our review of the evidence thus far points to primary prevention and acute treatment as the main determinants of cardiovascular disease mortality. Scientists have also put forward a host of other reasons for cardiovascular mortality. We discuss three of these alternative explanations: changes in distribution of birth weight, changes in education levels, and changes in occupational class. We conclude that the evidence for these theories is often strong, but they are quantitatively not very important in the time period we examine.

Birth Weight

There is some evidence that birth weight is an independent predictor of heart disease mortality at older ages. Biological evidence for this theory rests on the idea of "programming." As defined by the leading proponent of the link between birth weight and cardiovascular disease, programming is the "principle that the nutritional, hormonal, and metabolic environment afforded by the mother may permanently program the structure and physiology of her offspring" (Barker, 1998: 13). Experiments with animals and studies of infants have suggested that programming has an affect on the development of important organs such as the brain, lungs, liver, pancreas, and kidneys, and processes such as lipid metabolism and blood pressure regulation. Within this framework, birth weight has become the accepted measure of evaluating the extent to which an infant has been "programmed." Consequently, we consider whether changes in birth weight in the early part of the twentieth century contributed to the decline in cardiovascular mortality in the later half of the century. Since we are examining changes in cardiovascular mortality of 45- to 74-year-olds from about 1960 to about 1990, we are interested in changes in birth weights of people born between 1886 and 1945.

Data on birth weight from the early part of the twentieth century are limited. There are scattered records from individual hospitals in specific regions of the United States, but no national data. Ward (1993) analyzes data from the New England Hospital for Women and Children (NEHWC) and the inpatient and outpatient clinics of the Boston Lying-In Hospital between 1872 and 1890. In the NEHWC data, Ward shows that mean birth weight is relatively constant at about 3,500 grams for much of the time span and that birth weight decreases over the final few years. This would imply an increase in cardiovascular disease risk over time. The Boston Lying-In sample shows an increase in birth weight, but not a large one. Perhaps more important than overall birth weight, Ward shows that the share of low-birth-weight babies (defined as those weighing less than 2,500 grams) is relatively constant over time.

Costa (1998) presents birth weight data for the New York Lying-In Hospital for the 1910–30 period. Mean birth weight for the entire sample is 3,463 grams and the share of infants who had low birth weight is 5.5 percent. Time trends are not presented in this data, as the sample sizes for any given year are small. But these birth weight means are close to calculations from recent data. The mean birth weight for the 1988 National Maternal and Infant Health Survey is 3,454 grams and the share of infants that had low birth weight is 4.4 percent.

Both the Boston and New York data therefore suggest little change in birth weight over these periods. This implies that changing birth-weight is not an important factor in the U.S. decrease in cardiovascular disease mortality in the latter half of the twentieth century.

Education

The relationship between education and health outcomes has been long studied. It is well known that the more educated are in better health than the less educated. For 1996, among the 25- to 64-year age group, the death rate for individuals having less than 12 years of education is 556 per 100,000 people. For the group having just 12 years of high school, this figure falls to 472 deaths per 100,000; for individuals having a minimum of 13 years of education, the death rate is 230 deaths per 100,000, less than half that of the group whose education ended at high school. There are multiple channels through which education can affect health. It may help people process new information faster and at a more comprehensive level. For example, when the Surgeon General's report on smoking and health was released in 1964, quit rates among college-educated smokers were higher than among those without a high school education. While this gap between these two populations of smokers has narrowed, it exists to this day.

For purposes of our research, the question is not whether education affects health, but whether it does so *once we adjust for other risk factors*. That is, we care about whether education is a separate risk factor from blood pressure, cholesterol, smoking, obesity, and diabetes. To test this hypothesis, we use data from the Framingham Heart Study, which contains information on risk factors and education level. We regress incidence of cardiovascular disease and 90-day mortality conditional on having a cardiovascular disease episode on demographics, risk factor levels, and dummies for different education levels (see Cutler and Kadiyala, 2001). Results from these regressions indicate that while the signs on the coefficients are in the anticipated direction (more-educated people have lower risks), the coefficients are small and not statistically significant. Thus, education does not materially affect cardiovascular disease risk once the other risk factors are accounted for.

Occupation

Occupational class has also been hypothesized as a risk factor for cardiovascular disease (Pocock et al., 1987). Numerous studies have found that people in blue-collar jobs have higher cardiovascular disease incidence and mortality than those in white-collar ones. Moreover, at least in the earlier part of the century, farmers had a lower incidence of cardiovascular disease than either blue- or white-collar workers. Direct physical implications of manual labor may be important in this regard.

Similar to the relationship between education and mortality, occupation has the potential to affect mortality through a variety of channels. One channel might be that persons in blue-collar professions are more likely to experience high levels of stress than those in white collar positions, leading to an increase in cardiovascular disease incidence. But again, we are not as interested in examining these channels on their own as we are in identifying whether occupational class has an effect on mortality beyond its link to risk factors such as smoking, cholesterol, blood pressure, obesity, and diabetes.

To test this, we use the NHANES data, as this survey has information on the current occupation of the respondent and other risk factors. We restrict our sample to blacks and whites aged 45–64 years who do not have a prior cardiovascular incident, since most of this group is working. Occupations are classified into four categories: farmers, white-collar, blue-collar, and unknown. Approximately 34 percent of the sample are white-collar workers, 30 percent blue-collar are workers, 34 percent are unknown, and 2 percent are in the farming industry. Logistic regression of cardiovascular disease death within 10 years on demographic variables such as age, sex, risk factor, and occupation shows that occupation does not have an independent effect on cardiovascular disease death once the other factors are controlled for. In fact, contrary to expectations, once we adjust for the medical risk factors blue-collar workers are *less* likely than white-collar workers to die from cardiovascular disease, although again this point estimate is not significant. We thus conclude that occupational changes are not a major factor in reduced cardiovascular disease risk.

Summary

Our evidence thus indicates two factors as being particularly important in lower cardiovascular disease mortality. The first is intensive treatment of heart disease. We assign approximately one-third of the total mortality reduction to this factor. The remaining two-thirds we attribute to better control of hypertension, high cholesterol, and smoking. This risk factor control is a result of both medical and nonmedical advances. In the next three sections, we examine how and why these risk factors have changed.

III. Smoking

Smoking has a wide variety of deleterious effects on the human body. It contains more than 50 known carcinogens, adversely affects the functioning of the cardiovascular system, causes a variety of respiratory infections, and leads to low-birth-weight babies. We concentrate here on effects on the cardiovascular system.

Tobacco smoke contains high levels of carbon monoxide, a molecule that binds to hemoglobin, thus displacing oxygen molecules that are carried by the hemoglobin. This leads to a deficiency in the amount of oxygen transported to different tissues in the body and to an overall reduction in systemic oxygen transport. Smoking also causes an increase in the levels of low-density lipoprotein cholesterol and a decrease in the levels of high-density lipoprotein cholesterol. Both of these changes increase cardiovascular disease risk (more discussion on this in the next section). Further, smoking damages the inner lining of blood vessels which leads to an accumulation of materials such as fats and cholesterol at the damaged sites. Finally, carbon monoxide and nicotine derived from smoking also increase the "stickiness" of platelets found in blood. In the long-run these changes lead to blockages of blood flow, resulting in heart attacks and strokes.

Awareness of the dangers of smoking was present in the general media as early as 1953. A prominent publication called the *Sloan Kettering Report,* linking smoking and lung cancer, was reprinted in popular magazines such as *Reader's Digest* and *Consumer Reports*. Between 1953 and 1959, *Reader's Digest* ran 12 articles discussing smoking and health risks (Viscusi, 1992). While these stories generated some attention, the impact on public consciousness was relatively small. For example, a 1957 Gallup Poll questioned 1,520 people on whether they read or heard about a recent report by the American Cancer Society that detailed the effects of cigarette smoking. Seventy-eight percent of those interviewed said they had read or heard about the report. But of the 640 smokers who had, only 4 percent quit smoking. When the smokers who did not quit were questioned as to why[4] they continued to use tobacco, 15 percent believed the "reports not proven," 8 percent felt "they don't smoke enough to make any difference," and 30 percent said they "don't want to stop, not concerned enough, enjoy it."

This all changed with the *Report of the Advisory Committee to the Surgeon General on Smoking and Health*. The 1964 report stated that smoking causes lung and laryngeal cancer in men, is the primary cause of chronic bronchitis, and is associated with esophageal cancer, bladder cancer, coronary artery disease, emphysema, peptic ulcer, and low-birth-weight babies. The report concluded that "[c]igarette smoking is a hazard to health of sufficient importance in the U.S. to warrant appropriate remedial action."

The Surgeon General's report generated enormous media attention and was the lead story in newspaper and television broadcasts. Since the initial report in 1964, 25 additional Surgeon General's reports have refined and added to its conclusions. The 1983 Surgeon General's report was the first to causally link smoking and cardiovascular disease, estimating that smoking increases risk of death from coronary heart disease approximately threefold for people below age 65. The 1986 report concentrated on the dangers of passive or second-hand smoke, and the 1988 report pronounced nicotine an addictive substance comparable to cocaine and heroin in its physiological effects.

Changes in public actions affecting smoking came rapidly. Figure 4.3 shows a time line of major events concerning tobacco; a more complete listing of information and legislation related to smoking is contained in appendix table 4A1. The first phase of public action was to provide information about the dangers of tobacco. In 1965, Congress passed the Federal Cigarette Labeling and Advertising Act, which required the following warning on all cigarette packages: "Caution: Cigarette Smoking May be Hazardous to Your Health."[5] In 1967 the Federal Communications Commission (FCC) required that radio stations broadcasting cigarette commercials must provide equal airtime for smoking prevention messages. The Fairness Doctrine, in effect from 1967 through 1970, mandated equal time for anti-smoking commercials on television and radio. The Public Health Cigarette Smoking Act of 1969 banned cigarette advertising on television and radio altogether and required a stronger health warning on cigarette packages.

After the public information campaigns, public action turned increasingly toward raising the price of cigarettes. Real cigarette taxes increased

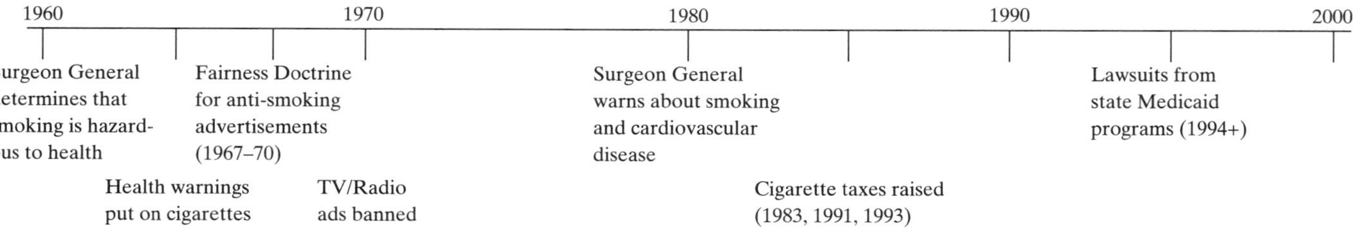

FIGURE 4.3: Public action and information about smoking

from an initial value of 44 cents per package in 1960 (in today's dollars) to 49 cents per package by 1970 (an 11 percent increase). The tax was fixed nominally, however, and over time inflation eroded its real value. By the end of 1982, taxes were much lower in real terms, falling by almost 55 percent from the 1970 value. Since then, however, taxes have again increased. Cigarette taxes increased by almost 50 percent from 1982 to 1983, and increased again in 1991 and 1993. Today, formal taxes are approximately 40 cents per pack. There are implicit taxes on cigarettes as well, with the most important of these being the recent settlement of lawsuits filed by state governments against tobacco companies over costs of smoking to the Medicaid program. Settlement of these lawsuits in 1999 resulted in real cigarette price increases of about 42 cents per pack (Cutler et al., 2000).

The anti-tobacco campaign has occurred both within and beyond the government sector. Soon after the report by the Surgeon General's Advisory Committee, the federal government established the National Clearinghouse for Smoking and Health (later renamed the Office on Smoking and Health) to consolidate and release information concerning the dangers of smoking. In addition to disseminating smoking-related research and information, the OSH works in schools and communities across the nation to develop anti-smoking programs. Hundreds of not-for-profit organizations and public health coalitions, such as the American Cancer Society, the American Heart Association, and the American Lung Association, have also developed campaigns against smoking..

The question for our research is how successful these activities were in reducing smoking. Figure 4.4 shows annual data on per-capita cigarette consumption from 1900 to 1998. Cigarette consumption increased 8,000 percent between 1900 and 1963, from 54 cigarettes per adult per year to 4,345 cigarettes per adult per year (about 12 cigarettes per day).[6] The increase was fairly continuous and, after the release of the 1964 Surgeon General's report, annual per-capita consumption stabilized at about 4,000 cigarettes per adult per year until 1976,a significant change in the trend. In the late 1970s, cigarette smoking began a downward consumption trend. By 1998, consumption fell to 2,261 cigarettes per person per year, a 48 percent decline from the 1963 level.

Figure 4.5 decomposes the post-1965 smoking reduction into the share of adults who are current smokers, former smokers, and never smokers.[7] In the first few years after the Surgeon General's report, the share of people who quit smoking rose significantly, by about 5 percentage points. This trend continued so that by 1995, half the people who ever smoked had

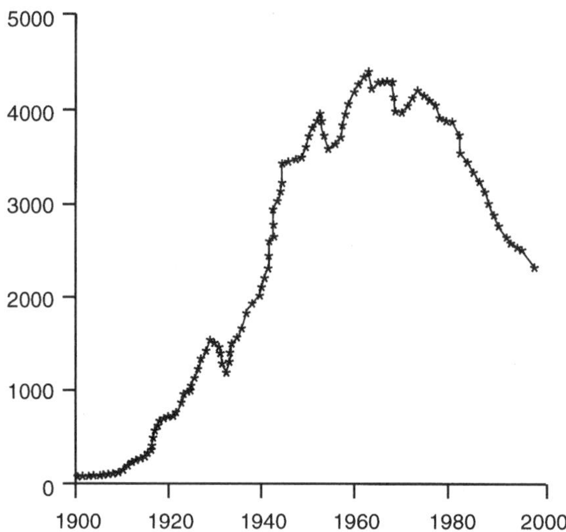

FIGURE 4.4: Annual per-capita cigarette consumption
SOURCE: U.S. Department of Health and Human Services, Centers for Disease Control and Prevention

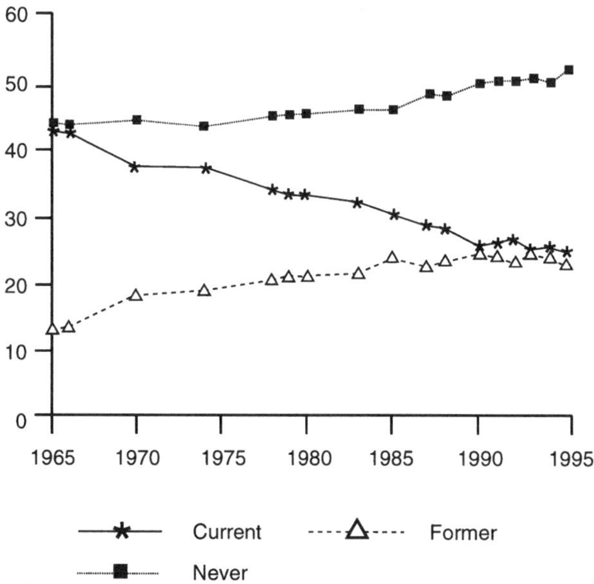

FIGURE 4.5: Smoking prevalence over time
SOURCE: National Health Interview Surveys
NOTE: Sample includes ages 18+ years.

quit. Furthermore, over time fewer people took up smoking. The share of never smokers rises particularly in the late 1970s and 1980s. Between 1980 and 1995, the share of never smokers rose from 46 percent to 52 percent.

The reduction in smoking is almost entirely a result of individual behavior, not medical technology, although nicotine gum was introduced in 1984, and nicotine patches began to be sold in December 1991. Approximately 10 percent of the smoking population tries these smoking cessation aids annually: about 5 million smokers each year try the nicotine patch and 2 million smokers try the gum. However, given that most of the people who attempt to quit do not succeed, the contribution of these aids to the reduction in smoking is likely small.

Evidence supporting the role of information in influencing smoking decisions comes from surveys of public knowledge and attitudes about smoking. A variety of surveys have been conducted over the years that allow one to track changes in public awareness of smoking risks. The three primary sources are the Gallup Polls (1949, 1954, 1957, 1958, 1960, 1969, 1977, 1981, 1990, and 1999), the Adult Use of Tobacco Surveys (AUTS, sponsored by the National Clearinghouse for Smoking and Health in 1964, 1966, 1970, 1975, and 1986), and the Roper surveys (Viscusi, 1992). The Gallup Polls sampled a minimum of 1,000 people; the Adult Use of Tobacco Surveys, about 3,000; and the Roper surveys, about 2,000.

Table 4.5 contains information on the public's changing awareness of smoking risk. The 1949 and 1954 Gallup Polls asked, "Do you think cigarette smoking is harmful or not?", with possible responses of "yes," "no," and "no opinion." Sixty percent of people in 1949 and 70 percent of people in 1954 believed that cigarette smoking is harmful to health. Moreover, there is a clear trend toward an increasing knowledge of the damage from cigarettes even before the Surgeon General's report, and not just among smokers. In 1949, 24 percent of nonsmokers and 45 percent of smokers claimed that cigarettes are not harmful to health. From the AUTS surveys the share of smokers who said that smoking is harmful to health rose from 70 percent in 1964 to 81 percent in 1975. Over the same time period, the share of nonsmokers who said that smoking is harmful increased from 89 percent to 95 percent.

The AUTS surveys ask questions that are similar to those used in the Gallup Polls ("Smoking cigarettes is harmful to health"), but more responses are allowed ("strongly agree," "mildly agree," "no opinion/don't know," "mildly disagree," and "strongly disagree"). Thus, although no exact comparison between responses in the two surveys can be made, the trends within each survey are informative. Furthermore, the AUTS surveys span

TABLE 4.5 Changes in Public Knowledge about Risk of Smoking

Survey	Year	Question	Response	% Agree
Gallup	1949	Do you think cigarette smoking is harmful	Yes, No, No opinion	60%
Gallup	1954	"	"	70
AUTS	1964	Do you think smoking cigarettes is harmful to health	Strongly agree, Mildly agree, No opinion, Mildly disagree, Strongly disagree	81 (strongly/mildly)
AUTS	1966	"	"	85 (strongly/mildly)
AUTS	1970	"	"	87 (strongly/mildly)
AUTS	1975	"	"	90 (strongly/mildly)
Gallup	1977	Do you think cigarette smoking is harmful to your health	Is, Is not, No opinion	90
Gallup	1981	Do you think cigarette smoking is harmful to your health	Is, Is not, Don't Know	91
Gallup	1990	"	"	96
Gallup	1999	Do you think cigarette smoking is harmful	Yes, No, No opinion	95

SOURCE: Partially from Viscusi (1992).
NOTE: AUTS—Adult Use of Tobacco Surveys.

the Surgeon General's report, making them particularly informative about the impact of this information on the public. Between 1964 and 1975, there was another large increase in the share of respondents who believed that smoking is harmful to health. In 1964, 81 percent of those surveyed strongly or mildly agreed that smoking is harmful to health; by 1975, the figure rose to 90 percent. From the late 1970s through 1999, the share of people believing that smoking was harmful to health increased again, to 95 percent.

This rising awareness over the course of 50 years—from 60 percent of people believing that cigarettes are harmful to essentially the entire population believing this—is impressive. The trend is sufficiently constant over time, so that no one piece of information—even the landmark 1964 Surgeon General's report—can be said to have changed the public perception by itself. But it is clear that the cumulative information from many sources had a large impact on public beliefs about the dangers of smoking.

TABLE 4.6 The Amount of Smoking That Is Hazardous to Health

Survey	Year	Question	Response	% Any amount
Roper	1970	How hazardous is smoking?	Any amount, only heavy smoking, not hazardous don't know	47% (any) 45% (heavy)
Roper	1972	"	"	48 (any) 42 (heavy)
Roper	1974	"	"	54 (any) 39 (heavy)
Roper	1976	"	"	54 (any) 38 (heavy)
Roper	1977	Here are some things that people have said are bad for your health. Not everyone agrees that these things are harmful to health. Would you tell me whether you think any amount of it is harmful to health, or only harmful if you do it to excess, or not really harmful at all?	Any amount harmful, Harmful only in excess, Not harmful, Don't know	59 (any) 38 (heavy)
Roper	1978	Same as 1970 survey	Same as 1970 survey	61 (any) 31 (heavy)
Roper	1979	Same as 1977 survey	Same as 1977 survey	58 (any) 39 (heavy)
Roper	1981	Same as 1977 survey	Same as 1977 survey	63 (any) 35 (heavy)
Roper	1987	Same as 1977 survey	Same as 1977 survey	71 (any) 26 (heavy)

SOURCE: Partially from Viscusi (1992).

In addition to overall awareness of the dangers of smoking, the intensity of smoking believed to be harmful has changed. Table 4.6 contains information from Roper surveys from 1970 to 1987 on the amount of smoking considered a health hazard. In 1970, less than half the population thought that any amount of smoking is harmful to health; many people thought only heavy smoking is hazardous. By 1987, more people overall believed that smoking is harmful, and the share indicating that any smoking is harmful was more than double the share indicating that only heavy smoking is dangerous.

TABLE 4.7 Knowledge of Relationship between Smoking and Health

Survey	Year	Question	Response	Heart Disease	Lung Cancer
Gallup	1957	What is your opinion: do you think cigarette smoking is one of the causes of . . .	Yes, No, Don't know	37%	50%
Gallup	1958	Do you think that cigarette smoking is or is not one of the causes of . . .	Is, Is not, Don't know	33	44
Gallup	1960	"	"	34	50
Gallup	1969	"	"	60	71
Gallup	1977	"	"	68	81
Gallup	1981	"	"	74	83
Gallup	1990	What is your opinion: do you think cigarette smoking is one the causes of . . .	Yes, No, No opinion	85	94
Gallup	1999	"	"	80	92

SOURCE: Partially from Viscusi (1992).

One issue in these campaigns is determining whether people understand the details of the adverse relationship between smoking and health, or simply learn that some activity is harmful without knowing truly why. As noted above, professional knowledge of the harm caused by smoking has changed over the years. The original Surgeon General's report on smoking in 1964 focused predominantly on the link between smoking and cancer. It noted an association between smoking and cardiovascular disease, but did not present evidence for causality. It was not until 1983 that the Surgeon General's report concluded that smoking caused cardiovascular disease as well.

To depict what the public knows about the dangers of smoking, table 4.7 lists the share of people who think that tobacco use causes heart disease and cancer. The data are from various Gallup Polls asking questions of the form "What is your opinion—do you think cigarette smoking is one of the causes of . . . {heart disease, lung cancer}." Their significance is mixed. On the one hand, people appear to have a good deal of specific knowledge. For example, they widely cite lung cancer as a consequence of smoking, along with cardiovascular disease, and their awareness of both risks increases over time. On the other hand, the differentiation between adverse outcomes is not as precise in this case as is its depiction in the medical literature. For example, after the 1964 report, the share of people believing that smoking causes heart disease rose just as much as the share associating smoking with lung cancer, even though the report stressed the implications for cancer. Indeed, heart disease and lung cancer as outcomes of smoking appear to track each other well over the time period, with roughly 10 percent more people in all years believing that smoking causes lung cancer as believe that it causes heart disease. There is little differentiation among adverse outcomes over time.

Overall, the results of tobacco surveys demonstrate a clear point: public information, and public actions such as higher taxes, have had a major impact on people's knowledge and behavior. Prior to the widespread information campaigns about smoking, cigarette consumption was increasing steadily since the start of the twentieth century. Immediately after the information was provided, knowledge and consumption patterns changed. The number of smokers decreased by one-half over the next 30 years, and essentially everyone in the population now believes that smoking is harmful to health.

IV. Cholesterol

Cholesterol is a fatlike substance that performs a variety of functions in the human body. It composes cell membranes, insulates nerve fibers in the central nervous system, helps in the formation of bile (an enzyme that digests fats), and serves as a precursor to certain adrenal and sex hormones. The liver naturally produces cholesterol. But too high a level of serum (also called blood) cholesterol leads to a hardening and occlusion of blood vessels, resulting in cardiovascular disease.

Physicians hypothesize that cholesterol deposits form a plaque on the walls of blood vessels, causing atherosclerosis, commonly called hardening of the arteries. When a large enough quantity of cholesterol builds up on the inside of the walls, it can protrude into the blood vessel and impede the flow of the blood, which can lead to a heart attack or stroke. Research has identified saturated fats (contained in foods such as red meat, butter, and lard) as contributing the most to increases in serum cholesterol, while obesity, low physical activity, and smoking are also likely to adversely affect serum cholesterol levels.

Little was known about the link between diet and health in the first half of the twentieth century. The first edition of *Harrison's Principles of Internal Medicine* noted that populations with high cholesterol and fat intake suffered atherosclerosis more commonly than populations with low cholesterol and fat intake. The populations studied, however, were frequently animal species, or human populations at the extremes of cholesterol intake. No values were given for healthy and unhealthy levels of cholesterol.

Knowledge of the relationship between diet and health was substantially expanded in the 1950s, with major increases in information continuing to today. Figure 4.6 delineates the major developments concerning this topic. In 1957 the epidemiologist Ancel Keys argued for the importance of dietary factors in explaining variations in disease incidence; in two different studies Keys demonstrated a linear relationship between serum cholesterol level and heart disease. A first study comparing three different communities in North Africa (Bantus, Cape Coloreds, and Europeans) indicated that high cholesterol levels are associated with heart disease, with the Europeans consuming the most fats and thus having the highest cholesterol levels and heart disease. Keys then went on to compare males of Japanese ancestry living in Japan, Hawaii, and Los Angeles, and again found a relationship between diet, serum cholesterol counts, and heart disease.

Keys followed up these initial forays with the Seven Countries study (Keys, 1970), the first large-scale analysis of relationships between diet and rates of disease across an array of populations. Men aged 40–59 years were surveyed in 18 areas across 7 countries (Yugoslavia, Italy, Greece, Finland, the Netherlands, Japan, and the United States) where there were known differences in diet. Results from the study showed a strong correlation between serum cholesterol levels and coronary heart disease death, and high blood pressure and coronary heart disease death. Variations in cholesterol accounted for more than 40 percent of the variation in the coronary heart disease death rate.

Early results from the Framingham Heart Study confirmed these relationships. The study began surveying a group of over 5,000 residents of Framingham, Massachusetts, in 1948. Clinical examinations have been conducted every two years, and major cardiovascular disease incidents (including death) are recorded. The 1971 study showed a strong correlation between serum cholesterol and coronary heart disease for men across all ages, and a correlation between serum cholesterol and coronary heart disease in younger (ages 30–40 years) women.

Following up these pieces of evidence (the Framingham study was cited explicitly), the 1970 volume of *Harrison's Principles of Internal Medicine* was the first to identify a level of high cholesterol, noting increasing health risk above 220 mg per 100 ml of blood. Still, the proposed guidelines were loose; treatment was recommended only for people with high cholesterol

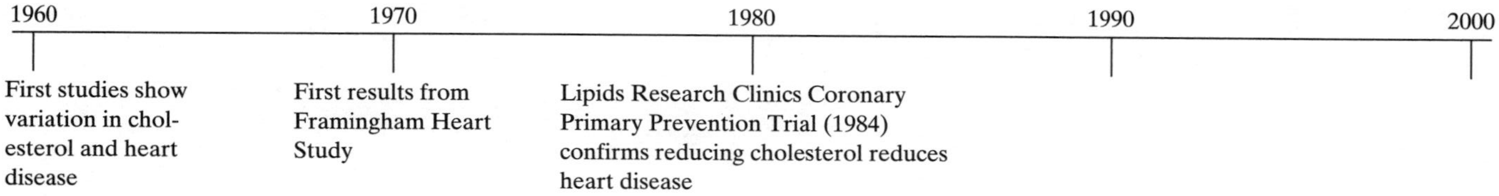

1960	1970	1980	1990	2000
First studies show variation in cholesterol and heart disease	First results from Framingham Heart Study	Lipids Research Clinics Coronary Primary Prevention Trial (1984) confirms reducing cholesterol reduces heart disease		

FIGURE 4.6: Public information about cholesterol

(above 250 mg per 100 ml), and in some cases treatment was recommended only for those whose cholesterol was 2 standard deviations above or below the age-specific mean—a level as high as 330 for 50- to 59-year-olds.

Popular publications help trace the spread of this knowledge through the general population. Articles about cholesterol began to appear with increasing frequency in the late 1950s, including "Are You Eating Your Way to a Heart Attack" in the December 1, 1956, edition of the *Saturday Evening Post* and "The Perilous Fat of the Land" in the April 1961 edition of *Reader's Digest*. Keys' initial research in 1957 generated publicity and regular newspaper coverage. In 1959 Keys and his wife wrote *Eat Well and Stay Well, the Mediterranean Diet* (Keys and Keys, 1959), which advised people to "eat less fat meat, fewer eggs and dairy products. Spend more time on fish, chicken, calves' liver, Canadian bacon, Italian food, Chinese food, supplemented by fresh fruits, vegetables, and casseroles." The book, which was translated into Finnish, Spanish, Italian, German, Japanese, and Portuguese, caused a columnist from the *Minneapolis Tribune* to lament the loss of the "mad, carefree past—the world as we knew it before Ancel Keys came along." The following year, Keys appeared on the cover of *Time* and opined that "Americans have Sunday dinner every day."[8]

These findings were convincing to some, but not all, medical researchers. The Framingham evidence and international studies showed a *correlation* between cholesterol and diet, but some scientists did not believe the link was *causal* without the corroborating evidence from a clinical trial. A 1980 report by the Food and Nutrition Board of the National Academy of Sciences supported this view, and concluded there was no reason to recommend that Americans lower their cholesterol. The director of the National Heart Lung and Blood Institute, Robert Levy, responded, "It's true that not all the facts are in. But to recommend doing nothing in the meantime is inappropriate. The existing information indicates that Americans should hedge their bets and seek a diet lower in saturated fats and cholesterol, at least until more evidence is available."

In 1984 the results of a randomized trial were reported. The Lipid Research Clinics Coronary Primary Prevention Trial (LRC-CPPT) had studied 3,806 men aged 35 to 59 years whose total cholesterol levels exceeded 265. Participants were split into two groups: one was given a cholesterol-reducing drug and put on dietary therapy while the other group received a placebo pill and dietary therapy. Over a 7- to 10-year follow-up period, results from the study showed a 2 percent reduction in coronary heart disease for every 1 percent decrease in serum cholesterol level. Furthermore, the coronary heart disease death rate in the drug group was 24 percent lower than the coronary heart disease rate in the placebo group (Anonymous, 1984).

The LRC-CPPT trial generated substantial amounts of media interest and appeared to galvanize opinion about the dangers of high cholesterol. Reporting on the trial's results, a story published in *Newsweek* in 1984 began, "Most people know that lowering cholesterol levels will prevent heart attacks. Or do they?" Numerous articles in the *New York Times* and the *Washington Post* also discussed the results of the LRC-CPPT. The headline of a *New York Times* front-page story read, "Study Backs Cutting Cholesterol to Curb Heart Disease Risk," while a *Washington Post* headline from the same day announced, "NIH Study Backs Low Cholesterol." Articles in the coming weeks included "Personal Health: Lowering Cholesterol in Blood" and "Cholesterol: Linking Diet, Heart and Health." One study found that eight major-market U.S. daily newspapers and three television networks[9] averaged between 30 and 40 heart disease stories per month over the 1980–90 time period. Toward the end of 1984 the combined total of such stories rose to over 400 per month (Finnegan et al., 1999).

The LRC-CPPT also led to the creation of national guidelines and a panel formed to standardize the definition of high cholesterol. The cutoff between moderate and high cholesterol was lowered to 200 mg per 100 ml of blood, and treatment was recommended once the level reached 240 mg per 100 ml. In addition, public and private efforts brought out the LRC-CPPT results and developed new definitions. In 1984 the National Cholesterol Education Program (NCEP) was established to educate physicians and the public about cholesterol. The NCEP program was designed to lower cholesterol levels and "to urge the public to have their cholesterol levels checked, to know their cholesterol levels and to understand the implications of their cholesterol reading." It broadcast public service announcements on television and radio and distributed pamphlets, including "Cholesterol Counts," designed for health professionals to treat patients; and "Fact Sheet on Blood Cholesterol" and "Facts about Blood Cholesterol," both describing basic facts about cholesterol.

There also were numerous private efforts toward spreading information about the dangers of cholesterol. The American Heart Association (AHA) recommended regular cholesterol screening and reductions in cholesterol levels. It also published pamphlets such as "Cholesterol and Your Heart," which recommended that people decrease total fat levels in their diets, as well as cut saturated fats from meat and dairy products while increasing the consumption of unsaturated fats. Numerous guides to eating well also were published at this time by the AHA and other organizations: "The

TABLE 4.8 Development of Pharmaceutical Therapy for Hypertension and Hypercholesterolemia

Hypertension	Year of Development	Hyperlipidemia	Year of Development
Vasodilators	1946	Nicotinic acid	1955
Peripherally acting agents	1953	Bile acid sequestrants	1964
Diuretics	1958	Fibric acid derivatives	1967
Centrally acting agents	1962	HMG-CoA reductase inhibitors (statins)	1987
Beta-blockers	1962		
Alpha blockers	1968		
Calcium channel blockers	1971		
ACE inhibitors	1979		
Angiotensin receptor antagonists	1995		

NOTE: Dates are FDA approval dates for the new molecular entity. In some cases (nicotinic acid, for example) the molecular entity is not new, and the date represents the first approval of a drug using the therapy.

Rutgers Guide to Lowering Your Cholesterol," "The Living Heart Diet," and "The American Heart Association Cookbook."

Research since the LRC-CPPT has highlighted the types of cholesterol and their differing impact on cardiovascular health. While the literature contained some discussion regarding cholesterol types as early as the 1970s, it has expanded dramatically. Medical textbooks and public discussion now differentiate between high density lipoproteins (HDL, or "good cholesterol") and low density lipoproteins (LDL, or "bad cholesterol"). LDL cholesterol is positively related to heart disease, while HDL is inversely related.

Over this time period, serum cholesterol levels in the U.S. population fell. Table 4.4 shows a 13 percent decline—from 43 percent to 30 percent—in rates of hypercholesterolemia between the early 1970s and the early 1990s. This change might result from either medical treatment changes or behavioral changes. Throughout this period, some pharmaceutical therapy for high cholesterol was being utilized (table 4.8). In the 1950s and 1960s, nicotinic acid was the common prescription, although it had substantial side effects that included ulcers and gout. Then in the late 1960s, the FDA approved the first bile acid sequestrants and fibric acid derivatives. Bile acid sequestrants are a class of drugs that bind bile acids and carry them out of the body, thereby forcing the body to create from cholesterol more bile acids, which are molecules essential to the digestive process. This process thus leads to a reduction in the cholesterol in the bloodstream. Fibric acid derivatives lower triglyceride levels and increase levels of HDL. While these two therapies have existed for some time, diet was still the first line of treatment. Bile acid sequestrants and fibric acid derivatives were used sparingly, as knowledge about their safety and efficacy was limited.

The first truly effective therapies were developed in the 1980s, with a new class of drugs called the statins. Statins inhibit a liver enzyme that is essential for the production of cholesterol. The consequent reduction in cholesterol production also leads to a reduction in LDL levels and to an increase in the HDL levels. The FDA approved four such drugs by 1993, and they are the most commonly prescribed anticholesterol medications today. Until the statin revolution, the share of people using cholesterol-lowering drugs was small. The early surveys in table 4.4 do not question people about whether they were taking such medications. But in the 1988–94 survey, only about 3 percent of the respondents had cholesterol below guideline levels and reported taking anticholesterol medication. Therefore compared with the 13 percent reduction in rates of high cholesterol overall, at least 77 percent of the decline in high cholesterol rates from the early 1970s through the early 1990s was the result of dietary change, including reduced fat and cholesterol intake and increased recreational exercise.

The most obvious explanation for reduced cholesterol in this time period is increased awareness of cholesterol risks and knowledge about health-improving behavior. To understand whether this explanation is plausible, we again use survey data to track the evolution of public knowledge of the relationship between cholesterol and heart disease. Data on knowledge about cholesterol are particularly good because of a series of studies conducted by the Food and Drug Administration, the Health and Diet Surveys (Guthrie, Derby, and Levy, 1999). The Health and Diet Surveys studied between 2,000 and 5,000 people in 6 years: 1982, 1984, 1986, 1988, 1994, and 1995. The first two surveys predate the LRC-CPPT trial that generated so much attention; the latter four surveys allow us to track responses after that influential study. In addition, the Health and Diet Surveys asked open-ended questions of the form "As you understand it, what are the major causes of heart disease or heart problems? Are there any others you can think of?" This type of questioning avoids some of the issues that may affect other surveys, such as respondents inferring from the question whether something is supposed to be good or bad.

Figure 4.7 reports the share of people naming cholesterol or fat as the most important risk factor for heart disease. The effect of the LRC-CPPT trial on this data is apparent. In the 1982 and 1984 surveys, only about one-quarter of the respondents believed that either cholesterol or fat was

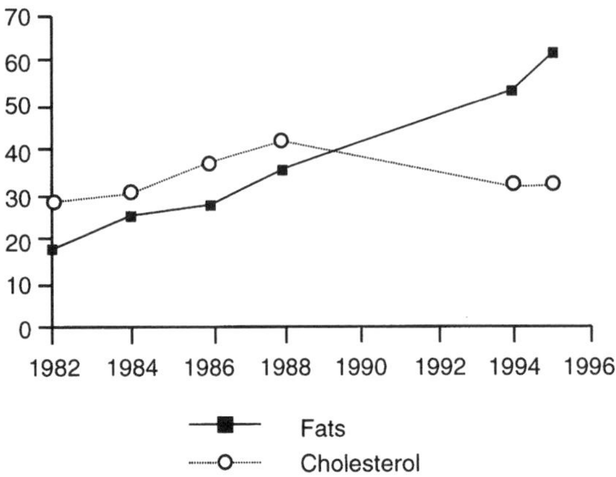

FIGURE 4.7: Awareness of diet/heart disease links
SOURCE: Health and Diet Surveys (1982, 1984, 1986, 1988, 1994, 1995); Guthrie, Derby and Levy (1999)
NOTE: Question asks respondents to name the most important dietary risk for heart disease.

related to heart disease. Between 1984 and 1998, however, the share of people mentioning cholesterol as a source of heart disease rose by 12 percentage points, or nearly 40 percent. In the late 1980s and particularly the 1990s, concern shifted from cholesterol to fat. By 1995, 60 percent of the survey participants identified fat as a factor in heart disease, three times the response of just a decade earlier. This response echoes the medical literature, which has suggested that fat intake is more important than dietary cholesterol intake in raising the body's serum cholesterol level.

Consistent with an increase in knowledge of the link between cholesterol and heart disease is an increase in consumers' attention regarding the amount of cholesterol they consume. Table 4.9 contains questions from Roper surveys from 1976, 1978, 1980, 1983, and 1985 which asked people to rate how important different food concerns were to them. The share of respondents who said that the cholesterol content was either very or fairly important rose from 63 percent in 1976 to 70 percent in 1985. The increase, while not enormous, is present, and occurred mainly in the last couple of years of the survey. Surveys from 1982, 1984, and 1986 also questioned people about how concerned they were about the level of cholesterol they consume. The share of people who said they were very or somewhat concerned increased from 58 percent in 1982 to 66 percent in 1986.

TABLE 4.9 Public Concern about Cholesterol

Survey			1976	1978	1980	1983	1985
Roper	When it comes to food, different people are concerned about different things. Tell me whether [cholesterol] is__ to you.	Very important	36%	36%	32%	36%	39%
		Fairly important	27	31	29	30	31
		Not too important	23	23	27	25	23
		Not at all important	13	9	11	8	6
		Don't know	1	1	1	1	1
			1982		1984		1986
Roper	Would you tell me for each one how__you personally are about the amount you use of each of them ?	Very concerned	20%		32%		30%
		Somewhat concerned	38		33		36
		Not at all concerned	35		33		31
		Don't use	1		1		2
		Don't know	1		1		1

More impressive are individual responses to the surveys. Figure 4.8 shows information from the Cholesterol Awareness Surveys of 1983, 1986, 1990, and 1995, which measured how informed adults over the age of 18 were about their own cholesterol. (The LRC-CPPT was released between the 1983 and 1986 surveys.) The first bars report the share of adults who have ever heard of high blood cholesterol. Not surprisingly, this share rises, from 77 percent in 1983 to 93 percent in 1995. Adults' actions responded even more dramatically, however. In 1983, just 3 percent of adults knew their cholesterol level; by 1995, half the population knew their level. And adults know what standard to use as well. Only 16 percent of adults in 1986 thought a blood cholesterol level below 200 (then the national recommendation) was desirable. By 1995, more than two-thirds of adults believed this was true.

Other research indicates that people are becoming more aware of which foods do and do not contribute to the serum cholesterol level, and more knowledgeable about remedies for high cholesterol levels (Schucker et al., 1991). For example, the share of people who said that saturated fat is found primarily in animal products (the correct answer) increased from 55 percent in the 1983 survey to 69 percent in the 1990 survey. The share of people who believed that getting regular exercise would help someone

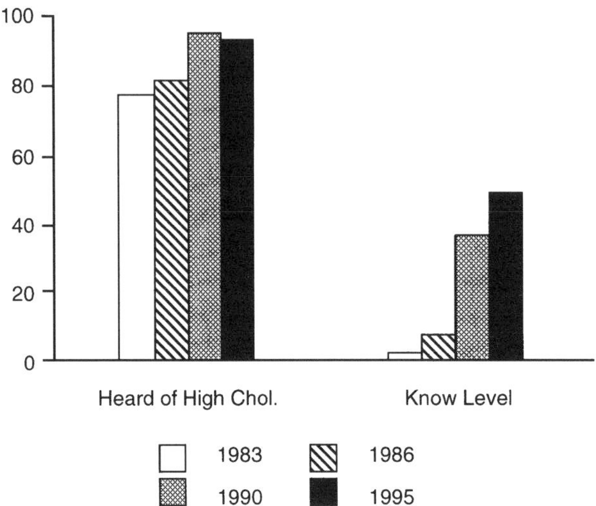

FIGURE 4.8: Knowledge of cholesterol
SOURCE: Cholesterol Awareness Surveys
NOTE: Sample includes ages 18+ years.

control their serum cholesterol (also a correct answer) increased from 40 percent to 66 percent.

The evolution in knowledge and practice concerning cholesterol risk has led to major changes in consumer dietary habits. Stephen and Wald (1990) assessed the share of energy intake composed of total fat and saturated fat consumption over much of the twentieth century. The data (fig. 4.9) are an amalgamation of dietary intake studies (generally, either 24-hour food recall studies, or 3- to 7-day records of all foods consumed by the surveyed individuals) conducted throughout the time period.[10] Stephen and Wald found that the percentage of energy coming from fat increased from 38 percent in the 1940s to 41 percent in the 1950s. It then fell slightly, to 40 percent, in the 1960s and then more rapidly, to 38 percent, in the 1970s and early 1980s. Saturated fat consumption mirrors this trend, with even more pronounced recent declines. The share of energy from saturated fat rose from 15 percent in the 1940s to 17 percent in the 1950s, and then fell to 16 percent in the 1960s, 14 percent in the 1970s, and 12 percent in the early 1980s.[11] More recently, Enns et al. (1997) have constructed similar measures of fat and saturated fat intake using data from the 1994–95 Continuing Survey of Foods (CSF II) data. About 3,000 men and women aged 20 years and over were sampled over the 1994–95 period. Results from this study follow the trend reported in the Stephen and Wald paper. Fat as

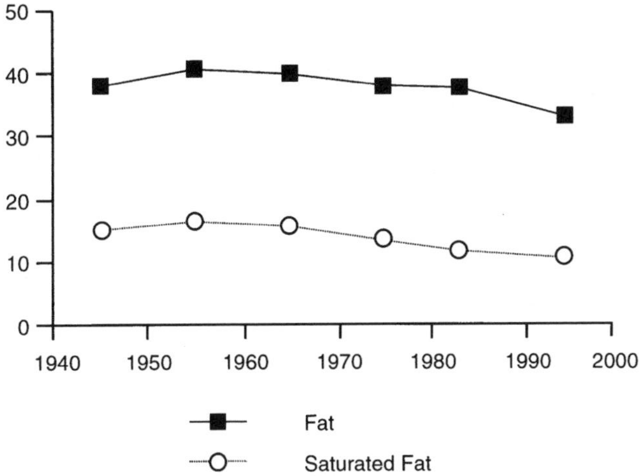

FIGURE 4.9: Fat and saturated fat as percentage of energy
SOURCE: Stephen and Wald (1990)
NOTE: Refer to notes 10 and 11 for description of data.

a percentage of energy continued to fall, from 38 percent for both men and women from the 1980–85 period to 32 percent for women and 34 percent for men in the 1994–95 period. Saturated fat as a percentage of energy fell, from 12 percent for men and women in 1980–85 to 11 percent for both in 1994–95.

A study by Ippolito and Mathios (1999) examines more recent trends in fat intake. They analyzed data on fat and dietary cholesterol consumption from surveys given in 1977, 1985, 1986, 1987/1988, and 1989/1990. Figure 4.10 reports their findings for males and females aged 18–50 years. Total fat, saturated fat, and cholesterol intake fell in both the 1977–85 and 1985–90 time periods, but much more so in the second period than in the first. Total fat intake (in grams per day) fell by 4.7 percent for men and 5 percent for women from 1977 to 1985; over the 1985–90 period, the rate of decrease increases to 14 percent for men and 11 percent for women. Similarly, from 1977–85, saturated fat intake fell by 2.5 percent for men and 3.8 percent for women over the first time period; again the rate of decrease increased to 17 percent for men and 14 percent for women. Ippolito and Mathios also show large decreases for the dietary cholesterol numbers over the two time periods (once more, there is a larger decrease from 1985 to 1990); figures for percentage of caloric intake of fat and saturated fat (see table 4.10) are comparable with the figures from Stephen and Wald.

TABLE 4.10 Average Daily Consumption of Fat and Dietary Cholesterol

	1977		1985		1987/88		1989/90	
Sex	M	F	M	F	M	F	M	F
Fat (grams/day)	112.8	73.3	107.5	69.6	94.1	63.9	92.6	62.1
Sat. fat (grams/day)	40.1	26.2	39.1	25.2	33.4	22.9	32.4	21.7
% Cal. from fat	41.7	40.9	36.6	36.8	36.9	37	35.8	35.3
% Cal. from sat. fat	14.8	14.6	13.2	13.3	13.0	13.2	12.4	12.3
Cholesterol (mg)	498.9	345.3	446.6	304.9	367.0	245.2	389	221.2

SOURCE: Ippolito and Mathios (1999).
NOTE: Sample includes ages 19–50 years.

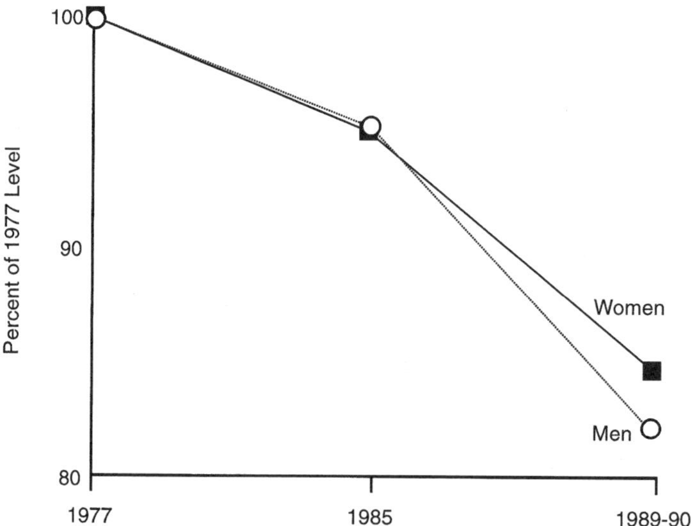

FIGURE 4.10: Changes in fat consumption
SOURCE: Ippolito and Mathos (1999)
NOTE: Sample includes ages 19–50 years.

Complementing the individual-level data on fat and saturated fat intake, Ippolito and Mathios also present trends from annual food supply data for foods with high fat and saturated fat content (table 4.11).[12] Per-capita consumption of red meat (a major source of fat and saturated fat) declined by 6 percent from 1977 to 1985, and fell another 10 percent between 1985 and 1990. Production of foods containing animal fat rose by 25 percent from 1977 to 1985, but then fell by 27 percent through 1990. Ippolito and Mathios also examine production trends in five other high-fat/dietary cholesterol foods: eggs, cream products, Italian cheese, all other cheese, and vegetable fats/oils. Production in four of the five food categories declined over the

TABLE 4.11 Per-Capita Food Supply of High Fat/Cholesterol Groups (lbs)

Year	Red Meat	Eggs	Cream Products	Italian Cheese	All Other Cheese	Animal Fats	Vegetable Fats/Oils
1977	132.2	34.3	5.0	3.7	12.3	10.6	42.7
1978	127.5	34.9	5.0	4.1	12.8	10.6	44.1
1979	124.4	35.5	5.1	4.2	12.9	11.5	44.9
1980	126.4	34.8	5.2	4.4	13.1	12.3	44.8
1981	125.1	34.0	5.3	4.5	13.7	11.7	45.7
1982	119.8	33.9	5.4	4.8	15.1	11.4	46.8
1983	123.9	33.5	5.7	5.3	15.3	12.1	47.9
1984	123.7	33.5	6.2	5.8	15.7	12.4	46.4
1985	124.9	32.9	6.7	6.5	16.1	13.3	50.9
1986	122.2	32.6	7.0	7.0	16.1	12.6	51.7
1987	117.4	32.7	7.1	7.6	16.5	11.1	51.8
1988	119.5	31.6	7.1	8.1	15.6	10.8	52.2
1989	115.9	30.4	7.3	8.5	15.3	9.9	50.5
1990	112.4	30.1	7.1	9.0	15.6	9.7	52.5

SOURCE: Ippolito and Mathios (1999).

1985–90 period (Italian cheese is the exception), in contrast with the 1977–85 period, where production of four out of the five items (exception is eggs) increased.[13]

It is clear that major changes in dietary habits occurred in the 1980s, resulting in lower fat and cholesterol intake. The reason for this also seems readily observable: research about the adverse effect of diet on health was translated to the public, leading to major changes in knowledge and behavior.

V. Hypertension

Hypertension is the medical term for high blood pressure. Blood pressure refers to the force (measured in millimeters of mercury) exerted by blood on the arteries as the blood is being pumped through the body by the heart. A blood pressure reading has two components: the top number is the systolic pressure (the pressure exerted on the arteries when the heart is beating [contracting]), and the bottom number is the diastolic pressure (the pressure exerted on the arteries when the heart is at rest [expanding]).

In the late 1940s and early 1950s, hypertension was thought to be related to cardiovascular disease, but the evidence of this link was not certain. The author of the 1950 edition of *Harrison's Principles of Internal Medicine,* for example, noted two schools of thought concerning this issue. Indeed, treatment of hypertension was often deemed rash and unjustified. A document titled "High Blood Pressure" produced by the Federal Security Agency remarked that in 90 percent of cases, the cause of hypertension is obscure. Treatment amounted to recommending that at "certain stages of the illness it might be necessary to rest at noon and to slow down in all activities" coupled with a possible reduction in diet, since it was thought that a person with hypertension "does better when his weight is average or a little below" (p. 4). Should the patient not respond to rest, mental relaxation, diet, and medicines, surgery was an option. The operation involved severing nerves close to blood vessels (sympathectomy)—a very dangerous procedure—and possible removal of the adrenal gland. Pyrogen therapy was also considered. In this therapy, bacteria was injected into the patient, with the hope of producing a fever that would lower blood pressure. As the 1948 publication noted, treatment was little better and potentially more dangerous than the "thousand and one advertised cures and remedies for hypertension" (ibid.) that it warned against.

Knowledge about the link between hypertension and cardiovascular disease has advanced considerably over time (fig. 4.11). During the 1950s and 1960s, numerous small-sample and nonrandomized treatment studies were conducted, documenting a positive relationship between blood pressure and cardiovascular disease. An early study, The Build and Blood Pressure Study of the Society of Actuaries in 1959, examined a sample of over 3.9 million life insurance policyholders. It concluded that higher mortality was predicted even by small increases above the average in systolic and diastolic blood pressure; mortality was shown to be high even for people who had what was then thought to be an acceptable blood pressure level.

Still, little was known about exactly what level of blood pressure should be considered dangerous. According to *Harrison's Principles of Internal Medicine* for 1962, for example, "[H]ypertension may be diagnosed if on repeated examinations the blood pressure is found to be above that considered normal for adolescents of similar racial and environmental background" (*Harrison's,* 1962: 1346). *Harrison's* also described a divergence of opinions in the medical community concerning appropriate treatment. One view held that the exact level of blood pressure has little clinical significance; that for a variety of reasons results from antihypertensive therapy are difficult to evaluate; and that side effects of specific therapy may be worse than the disease. The other view (recommended by the author) held that diastolic pressure is important in determining mortality and that attempts to lower blood pressure seem justified in *properly selected cases*. To take just one example where treatment would be administered immediately if the patient came to a physician's attention today, the author concludes, "A woman who has tolerated her diastolic pressure of 120 for 10 years

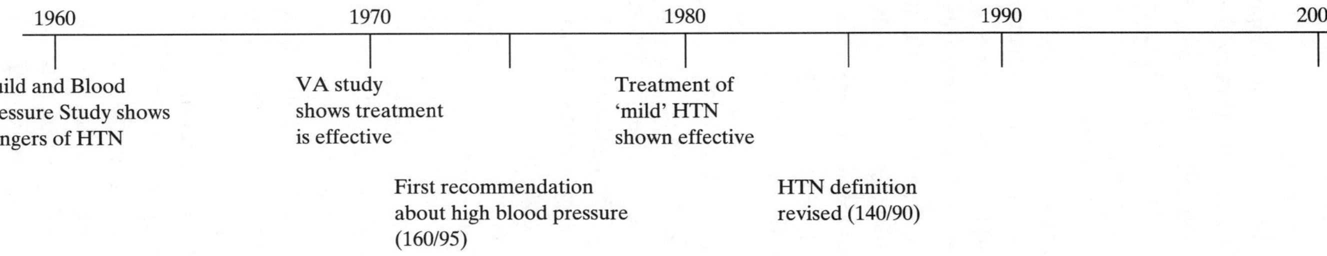

FIGURE 4.11: Public information about hypertension

without symptoms or deterioration does not need immediate specific treatment for hypertension."

Effective drug therapies began to be developed about this time (table 4.8). In 1954,[14] the only FDA-approved drug therapies for hypertension were vasodilators and peripherally acting agents.[15] Both of these drugs have very widespread effects, with many adverse side effects; moreover, their effectiveness diminishes over time. Consequently, today they are only used in emergency situations. In the late 1950s, diuretics, the first modern pharmaceutical antihypertensive therapies, were developed. These drugs work by inhibiting sodium and water reabsorption in the kidney, thus reducing the blood volume and hence blood pressure.

Randomized trials of these new therapies followed. The Veterans Administration Cooperative Study of 1967 was the first large prospective experiment to study the effectiveness of antihypertensive agents. A total of 523 people having a diastolic pressure of 90–129 were selected and split into two groups, a higher blood pressure group (115–129) and a lower blood pressure group (90–114). Within each group there was a treatment (with antihypertensives) and a control group, which were similar in age, racial distribution, and blood pressure. Within $1\frac{1}{2}$ years, major differences were noted between the control and treatment group within the higher blood pressure group (27 complications in the placebo group versus 2 complications in the treatment group). The trial for this group was stopped because it was not deemed ethically appropriate to withhold treatment from the placebo control group. There was also some evidence of a positive treatment effect in the lower blood pressure group, as the risk of morbid events due to hypertension was 37 percent less in the treatment group. Overall, results from the study proved conclusively the beneficial effects of treating people with high blood pressure, but there was still debate over the benefits of treating people at the lowest levels (90–114 diastolic).

While the Veterans Study was in progress, results from a Framingham study in 1969 showed a relationship between blood pressure and coronary heart disease. The paper analyzed men and women aged 30–62 years based on their blood pressure at initial examination. Participants were divided into three categories: hypertensive (blood pressure $\geq$ 160/95), normotensive (blood pressure $\leq$ 140/90), and borderline (not hypertensive and not normotensive); risk of coronary heart disease was examined for each. The result showed that people in the borderline and hypertensive categories were much more likely to suffer from coronary heart disease over the course of 14 years. This relationship existed among men and women and across the two age groups analyzed ($<$ 50 and $\geq$ 50).

Results from the Veterans Study along with the evidence from the Framingham study led to the first guidelines for hypertension diagnosis. The National High Blood Pressure Education Program (NHBEP), established in 1972, recommended that people whose systolic pressure was above 160 mm HG or whose diastolic pressure was above 95 mm HG be diagnosed as being hypertensive. Treatment with antihypertensives was recommended for those whose diastolic pressure was greater than 105 mm HG. Observation and management without drugs was recommended for people whose diastolic pressure was between 95 to 105 mm HG.

Appropriate therapy for people with more moderate hypertension was still a concern. To address this issue, the Hypertension Detection and Follow-up Program trial was conducted in the mid-1970s. Results reported in 1979 showed that treatment was effective in preventing cardiovascular disease even in people having "mild" levels of hypertension (diastolic pressure between 95 and 104).

Based on the results of these studies, the definition of hypertension was lowered, so that people whose systolic pressure was above 140 or whose diastolic pressure was above 90 were considered hypertensive. The 1984 report from the NHBEP advised physicians to treat all patients whose diastolic pressure was between 95 and 104 with antihypertensive medication, and to treat patients whose diastolic pressure was less than 95 but who were otherwise at high-risk (for example, patients with diabetes mellitus or with other cardiovascular risk factors) the same way. For people with high blood pressure and no other risk factors, nonpharmacologic therapy was recommended. If diastolic blood pressure remained above 90 after attempting nonpharmacologic treatment, then treatment with drugs became an option.

In addition, new antihypertensives were being developed. Perhaps the most important advance was the introduction in 1962 of beta-blockers, which reduce the speed of conduction and the strength at which the heart contracts, hence lowering blood pressure. This development was followed by that of calcium channel blockers in 1971, ACE inhibitors in 1979, and angiotensin receptor antagonists in 1995.[16]

Nonpharmacologic treatments also have been emphasized over the last two decades. Initial recommendations specified only weight and salt control as contributing to hypertension. By 1984, lack of exercise and heavy alcohol intake also were recognized as factors. More recent research has suggested an inverse relationship between potassium consumption and hypertension (Stamler, 1997).

A variety of sources measure public knowledge about the relationship between hypertension and cardiovascular disease, and the different factors that might affect one's blood pressure. The National Heart, Lung, and Blood Institute of the National Institutes of Health conducted a survey, The Public and High Blood Pressure, in 1973 and 1979. Each survey sampled the population aged 17 years and older using a variety of questions relating to hypertension. The 1973 sample interviewed about 4,000 people, and the 1979 sample interviewed approximately 5,000. Because both surveys were taken after the VA trial and the beginning of widespread coverage of the dangers of hypertension, we view these studies partly as evidence of how informed people became, and partly as evidence of the spread of information.

Table 4.12 shows the results of these surveys. The first panel indicates the health conditions people thought were the consequences of high blood pressure; the second panel gives the percentage of respondents indicating a particular condition. Public knowledge overall is high. In response to questions about the consequences of high blood pressure, people in both survey years put strokes and heart attacks (the two most important complications) near the top. In 1973, 87 percent of respondents said that high blood pressure causes stroke; 91 percent said the same in 1979. Eighty-one percent of people in the 1973 survey said that heart attacks are caused by high blood pressure; this figure rose to 89 percent in 1979. Further, respondents did not associate hypertension with all health problems. They did not link high blood pressure with pneumonia, arthritis, or anemia (none of which are true clinically). The only major change in this time period is a doubling of the share of people associating high blood pressure with diabetes.

Knowledge of the causes of hypertension is less accurate but still reasonable. In both survey years, respondents associated hypertension primarily with worrying, stress, tension, and obesity. The first three factors are still being debated in the medical community; the fourth conforms with clinical evidence. There were large increases over the decade in the share of respondents who associated hypertension with eating too much salt, smoking, heredity, and a sedentary lifestyle. Only three of these factors are correct; while smoking increases blood pressure in the short-term, it is not associated with long-term increases in blood pressure. Finally, few people associate hypertension with either too much blood in the system or regular exercise.

Data suggest that hypertension information had a large effect on people, both in terms of their knowledge about the condition and their consequent health choices. Figures 4.12 and 4.13 show data from the National Health and Nutrition Examination Surveys on changes in awareness and treatment of hypertension in the population. Figure 4.12 reports the share of "at-risk" hypertensives—people who have elevated blood pressure or those

TABLE 4.12 Knowledge about Hypertension

		1973	1979
Consequences of High Blood Pressure			
Is a stroke caused by high blood pressure?	Caused by	87%	91%
	Not caused by	4	3
	Not sure	9	6
Is dizziness caused by high blood pressure?	Caused by	86	91
	Not caused by	7	4
	Not sure	7	5
Is a heart attack caused by high blood pressure?	Caused by	81	89
	Not caused by	9	5
	Not sure	10	6
Is a headache caused by high blood pressure?	Caused by	75	81
	Not caused by	15	11
	Not sure	10	8
Is a nosebleed caused by high blood pressure?	Caused by	65	67
	Not caused by	20	12
	Not sure	15	21
Is hardening of arteries caused by high blood pressure?	Caused by	50	53
	Not caused by	28	27
	Not sure	6	20
Is diabetes caused by high blood pressure?	Caused by	15	35
	Not caused by	63	39
	Not sure	22	26
Is anemia caused by high blood pressure?	Caused by	12	15
	Not caused by	67	60
	Not sure	21	20
Is arthritis caused by high blood pressure?	Caused by	6	9
	Not caused by	78	73
	Not sure	16	18
Is pneumonia caused by high blood pressure?	Caused by	5	7
	Not caused by	80	75
	Not sure	15	18
Causes of High Blood Pressure			
Is worrying, stress, and tension a possible cause of high blood pressure?	Definite cause	72%	73%
	Possible cause	23	23
	Not a cause	3	2
	Not sure	2	1
Is being overweight a possible cause of high blood pressure?	Definite cause	65	66
	Possible cause	29	30
	Not a cause	3	2
	Not sure	3	2

continued

TABLE 4.12 *continued*

		1973	1979
Is eating fatty foods a possible cause of high blood pressure?	Definite cause	52	57
	Possible cause	33	32
	Not a cause	8	6
	Not sure	7	4
Is eating too much salt a possible cause of high blood pressure?	Definite cause	37	52
	Possible cause	35	34
	Not a cause	15	7
	Not sure	13	7
Is smoking a possible cause of high blood pressure?	Definite cause	38	45
	Possible cause	33	34
	Not a cause	17	13
	Not sure	12	8
Is heredity a possible cause of high blood pressure?	Definite cause	28	37
	Possible cause	37	38
	Not a cause	24	16
	Not sure	11	8
Is not getting enough exercise a possible cause of high blood pressure?	Definite cause	20	28
	Possible cause	42	45
	Not a cause	26	19
	Not sure	19	8
Is old age a possible cause of high blood pressure?	Definite cause	26	25
	Possible cause	40	45
	Not a cause	25	23
	Not sure	9	6
Is too much blood in the system a possible cause of high blood pressure?	Definite cause	14	14
	Possible cause	19	20
	Not a cause	44	40
	Not sure	23	26
Is regular hard exercise a possible cause cause of high blood pressure?	Definite cause	10	10
	Possible cause	22	21
	Not a cause	56	60
	Not sure	12	10

SOURCE: U.S. Department of Health and Human Services et al., 1986.

taking medication who have their blood pressure under control—who are aware they have high blood pressure. This share increases dramatically, from only half of the at-risk group in the late 1950s and early 1960s, to over two-thirds by the early 1990s. This change has occurred despite the fact that the current pool of hypertensives includes many people with more moderate blood pressure than in previous years. Among those aware of their hypertension, treatment rates have increased as well. The combination of these two factors means that the share of all hypertensives taking

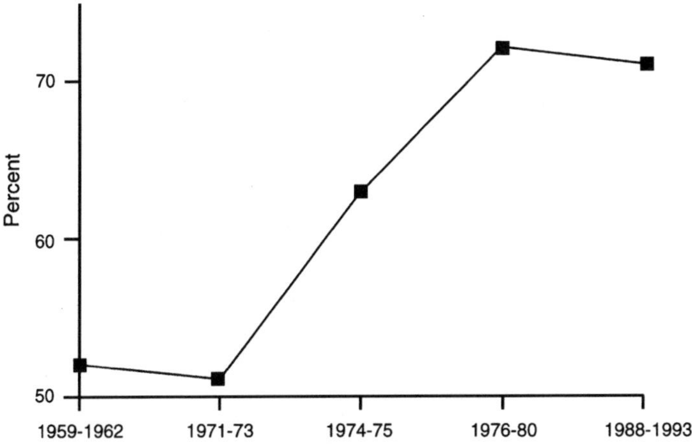

FIGURE 4.12: Share of hypertensives aware of condition
SOURCE: National Health and Nutrition Examination Surveys
NOTES: Samples in various years include blacks and whites, aged 45–74 years, who have not had a cardiovascular disease incident and who are hypertensive. Hypertension is defined using knowledge at time of survey.

medication rose from 33 percent in the late 1950s-early 1960s to over 50 percent in the late 1980s-early 1990s. Figure 4.13 presents this data.

Other surveys show similar findings. The Hypertension Detection and Follow-Up Program screened nearly 32,000 people aged 30–69 years in 1973–74, to find those appropriate for the clinical trial (Apostolides et al., 1980). The screening was conducted in three cities: Baltimore, Maryland; Birmingham, Alabama; and Davis, California. A subsequent follow-up study of 12,000 people was conducted in those cities in 1977–78, using the same selection criteria but different participants. The follow-up found considerable increases in awareness of hypertension over this time period. Conditional on having hypertension, the share of people who knew they were hypertensive increased by 9 percent on average, and within every age/sex group. The percentage of those who were treated also increased, by 14 percent on average.

Behavioral changes were encouraged as well. In the late 1970s and early 1980s, research studies highlighted the role of sodium in raising blood pressure. While sodium was known for some time to be a risk factor for hypertension, more and more evidence was being generated regarding this connection, leading to a variety of agencies throughout the 1970s recommending reduced salt intake. The Committee on Nutrition of the American Academy of Pediatrics in 1974 recommended that children reduce or avoid

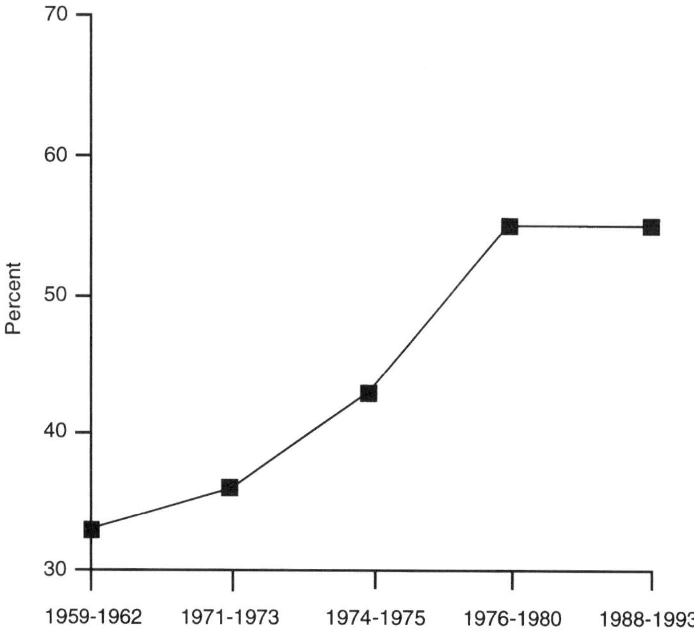

FIGURE 4.13: Share of hypertensives taking antihypertensive medication
SOURCE: National Health and Nutrition Examination Surveys
NOTES: Samples in various years include blacks and whites, aged 45–74 years, who have not had a cardiovascular disease incident and who are hypertensive. Hypertension is defined using knowledge at time of survey.

increasing salt intake. In 1977, the U.S. Senate Select Committee on Nutrition and Human Needs recommended reducing intake of salt to 5g per day. In 1972, the Federation of American Societies for Experimental Biology (FASEB), under the auspices of the FDA, began to review available safety data on generally regarded as safe (GRAS) substances. The final report in 1979 from a panel created by the FASEB concluded that "evidence on sodium chloride [salt] is insufficient to determine that the adverse effects reported are not deleterious to the health of a significant portion of public when it is used at levels that are now current and in the manner now practiced." The committee further recommended that sodium chloride intake be lowered; that guidelines be developed for restricting salt in processed foods; and that labeling of sodium content of foods be developed to help meet these objectives. This was supposedly the second most negative conclusion that could have been reached by the panel during the review. The degree of public concern is highlighted by the appearance on the best-seller list of a book titled *Killer Salt* (Whittlesey, 1977). Given the circumstances, the FDA and the NHBEP began to stress the relationship between salt and hypertension in their media campaigns. Responding to this information, the share of people who said they were purchasing low-salt food rose from about 13 percent in the early 1980s to about 19 percent in the 1990s. The amount of salt in the average diet also fell, by 22 percent, largely as a result of a decreased use of table salt (Engstrom, 1997).

Changes in knowledge and therapy together had a dramatic effect on the incidence of hypertension. Table 4.4, developed from the NHANES surveys, shows that the share of people who had high blood pressure decreased nearly by half between the early 1970s and the early 1990s. The importance of medication in this change is shown in the penultimate row of the table. The share of the population having medically controlled blood pressure rose from 3 percent in the early 1970s to 10 percent about 1990. While this 7-percentage-point change is significant, it is nowhere near as large as the 26-percentage-point overall reduction in the share of people having elevated blood pressure. Indeed, these data suggest that only one-quarter ($\frac{7}{26}$) of the decline in hypertension rates is attributable to medication.

But this estimate understates the role of pharmaceuticals in blood pressure reduction. Some of those taking medication have lowered, but not controlled, their hypertension. This reduces disease risk, albeit not as fully as full control does. We address the contribution of medication and behavioral changes to better health more completely in the next section.

VI. The Return to Medical Research

A central empirical question is to separate out the role of medication and behavioral change in improved control of hypertension and high cholesterol, and to value the changes in medical knowledge and treatments that produce them. We have attempted such a decomposition. Our methodology is described in more detail in our other work (Cutler and Kadiyala, 2001); we summarize it briefly here. We studied data on blood pressure and cholesterol for people taking medication and people not taking medication, and used that information to infer the effect of medication on risk factor levels. We then combined these estimates with data on the share of the population taking medication, to arrive at an estimate of the effect of medication on changing the risk of cardiovascular disease. The residual is attributable to behavioral factors.

Our results suggest that approximately one-half of the reduced disease risk is a result of increased medication use and effectiveness, and the other half results from behavioral change. Some medication use eliminates risk entirely, while more extensive use reduces risk levels, even though risk levels are still elevated.

Combined with our earlier estimate of the importance of acute treatment changes, this assessment of medical and behavioral factors allows us to estimate an overall decomposition of reduced cardiovascular disease mortality. As noted previously, we estimate that approximately one-third of reduced mortality results from better intensive treatment of acute incidents, particularly heart attacks. Half of the remainder, or one-third of the total change, results from increased use and effectiveness of medication for hypertension and high cholesterol. The final third is a result of behavioral change: reduced smoking, lower fat intake, reduced alcohol and salt use, and the like. Put another way, the contribution of medical care to better health—both intensive care and preventive pharmaceuticals—is approximately two-thirds of the total, and behavioral change comprises approximately one-third.

There is naturally uncertainty about these exact shares, but our final results are not particularly dependent on specific values.

The Rate of Return to Treatments and Knowledge

Medical research and treatments have costs as well as benefits; both need to be compared to determine whether the increase in spending is worthwhile.

The value of medical research is longer, healthier lives. As noted in the introduction to this chapter, the average 45-year-old will live $4\frac{1}{2}$ years longer today than he or she would have in 1950, solely because cardiovascular disease mortality has decreased. About two-thirds of this change, or 3 years, results from improved medical treatment; one-third, or $1\frac{1}{2}$ years, results from behavioral change.

Measuring the benefits of this additional survival requires valuing the life extension in dollars. A typical estimate in the literature (Viscusi, 1993; Tolley et al., 1994; Cutler and Richardson, 1997, 1998, 1999; Murphy and Topel, this volume) is that each year of life in perfect health is worth about \$100,000. This number is not exact, but reflects a rough midpoint of common estimates. We use a value of 100,000 for our calculations. We further discount these benefits at a 3 percent real discount rate. Using these estimates, the value of medical treatments is about \$120,000. Similarly, the value of behavioral changes is \$30,000.[17]

These benefits must be balanced against the costs of achieving them. The cost of the medical treatments is the money spent on those therapies.

The typical 45-year-old can expect to spend about $30,000 in present value on cardiovascular disease care over his/her remaining lifetime. Spending on cardiovascular disease in 1950 was negligible, so the increase is about $30,000. Compared with the $120,000 of benefits, it is clear that this spending increase is worth its cost. We estimate a rough rate of return of 4 to 1 for medical treatment changes. Typically, society is happy with rates of return of about 1.1 to 1. The rate of return we estimate is an order of magnitude higher.

The cost of behavioral change is the money spent on researching these behaviors and conveying findings of that research to the public. From 1953 to 1997, NIH spending on all factors related to cardiovascular disease—including behavioral knowledge and other research—amounted to about $3 billion annually, or $10 per person per year. For a person with a 50-year tax-paying span, this amount comes to about $500 over his/her lifetime (ignoring discounting). There are also costs of disseminating research findings to the public, but these costs are not large. Some information is conveyed by physicians, and much is conveyed by newspapers, TV, and radio. No firm data on these costs is available. As a rough guess, we assume such costs amount to about 10 doctor visits per person. At a cost of $50 per visit (in today's dollars), this is another $500 of expense. Total costs of behavioral change are therefore about $1,000 per person. Comparing the costs and benefits of behavioral change yields a very clear conclusion. Research and dissemination costs of about $1,000 per person brought benefits of about $30,000 per person, for a 30-to–1 return. This rate is even greater than the return to medical treatments.

It is clear in examining these estimates that the uncertainty in our various calculations does not have a meaningful impact on our conclusions. For example, medical treatment changes would be worth the cost even if only one-sixth of mortality reductions resulted from medical intervention, far below our best guess of two-thirds. Similarly, research on behavioral knowledge would be worth it even if such knowledge contributed only 1 percent to better health, compared with the 33 percent we allocate to it. The conclusion is clearly and unequivocally that medical research is worth the cost.

While we have shown a considerable decrease in risk factors due to changes in treatment and behavior, our analysis leaves a number of puzzling questions unaddressed. Obesity is also a risk factor for cardiovascular disease, and most surveys indicate that people are aware of this fact. Yet over the last few decades, obesity has been on the rise. Investigating why people responded to information about smoking, blood pressure, and cholesterol but not obesity would be very useful. So too would repeating this calculation for other diseases. We leave each of these topics for future research.

Appendix: Table 4A.1 Time Line of Important Smoking-Related Events and Legislation

1964 *Smoking and Health: Report of the Advisor Committee to the Surgeon General* is published. The report concludes that cigarette smoking is a cause of lung cancer in men and a suspected cause in women.

American Medical Association calls smoking "a serious health hazard."

1965 Federal Cigarette Labeling and Advertising Act is passed and requires the following health warning on all cigarette packages: "Caution: Cigarette Smoking May Be Hazardous to Your Health."

1967 Fairness Doctrine is instituted by the Federal Communcations Commission. Requires stations broadcasting cigarette commercials to give free airtime to smoking-prevention messages.

1969 Public Health Cigarette Smoking Act of 1969 bans cigarette advertising on TV and radio; requires stronger health warning on cigarette packages. New warning: "The Surgeon General Has Determined that Cigarette Smoking Is Dangerous to Your Health."

1972 Surgeon General's report determines that second-hand smoke is a health risk.

1973 Civil Aeronautics Board requires nonsmoking sections on all commercial airline flights.

Arizona is the first state to restrict smoking in public places, and the first to do so because second-hand smoke is deemed a public health hazard.

1977 American Cancer Society sponsors the first national Great American Smokeout.

1981 Surgeon General's report concludes that no cigarette or level of tobacco consumption is safe.

1983 Congress doubles the federal excise tax on cigarettes.

Surgeon General's report focuses on the relationship between smoking and cardiovascular disease.

1984 Congress passes the Comprehensive Smoking Education Act, which requires that the rotation of four different health warnings on cigarette packages and advertisements.

1986 Congress permanently extends the 16-cents-per-pack federal excise tax on cigarettes.

1990 Airline smoking ban goes into effect. No smoking is permitted on all scheduled domestic flights lasting 6 hours or less.

1991 Federal cigarette excise tax increases.

1992 Federal legislation requires states to adopt and enforce restrictions on tobacco sales to minors.

1993 Federal cigarette excise tax increases.

1994 FDA commissioner David Kessler testifies that cigarettes may qualify as drug delivery systems, bringing them under the jurisdiction of the FDA.

The State of Mississippi sues the tobacco industry to recover its Medicaid costs for tobacco-related illnesses.

Notes

1. Parts of this chapter are drawn from a longer paper (Cutler and Kadiyala, 2001) that contains more-detailed analysis.

2. See Cutler, McClellan, and Newhouse (1999) for more discussion. There has been much less progress in the treatment of strokes. We thus focus on heart disease in this discussion.

3. The rates of hypertension and hypercholesterolemia are based on present-day definitions of what would constitute high levels. These levels have fallen over time, as we discuss later in the chapter.

4. People were allowed multiple answers.

5. The warning has since changed. The first change, made in 1969, read, "Warning: The Surgeon General Has Determined That Cigarette Smoking Is Dangerous to Your Health." The newest version contains more-detailed information, for example that cigarette smoke contains carbon monoxide.

6. The 1900 figures are low in part because during that time many cigarettes were hand rolled.

7. Never smokers are defined as people who have consumed fewer than 100 cigarettes in their lifetime.

8. Keys also attributed the rise of heart disease to "the North American habit for making the stomach the garbage disposal unit for a long list of harmful foods."

9. Newspapers were the *New York Times, Washington Post, Detroit Free Press, Chicago Tribune, New Orleans Times Picayune, St. Louis Post-Dispatch, Los Angeles Times,* and the *San Francisco Examiner*. The TV networks were ABC, NBC, and CBS.

10. Overall, 20 studies from the 1940s, for a total of 4,178 individuals; 46 studies from the 1950s, 20,993 people; 28 studies from the 1960s, 11,239 people; 53 studies from the 1970s, 73,449 individuals; and finally, 20 studies from 1980–85, 1,492 individuals. This includes all studies of healthy individuals (except for vegans and vegetarians), regardless of whether the data comprised a random sample or whether the individuals surveyed came from specific groups, such as athletes.

11. The numbers of individuals used for the saturated fat calculation are smaller than for the total fat calculation because saturated fat was not reported in all the studies. The numbers from 1940–80 are 64, 3951, 3939, 61068, and 178.

12. Available food supply equals annual production plus imports minus exports, industrial nonfood uses, farm uses, and end of year inventories. One caveat concerning this data: it represents the food that is available rather than the food actually eaten. Wastage and spoilage would ideally be subtracted from this data. We do not have any evidence that wastage and spoilage have either increased or decreased over this time period, however.

13. These conclusions come from piecewise linear regression models that check to see whether there was a shift in trend after the 1985 period. These models use the data presented in table 4.11.

14. The FDA approval process for drugs began after World War II.

15. Vasodilators allow blood vessel walls to relax/widen so blood can flow more easily. Peripherally acting agents are drugs that inhibit the nerves from firing to contract blood vessel walls.

16. Calcium channel blockers block calcium from getting into the muscle in the walls of the blood vessels, so they contract less frequently. ACE inhibitors inhibit the formation of angiotensin, a substance that makes the arteries constrict, thus keeping the arteries open and consequently lowering pressure. Angiotensin receptor antagonists have effects similar to ACE inhibitors, with fewer side effects.

17. This estimate nets out the cost of behavioral change in terms of lower welfare from smoking, eating fatty foods, and other pleasurable behaviors (see Cutler and Kadiyala, 2001).

References

Anonymous. 1984. "The Lipid Research Clinics Coronary Primary Prevention Trial Results. I. Reduction in Incidence of Coronary Heart Disease." *Journal of the American Medical Association* 251, no. 3 (20 January): 351–64.

———. 1984. "The Lipid Research Clinics Coronary Primary Prevention Trial Results. II. The Relationship of Reduction in Incidence of Coronary Heart Disease to Cholesterol Lowering." *Journal of the American Medical Association* 251, no. 3 (20 January): 365–74.

Apostolides, Aristide Y., Gary Cutter, Jess F. Kraus, Albert Oberman, Thomas Blaszkowski, Nemat O. Borhani, and Greg Entwisle. 1980. "Impact of Hypertension Information on High Blood Pressure Control between 1973 and 1978." *Hypertension* 2, no. 5 (September-October): 708–13.

Barker, David J. P. 1998. *Mothers, Babies and Health in Later Life*. Edinburgh: Churchill Livingstone.

Costa, Dora L. 1998. "Unequal at Birth: A Long-Term Comparison of Income and Birth Weight." *Journal of Economic History* 58, no. 4 (December): 987–1009.

Cutler, David M., Jonathan Gruber, Raymond S. Hartman, Mary Beth Landrum, Joseph P. Newhouse, and Meredith B. Rosenthal. 2000. "The Economic Impacts of the Tobacco Settlement." NBER Working Paper no. 7760, June.

Cutler, David M., and Srikanth Kadiyala. 2001. "The Economics of Better Health: The Case of Cardiovascular Disease." Mimeo, Harvard University.

Cutler, David M., Mark McClellan, and Joseph P. Newhouse. 1999. "The Costs and Benefits of Intensive Treatment for Cardiovascular Disease." In *Measuring the Prices of Medical Treatments,* edited by Jack Triplett, 34–71. Washington, D.C.: Brookings Institution.

Cutler, David M., Mark McClellan, Joseph P. Newhouse, and Dahlia Remler. 2000. "Pricing Heart Attack Treatments." In *Medical Care Output and Productivity,* edited by David Cutler and Ernst Berndt. Chicago: University of Chicago Press.

Cutler, David, and Elizabeth Richardson. 1997. "Measuring the Health of the United States Population." *Brookings Papers on Economic Activity* 2:217–72.

———. 1998. "The Value of Health: 1970–1990." *American Economic Review Papers and Proceedings*: 97–100.

———. 1999. "Your Money and Your Life: The Value of Health and What Affects It." In *Frontiers in Health Policy Research*, vol. 2, edited by Alan Garber, 99–132. Cambridge, Mass.: MIT Press.

Dustan, Harriet P., Edward J. Roccella, and Howard H. Garrison. 1996. "Controlling Hypertension: A Research Success Story." *Archives of Internal Medicine* 156 (23 September): 1926–35.

Engstrom, Alta, Rosemary C. Tobelmann, and Ann M. Albertson. 1997. "Sodium Intake Trends and Food Choices." *American Journal of Clinical Nutrition* 65(suppl.): 704S–7S.

Enns, Cecilia W., Joseph D. Goldman, and Annetta Cook. 1997. "Trends in Food and Nutrient Intakes by Adults: NFCS 1977–1978, CSFII 1989–1991, and CSF11 1994–1995." *Family Economics and Nutrition Review* 10, no. 4: 2–15.

Finnegan, J. R., K. Viswanath, and James Hertog. 1999. "Mass Media, Secular Trends, and the Future of Cardiovascular Disease Health Promotion: An Interpretive Analysis." *Preventive Medicine* 29:S50–S58.

Goldman, Lee, and E. Fran Cook. 1984. "The Decline in Ischemic Heart Disease Mortality Rates: An Analysis of the Comparative Effects of Medical Interventions and Changes in Lifestyle." *Annals of Internal Medicine* 101:825–36.

Guthrie, Joanne F., Brenda M. Derby, and Alan S. Levy. 1999. "What People Do and Do Not Know about Nutrition." In *America's Eating Habits: Changes and Consequences,* edited by Elizabeth Frazao. Washington, D.C.: Food and Rural Economics Division, Economic Research Service, U.S. Dept. of Agriculture, Agriculture Information Bulletin no. 750 (AIB-750), May.

Harrison's Principles of Internal Medicine. Various editions. New York: McGraw-Hill.

Heidenreich, Paul, and Mark McClellan. 2000. "Trends in Heart Attack Treatment and Outcomes, 1975–1995: Literature Review and Synthesis." In *Medical Care Output and Productivity,* edited by David Cutler and Ernst Berndt. Chicago: University of Chicago Press, 2000.

Hunink, Maria G., Lee Goldman, Anna N. Tosteson, Murray A. Mittleman, Paula A. Goldman, Lawrence N. Williams, Joel Tsevat, and Milton C. Weinstein. 1990. "The Recent Decline in Mortality from Coronary Heart Disease, 1980–1990: The Effects of Secular Trends in Risk Factors and Treatment." *Journal of the American Medical Association* 277, no. 7 (19 February): 535–42.

Hypertension Detection and Follow-Up Program Cooperative Group. 1979. "Five-Year Findings of the Hypertension Detection and Follow-Up Program I. Reduction in Mortality of Persons with High Blood Pressure, including Mild Hypertension." *Journal of the American Medical Association* 242, no. 23 (7 December): 2562–71

Ippolito, Pauline M., and Alan D. Mathios. 1999. "Health Claims in Food Advertising and Labeling." In *America's Eating Habits: Changes and Consequences,* edited by Elizabeth Frazao. Washington, D.C.: Food and Rural Economics Division, Economic Research Service, U.S. Dept. of Agriculture, Agriculture Information Bulletin no. 750 (AIB-750).

Keys, Ancel, and Margaret Keys. 1959. *Eat Well and Stay Well, the Mediterranean Diet.* Garden City, N.Y.: Doubleday.

Keys, Ancel, ed. 1970. *Coronary Heart Disease in Seven Countries*. New York: American Heart Association.

Pocock, S. J., A. Gerald Shaper, Derek G. Cook, Andrew N. Phillips, and Mary Walker. 1987. "Social Class Differences in Ischaemic Heart Disease in British Men." *Lancet* 2:197–201.

Schucker, Beth, Janet T. Wittes, Nancy C. Santanello, Steven T. Weber, David McGoldrick, Karen Donato, Alan Levy, and Basil M. Rifkind. 1991. "Change in Cholesterol Awareness and Action: Results from National Physician and Public Surveys." *Archives of Internal Medicine* 151 (April): 666–73.

Society of Actuaries. 1959. *Build and Blood Pressure Study*. Chicago: Society of Actuaries.

Stamler, J., A. W. Caggiula, and G. A. Grandits. 1997. "Relation of Body Mass and Alcohol, Nutrient, Fiber, and Caffeine Intakes to Blood Pressure in the Special Intervention and Usual Care Groups in the Multiple Risk Factor Intervention Trial." *American Journal of Clinical Nutrition* 67(suppl.): 338S–65S.

Stephen, Alison M., and Nicholas J. Wald. 1990. "Trends in Individual Consumption of Dietary Fat in the United States, 1920–1984." *American Journal of Clinical Nutrition* 52:457–69.

Sytkowski, Pamela A., Ralph B. D'Agostino, Albert J. Belanger, and William B. Karmel. 1996. "Sex and Time Trends in Cardiovascular Disease Incidence and Mortality: The Framingham Heart Study, 1950–89." *American Journal of Epidemiology* 143, no. 4:338–50.

Tolley, George, Donald Kenkel, and Robert Fabian, eds. 1994. *Valuing Health for Policy: An Economic Approach*. Chicago: University of Chicago Press.

U.S. Department of Health and Human Services, Public Health Service, and National Institutes of Health. 1986. *Public Perceptions of HighBlood Pressure and Sodium*. NIH publication 86-2730. Washington, D.C.: National Institutes of Health.

U.S. Public Health Service, Federal Security Agency. 1948. "High Blood Pressure." Washington, D.C.: Government Printing Office.

Veterans Administration Cooperative Study Group on Antihypertensive Agents. 1967. "Effects of Treatment on Morbidity in Hypertension: Results in Patients with Diastolic Pressures Averaging 115 through 129 mm Hg." *Journal of the American Medical Association* 202:1028–34.

Veterans Administration Cooperative Study Group on Antihypertensive Agents. 1970. "Effects of Treatment on Morbidity in Hypertension: Results in Patients with Diastolic Pressures Averaging 90 through 114 mm Hg." *Journal of the American Medical Association* 213:1143–52.

Viscusi, Kip W. 1992. *Smoking: Making the Risky Decision*. New York: Oxford University Press.

———. 1993. "The Value of Risks to Life and Health." *Journal of Economic Literature,* 1912–46.

Ward, Peter W. 1993. *Birth Weight and Economic Growth.* Chicago: University of Chicago Press.

Whittlesey, Marietta. 1977. *Killer Salt.* New York: Bolder Books.

CHAPTER FIVE

Biomedical Research and Then Some: The Causes of Technological Change in Heart Attack Treatment

Paul Heidenreich and Mark McClellan

I. Introduction

Recent research on trends in the health of the U.S. population has highlighted impressive gains over the past several decades. National mortality statistics have shown an increase in life expectancy from birth of approximately 8 years since 1950 (National Center for Health Statistics, 1999). A number of recent studies based on longitudinal surveys with consistent and relatively objective definitions of health status have also documented that, at least since the early 1980s, mortality improvements have been accompanied by lower, not higher, rates of functional impairment (e.g. Manton, Corder, and Stallard, 1997). Studies of functional health over longer time periods are also consistent with this conclusion (e.g. Costa, 2000). Several of the papers prepared for this conference volume highlight the social welfare implications of these health improvements. Murphy and Topel (this volume) estimate the value of the increased life expectancy from 1970 to 1990 at over $57 trillion, or close to $3 trillion per year; and Nordhaus (this volume) argues that health improvements over the past half century exceeded the value of all other measured improvements in U.S. economic output during the same period. Even though medical expenditures have risen substantially, current and future generations are enormously better off as a result of this improvement in health.

Paul Heidenreich is a practicing cardiologist in the Palo Alto Veterans Administration Health System and assistant professor of medicine at Stanford University. Mark McClellan is associate professor of economics and medicine at Stanford University and a research associate of the National Bureau of Economic Research.

We thank Mark Lo for outstanding research assistance; Victor Fuchs, Antonio Rangel, and seminar participants at NBER for helpful comments; and the National Institute on Aging and the Veterans Administration for financial support. All errors are our own.

While much of the long-term improvement in health prior to 1950 was associated with economic development (Fogel, 1994), the recent improvements in social welfare appear to be more strongly related to growth in public and professional biomedical knowledge (Hunink et al., 1997; Braunwald, 1997). The mortality improvements are largely the result of falling mortality for cardiovascular disease (NCHS, 1999),[1] a set of conditions that primarily affect the middle-aged and elderly. Biomedical research is widely viewed as the principal source of this increased knowledge, and the national accounts suggest that such research amounts to only a tiny fraction of the value of the health improvements that have occurred. As Murphy and Topel note, the *total* expenditures of around $36 billion on biomedical research and development in 1995—consisting primarily of National Institutes of Health (NIH) spending ($13 billion) and private pharmaceutical research ($14 billion)—are trivial compared with improvements in health, which have an average value of over $2 trillion per year.[2] Thus, a natural question is whether current spending on medical research and development (R&D) is too low, that is, whether additional direct government expenditures or financial incentives for private research will yield very high returns.

Answering this critical R&D policy question convincingly is very difficult. As Meltzer discusses in chapter 6 of this volume, it requires an analysis of the likely impact of incremental ("marginal") additional research on addressing disease mechanisms responsible for "premature" death. It also requires the diffusion of this biomedical knowledge into medical practice. Given the difficulty of this forward-looking undertaking, a variety of studies have examined past contributions of different factors, including medical treatments, behavior, and unexplained "residuals," to the observed improvements in health, especially for cardiovascular disease. We review some of these papers in the next section; they suggest that changes in treatment and behavior that result from increased medical knowledge can plausibly account for a large share of the improvements in cardiovascular disease mortality. Fewer studies have sought to link specific R&D activities to these changes in professional and public knowledge; doing so is very difficult. Virtually every technological change embodies knowledge acquired in a range of previous research studies, including both biomedical studies and innovations in other sciences and industries. In addition, biomedical R&D is global, with much of the participation and a portion of the research funding now coming from non-U.S. sources.

As a result, these previous studies have generally not provided direct evidence of the impact on health of specific research studies, or on the likely value of additional research funding. Rather, they conclude that the recent gains in health are extraordinarily valuable in comparison with the relatively modest past funding for "formal" biomedical research, which, as it is usually tabulated, consists of expenditures on "basic" laboratory studies, and "applied" research, primarily in the form of randomized clinical trials. This argument seems convincing. Indeed, the view that additional biomedical research is one of the federal government's most worthwhile investments undoubtedly underlies the bipartisan support in Washington for continuing to increase funding for the NIH. The goal of our chapter is to begin to provide some direct evidence to support this seemingly clear conclusion.

We conduct a detailed review of the literature on how technological change has actually occurred for one important component of treatment of cardiovascular disease: the care of heart attacks. We focus on this particular aspect of medical care because it is important—improvements in heart attack mortality have contributed significantly to the overall improvements in cardiovascular mortality—and because it seems to provide the best case for attributing changes in health outcomes to specific biomedical research studies. Over the past several decades, hundreds of randomized clinical trials have been performed on many aspects of the acute management of heart attacks. These trials were associated with major changes in heart attack treatment, and impressive improvements in heart attack survival. We focus on applied biomedical research—clinical trials—not because we view more basic research as unimportant, but because it is much easier to identify connections between these applied studies and changes in medical care and health. Moreover, these formal trials comprise the bulk of funding for formal biomedical research that is directly related to cardiovascular disease. Finally, as we discuss in more detail below, the medical treatments studied in these trials appear to account for most of the observed improvements in heart attack outcomes.

We reach several conclusions. First, we find that formal applied research studies, which are explicitly directed toward improving clinical practice, cannot alone explain much of the observed changes in practice that accounted for declining heart attack mortality. Rather, clinical practices generally "lead" the results of the trials, sometimes by many years, and also "lag" the results of the trials, often responding only slowly to new formal research findings. Our findings illustrate the importance of an understudied source of new biomedical knowledge and thus of technological change in health care: improvements in knowledge *outside* of the context of basic research and clinical trials, which we term "informal" R&D activities. A number of previous anecdotal studies have suggested that informal R&D

may play a major role in guiding formal research and mediating its impact on medical practice. But no study has assessed its importance systematically. This oversight may have important policy implications: in contrast with funding for formal biomedical research, public and private funding for such "informal" research activities is smaller and has declined in recent years. Both because of their potential importance and because of the large recent differences in public policies toward formal and informal R&D, understanding informal R&D activities may be a critical part of guiding public policies to increase the value of the biomedical knowledge base.

Second, our results help explain a fundamental puzzle of research in the health care industry: why, in an industry where technological change is clearly occurring at a rapid pace, are conventional measures of R&D spending only slightly above the average for the U.S. economy as a whole, and far below that of other "high-tech" industries? We find that informal activities are an important source of changes in biomedical knowledge that are not included in conventional measures of R&D spending. Thus, biomedical research properly measured may be much more extensive than the level of formal support might suggest. This conclusion seems plausible: unlike pharmaceuticals or computers, health care is a service industry. Medical consumers have extremely heterogeneous health problems, and medical production involves complex combinations of treatments that may benefit from considerable individualization. Thus, it seems likely that there is much room for improving welfare beyond what can be demonstrated in formal evaluations of specific treatments in specific patient populations. Our results suggest some directions for further investigation of how biomedical knowledge changes that complement much of the previous emphasis on the impact of formal research studies.

Finally, we provide new evidence of the impact of formal research studies in heart attack care. By examining the timing, findings, and impact of specific research studies, we are able to reach more specific conclusions about the likely value of additional applied research funding over the past several decades. While these conclusions are speculative, they suggest that additional formal research funding on several aspects of heart attack treatment might have led to better outcomes sooner. In particular, we find some evidence for greater lags in the formal evaluation of "informal" innovations in the use of generic drugs; as a result, the diffusion of these effective practices was delayed by some years. We find little evidence for significant lags in the performance of formal trials involving patented drugs. These results are consistent with some underfunding when biomedical knowledge is not embodied in private intellectual property rights, that is, when it is a public good. For innovation in procedures, we find little evidence that formal trials had much of an impact on development and use; here, the incremental innovation and "learning by doing" which are important components of informal R&D (and which are largely funded outside of formal R&D mechanisms) appear to be even more important in augmenting biomedical knowledge.

Section II provides some additional background on two key issues for our analysis: previous research on the sources of improvements in health outcomes for cardiovascular disease, and previous research on the causes of technological change. Section III reviews our methods for assessing the contributions of formal biomedical research and less-formal clinical development to the medical knowledge base, as reflected in medical practice. Section IV presents our empirical results on the relationship of changes in medical practice to the publication of relevant formal research. Section V discusses some implications of our findings and possible directions for further research.

II. Background

Causes of Improvements in Heart Disease Outcomes

Previous clinical reviews have evaluated the contribution of broad categories of explanatory factors to improvements in outcomes for ischemic heart disease (IHD). Risk factor reduction leading to primary and secondary prevention of fatal coronary events, including acute myocardial infarction (AMI) and ischemia-induced ventricular arrhythmias, appears to have been responsible for a majority of this decline up to the early 1980s. For example, Goldman et al. (1982) estimated that changes in risk factors leading to primary disease prevention accounted for 54 percent of the decline in IHD mortality between 1968 and 1976. Medical treatments such as greater utilization of antihypertensive drugs, as well as changes in behavior, contributed to these trends in risk factors. Medical interventions for patients with ischemic heart disease, including both acute treatment and secondary prevention, accounted for 40 percent of the decline in IHD mortality. Among these interventions, 13.5 percent of the decline was attributed to coronary care unit treatments, 4 percent to prehospital resuscitation, 7.5 percent to treatment of hypertension, 3.5 percent to coronary artery bypass surgery, and 10 percent to other medical treatments of IHD, particularly chronic use of beta-blocker drugs. (Many of these technologies are described in more detail below.)

Weinstein and colleagues developed the Coronary Heart Disease model, a sophisticated state-transition model of outcomes of ischemic heart disease for patients in the United States. The first study using the model concluded, like Goldman, that the majority of mortality improvements prior to 1980 resulted from primary prevention through improvements in risk factors (Weinstein et al., 1987). However, analyses of more recent periods indicated that risk factor reductions could explain less than 20 percent of the total reduction in heart disease mortality between 1980 and 1990 (Hunink et al., 1997). Moreover, primary and secondary prevention through risk factor reduction appears to be increasingly associated with medical treatment changes, such as increased use of cholesterol-lowering and antihypertensive agents that have better side-effect and compliance profiles. Thus, medical treatments rather than behavioral changes seem to be increasingly important in explaining IHD mortality improvements.

Our own research (Heidenreich and McClellan, 2000) has sought to determine the contribution of specific changes in medical technology within each of the two broad categories of risk factor reduction, leading to primary and secondary prevention, and acute treatment of major heart disease events. The most complete and reliable data by far exist for the acute treatment category, allowing us to analyze changes in acute treatment in the most detail. In an analysis of changes in this category between 1975 and 1995, we found that the number of new heart attacks remained roughly constant, at around 540,000 per year. The in-hospital (case) mortality rate declined from 23 percent to 14 percent, and the 30-day mortality rate declined from 27 percent to 17 percent. We reviewed specific changes in heart attack patient characteristics, changes in the acute treatment of heart attacks, and changes in other components of medical therapy (including pre-hospital care and secondary prevention) that could contribute to these trends. We found that changes in heart attack patient characteristics could explain as much as one-third of the decline in the average AMI mortality rate over the 1975–95 period. We also found that four therapeutic changes—greater use of aspirin, beta-blockers, thrombolytics, and primary angioplasty—accounted for a large share of the improvements in outcomes. Reductions in the use of certain drug treatments such as lidocaine, which are probably harmful in routine use after AMI, may also have accounted for a small share of the improvement.[3] Table 5.1 summarizes our conclusions about the specific treatment changes that contributed to improved acute outcomes for AMI.

The specific factors we have described—changes in AMI patient characteristics and changes in acute treatment—appear to explain approximately 80 percent of the total improvement in acute mortality for heart attacks that occurred between 1975 and 1995. The remaining 20 percent are presumably

TABLE 5.1 Reduction in AMI Mortality Explained (%) Due to Changes in Acute Treatment between 1975 and 1995*

Medications	Direct Effect	Indirect Effect (Interactions)**	Total Effect
Beta-blockers	6.6	−0.75	5.9
Aspirin	27.5	−1.83	26.5
Nitrates	4.2	−0.49	3.7
Heparin/anticoagulants	1.8	−0.17	1.6
Ca- Antagonists	−7.3	0.08	−7.2
Lidocaine	5.5	−0.09	5.4
Magnesium	−0.3	0.01	−0.3
ACE inhibitors	2.7	−0.33	2.4
Thrombolytics	16.1	−0.83	15.3
Procedures			
Primary PTCA	9.8	−0.83	8.9
CABG	0.7	−0.09	0.6

*Percentage of 1995–75 decrease in AMI 30-day mortality rates explained by observed increases in individual treatments from 1975 to 1995 levels. All other treatments are assumed to be used at 1995 levels. Indirect effects reflect negative interactions (substitution effects because of similar mechanisms of action) with other changes in drug therapy.

**Interaction effects are offsets because the mechanism of the treatment substitutes for other treatments that previously had been more widely used. For example, because aspirin has a modest effect on reducing blood clotting, it is likely that a small part of the net benefit of heparin (which also reduces blood clotting) would be reduced by the diffusion of aspirin, and conversely.

the result of other technologies that we have not studied in detail, and miscellaneous other factors. Unfortunately, published studies are not adequate for more than speculative discussion of the specific treatments responsible for primary prevention—avoidance of heart disease—and secondary prevention—improvements in post-acute mortality for heart disease patients. Studies have shown that diagnostic procedures for risk stratification (to guide further treatment more effectively), risk factor counseling, pharmacologic therapies, and invasive procedures may result in significant reductions in long-term mortality after heart attacks. But the research data on effectiveness of these long-term treatments is less extensive than for acute treatments,[4] and consistent data on the utilization of specific treatments over time is difficult to assemble. However, our broader analysis of trends in major treatment categories is consistent with changes in medical treatment explaining a substantial part of the observed risk factor reductions.

Taken together, the factors discussed here suggest that medical innovations in each of primary prevention, acute and post-acute management, and secondary prevention have led to substantial reductions in acute and long-term AMI mortality. Because the most precise biomedical research evidence on treatment effects exists for acute treatment of IHD events, our detailed analysis of the causes of these technological changes focuses on these treatments. We leave for future work a more qualitative discussion of the causes of technological change for primary and secondary prevention.

Contributions of Research and Development to Technological Change in Health Care

Many studies of technological change, in health care and other settings, envision a linear process of R&D such as that shown in figure 5.1. Knowledge progresses from basic to applied research to embodiment in new products and processes. Funding for formal biomedical research is unquestionably an important contributor to this process, and funding for basic research to further understanding of mechanisms of disease may have significant and fundamental long-term effects on biomedical knowledge. A large share of NIH research funding, as well as most funding from drug and device manufacturers, involves applied research in the form of randomized clinical trials. Eventually, in the linear models, the results of the formal R&D studies are translated into "downstream" practice applications, as new biomedical knowledge diffuses from leading clinicians at academic centers and elsewhere into routine practice.

In fact, however, technological change in most industries is far from a linear process. As Rosenberg (1994) notes, innovations in practice often reflect research findings in other fields or from some time in the past. For this reason, Rosenberg argues, most of the R&D expenditures in most industries involve D. This includes such innovations as incremental improvements in existing technologies, through greater experience ("learning by doing"), user-driven improvements in products and processes, and user-driven importation of technologies from other industries. Each of these particular innovations may appear modest, technical, and even obscure; collectively, however, they may lead to enormous increases in productivity that could not have been foreseen from the findings of the underlying research studies alone. They may also spur new directions in basic research.

On the surface, health care might appear to be an exception to Rosenberg's findings. Many health economists and other experts envision a "research pipeline" or "technological imperative," like the process outlined in figure 5.1, which begins with exogenous funding from the NIH and drug companies and eventually leads to new drugs and procedures. But the actual process is probably far less linear, as figure 5.2 suggests. While randomized clinical trials are the gold standard for demonstrating the efficacy of a new treatment and thus for "evidence-based" medicine, there are many reasons to doubt that they are the only major source of applied biomedical

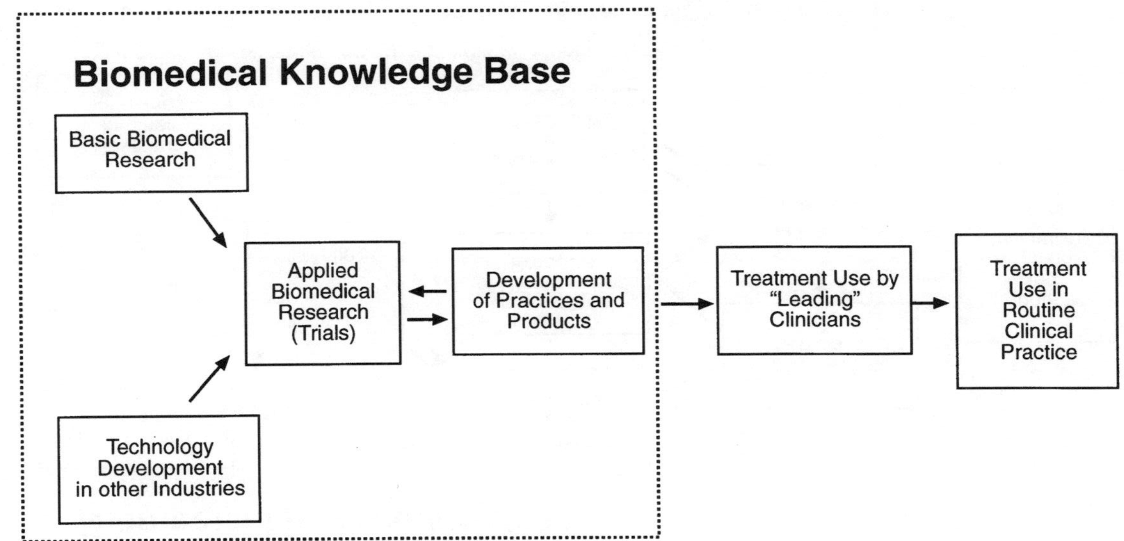

FIGURE 5.1: Linear model of impact of "formal" r + d on medical care

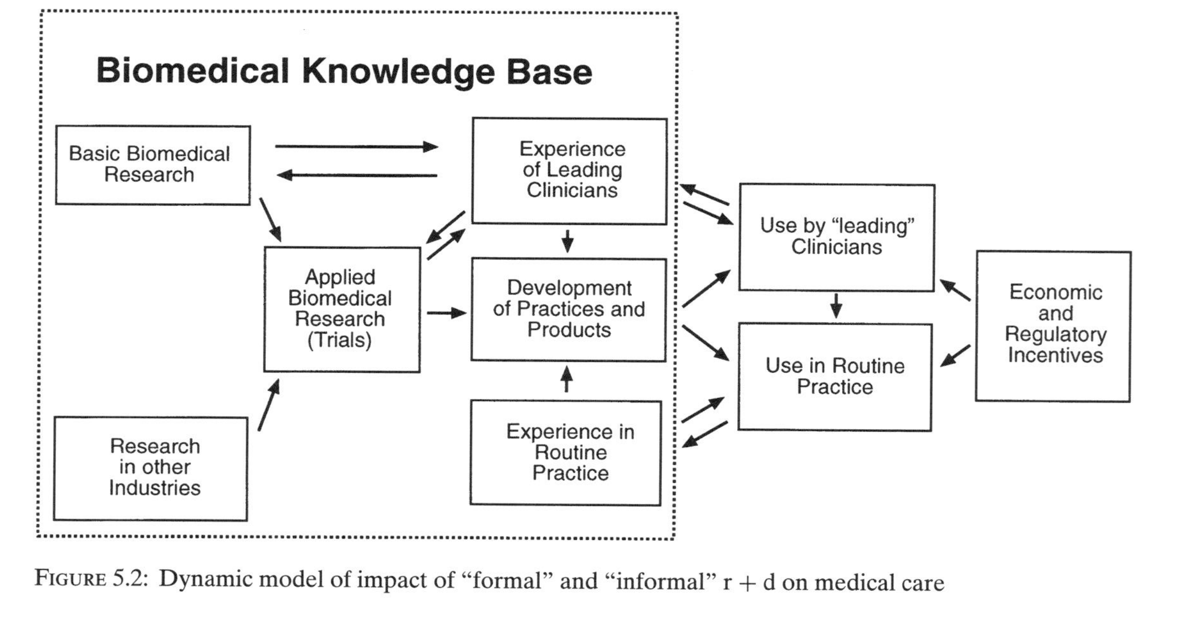

FIGURE 5.2: Dynamic model of impact of "formal" and "informal" r + d on medical care

knowledge. Clinical trials are expensive, because enough patients must be identified and enrolled to detect a clinically important treatment effect (or lack thereof), and then the patients must be treated according to an (often costly) protocol and monitored until the health endpoints of the study are reached—which may take years. As a result, they are not performed for all types of medical treatment decisions for all types of patients. In addition, trials generally reflect close connections between formal and less formal sources of knowledge. The principal investigators typically include leading clinicians who spend much of their time treating patients and discussing their treatment with other experts, and whose research ideas undoubtedly draw on these experiences. They may also be entrepreneurs involved in the development of new devices or other products related to their medical practice. Indeed, most applications for clinical research funding include a detailed discussion of clinical experience, typically based on nonrandomized populations or patient series, which suggest that the trial may or may not find an effect on outcomes.

These facts suggest a close but by no means unidirectional relationship between formal research, at least applied biomedical research, and informal insights and developments in actual clinical practice. Previous anecdotal studies also confirm the importance of medical innovations that occur primarily after basic research is completed and a drug or device is introduced into practice. Geljins and Rosenberg (1994) give a number of examples. They note that the first oral contraceptive pills on the market had significant adverse side effects, including problems of blood clots; guidance from users which suggested that lower dosages and "combination" estrogen-progesterone treatments reduced side effects inspired modifications in the formulation of OCPs. They also highlight the gradual but highly significant cumulative improvements in endoscopy procedures, which have led to the widespread use of minimally invasive surgery. Numerous more recent examples exist. Finasteride, a drug initially developed for treatment of prostate cancer, is now used much more widely to prevent hair loss. Indeed, many drugs are used frequently if not primarily for "off-label" indications, uses other than those for which initial FDA approval was given on the basis of randomized trials. Despite the absence of formal trials, the use of intensive cardiac procedures—including cardiac catheterization, bypass surgery, and angioplasty—has increased rapidly in the United States compared with many other developed countries such as Canada and Denmark, apparently as a result of differences in the financial and regulatory incentives for innovations in "high-tech" medical practices among these countries (McClellan and Kessler, 2002).

With these examples in mind, it is perhaps not surprising that biostatisticians have estimated that only 10 percent to 20 percent of medical practices are grounded in clear evidence of treatment effectiveness in the form of randomized trials (U.S. Congress Office of Technology Assessment, 1983; Eddy, 1996). Advocates of "evidence-based" medical practice point to this fact, along with the evidence of wide variations across areas and hospitals in many medical practices, to argue that treatments should be encouraged only when they have been demonstrated to be effective in formal trials. But the preceding discussion suggests that waiting for formal evidence of treatment effects has its own disadvantages. Patients may have to forego potentially beneficial treatments, and trial protocols cannot capture all the ongoing incremental improvements and hands-on clinical experience that may be important determinants of how and when particular treatments are used.

Thus, formal research and informal development of medical innovations may both be important components of the biomedical knowledge base that determines health care productivity. Although anecdotal evidence suggests that informal developments are quantitatively important in understanding technological change in health care, we know of no comprehensive studies of the role of formal and informal sources of biomedical knowledge in explaining the changes in outcomes for a common health problem.

To investigate this important question, we extend our previous research on the sources of improved outcomes for heart attacks in the past two decades. We consider two ways in which the contributions of informal practice developments to technological change can be distinguished from formal applied research. First, if informal practice developments influence clinical trials and are able to anticipate their results in most cases, then medical practice should "lead" clinical trials. This will occur, for example, if expert clinicians develop practice innovations that they expect to influence outcomes and then turn to randomized trials to confirm their expectations, after their new beliefs are already being implemented in practice and are diffusing to their colleagues. Second, if clinical trials are significantly removed from applicability to real-world community practice, then their publication should have minimal short-term effects on medical practices. Instead, medical practice would "trail" clinical trials, only gradually catching up with the implications of the studies as clinicians in routine practice settings gradually translate results into their own practices. Either finding would suggest that formal research studies alone do not determine the effective medical knowledge base, and that a complete accounting of the sources of improved biomedical knowledge must look beyond formal research funding alone. Conversely, if medical innovation is primarily a "pipeline" process that moves from basic research to specific clinical applications, then applied research should have a more significant impact on practices.

Some previous studies have investigated the impact of clinical trials on medical practice (Chalmers, 1974; Friedman et al., 1983; Fineberg, 1987; Lamas et al., 1992; Ketley and Woods, 1993; Col et al., 1996). For the most part, these studies have found results consistent with an important role of informal development of clinical practices, but they have some important limitations. Virtually all of them investigated only a single trial or a few trials in detail, and none conducted a comprehensive analysis of all the applied research that might influence technological change for a common illness. Thus, a finding that a trial had a limited impact on practice is difficult to interpret: it is possible that previous studies were more important influences on clinical knowledge. In addition, an examination of a few individual studies makes it difficult to reach broader conclusions about the impact of applied research. For example, if clinical experts do "lead" trial results in their practices, it is likely that they would not be infallible—they will make some errors in their expectations about treatment effects. Only by analyzing all the research evidence is it possible to determine whether such errors are common, and whether they are corrected over time as a result of new evidence from trials. Second, many of these previous studies evaluated practices in the 1970s and 1980s, and it is possible that the method by which technological change occurs in medical practice has itself changed over time. Our approach allows us to investigate these issues. The previous studies offer one important advantage: they typically involve a more detailed, exact analysis of the timing of effects of a particular trial than is possible in our broader study. For example, in order to provide comprehensive information on heart disease practices over a long time period, we have confined our measurement of medical practices to five-year intervals, so that we can only interpolate changes within these intervals. The detailed studies can help fill some of these gaps. We discuss some of the studies in more detail in the next section, where they provide some additional insights into how specific changes in medical practice have occurred.

III. Methods

Trends in Medical Practices

We performed searches of the entire MEDLINE database, and reviewed the bibliographies of review articles, to identify studies describing treatment for heart attacks and other forms of ischemic heart disease. We reviewed all identified studies that included information on population trends in the treatment of heart attacks, and also reviewed studies that reported on trends in teaching hospitals. We used population-based studies with at least a 10-year range whenever possible to determine changes in intervention rates during the 1975–95 period. Where possible, we used multiple sources of information; where the sources did not agree exactly, we averaged results. In most cases, our multiple sources showed similar rate trends. We also obtained estimates of treatment rates from large databases of Medicare patients, including the Cooperative Cardiovascular Project (CCP) and Medicare claims files. These data were the basis for our estimates of population trends in use of the following acute treatments that had been shown to be effective in randomized trials published since 1975: aspirin, thrombolytics, beta-blockers, angiotensin converting enzyme (ACE) inhibitors, and primary angioplasty. We also collected data on population trends in use of calcium channel blockers and lidocaine, which had been shown to be either ineffective or harmful during our study period. In addition, we collected data on other heart attack treatments for which the results of formal research were less clear. Our literature review and construction of treatment rate estimates are described in more detail in Heidenreich and McClellan (2000).

Publication of Relevant Clinical Trial Results

We also searched the entire MEDLINE database, and reviewed the bibliography of published review articles, textbooks, and metanalyses, to identify all major published randomized controlled trials related to these innovations in the treatment of heart disease since the early 1970s. Although they were not always consistent, metanalyses of clinical trials on particular aspects of AMI care published during this period were especially helpful for summarizing the significance and timing of research results. The metanalyses report not only the major findings of each particular study related to a given treatment, but also the impact of each incremental study on a cumulative measure of the state of knowledge about treatment effects from randomized trials. Using these data, we described the timing of important developments in research knowledge about each of the heart disease treatments.

Relationship of Clinical Practices to New Research Findings

We conducted descriptive analyses of the relationship of relevant new biomedical research developments to clinical practices, to determine whether "leading" and "trailing" effects of clinical practices were significant and the extent to which trends in practices were influenced by formal biomedical research studies.

IV. Results

SOURCES OF CHANGES IN HEART ATTACK TREATMENTS

In this section, we report on the results of our analysis of the contributions of formal applied research and informal development of clinical practices to technological change for the treatment of acute episodes of heart disease over the past 25 years. Treatment effects for acute coronary events, principally AMI, comprise perhaps the most extensive randomized trial evidence in the health care industry. In what follows, we review some of the major developments in treatment for AMI, to document the relationship of changes in practice to the development of evidence from clinical trials. Table 5.2 describes changes in the various dimensions of acute AMI treatment between 1975 and 1995.

Aspirin

Biomedical insights that aspirin might influence the outcomes of AMI date well before the 1970s. The importance of thrombosis (formation of a clot within a blood vessel supplying the heart) in the pathogenesis of acute coronary events was long appreciated by clinical experts. Beginning with the Cardiff-1 Trial (Elwood et al., 1974), a series of at least seven major randomized trials mostly performed outside the United States investigated whether aspirin therapy initiated shortly after AMI led to reductions in short-term outcomes like in-hospital mortality as well as longer-term AMI recurrence and mortality (Coronary Drug Project Research Group, 1976; Elwood and Sweetnam, 1979; Aspirin Myocardial Infarction Study Research Group, 1980; Persantine-Aspirin Reinfarction Study Group, 1980; Klimt et al., 1986). None of these trials, which enrolled a minimum of over 1,200 patients and had follow-up periods of at least 6 months and sometimes much longer, detected a statistically significant mortality reduction in patients randomized to aspirin treatment. Indeed, the AMIS trial, which was by far the largest of the early aspirin trials, with over 4,500 patients enrolled, demonstrated a trend toward *higher* mortality in the aspirin group.

The clinical uncertainty was largely resolved with the Second International Study of Infarct Survival (ISIS-2, 1988), which enrolled over 17,000 AMI patients in a large number of participating countries. ISIS-2 documented a 36 percent reduction in one-month mortality after AMI in the aspirin group, and is widely regarded among cardiology experts as settling the issue of whether aspirin is an effective acute treatment.

However, it is worth noting that the application of conventional met-analysis techniques to pooled results from *all* these trials would not lead to the conclusion that aspirin use significantly reduces long-term mortality

TABLE 5.2 Trends in Treatment of Acute Myocardial Infarction (% of Hospitalized AMI Patients Receiving Treatment)

Treatment	1975	1980	1985	1990	1995	Key Sources/Comments
Therapies with clear mortality benefit demonstrated in randomized trials						
Aspirin[†]	5	6	30	62	75	Goldberg et al., 1999; Burns, 1997; Rogers, 1994
Beta-blockers	21	42	48	47	50	Goldberg et al., 1999; Gurwitz, Col, and Avorn, 1994; McLaughlin et al., 1996
Thrombolytics	0	0	9	25	31	Chandra, 1997; Rogers, 1996
ACE inhibitors	0	0	0	13	21	Goldberg et al., 1999; Heidenreich and McClellan, 1999
Primary PTCA	0	0	0	3	9	Rogers, 1996; Medicare and California discharge data
Other therapies						
Ca- Antagonists	0	na	64	59	31	McGovern, 1992; Pashos et al., 1994; Gurwitz, Col, and Avorn, 1994; Rogers, 1996
Heparin/ anticoagulants	53¶	53¶	53	75	70	Rogers, 1994; McGovern, 1996
Lidocaine	30	48	47	34	16	Goldberg, 1987; Chandra, 1996
Magnesium	0	na	na	na	8.5	Ziegelstein, 1996
Nitrates	56	83	93	93	93	Goldberg, 1987 [1990–95 values are assumed equal to 1985]
Urgent CABG	3**	6	8	10	14	McGovern, 1992, 1996; Medicare discharge data

na = no available data.
*In hospital or 30-day use.
[†]includes persantine and sulfinpyrazone.
¶Assumed equal to 1985 values in base case analysis. No evidence in literature of significant diffusion, but no reliable estimates could be obtained.
**Average of 1970 and 1979 values.

after AMI at conventional levels of statistical significance ($p < .05$) (Lau et al., 1992). Statistical significance would be achieved if the AMIS trial were excluded; biostatisticians and many clinical experts have argued that this is a reasonable step because of a significant imbalance in baseline risk factors favoring the control group in that trial. Despite the limitations of the formal knowledge base, both immediate and long-term treatment with aspirin or other antiplatelet agents unless contraindicated (e.g., by bleeding problems) is a consensus treatment recommendation among cardiologists today.

Substantial use of aspirin in the management of AMI predated the evidence of its effectiveness in randomized trials. Aspirin was occasionally used in 1975 and 1980 (table 5.2), and it was used in about 30 percent of AMI cases nationwide by 1985, well ahead of the publication of a statistically significant effect in ISIS-2. Moreover, rates of use in academic centers were already much higher by this time. Kizer et al. (1999) note that 74 percent of patients enrolled in the Thrombolysis in Myocardial Infarction—phase 1 trial (TIMI-1), which enrolled patients from 1984–85, and 89 percent of patients enrolled in the Thrombolysis in Myocardial Infarction—phase 2 (TIMI-2), which enrolled patients between 1984 and early 1988, received aspirin during their AMI hospitalization and at discharge. This high rate of aspirin use among treating physicians at leading academic centers ahead of publication of ISIS-2 was in part due to the decision of the trial designers to recommend aspirin use unless contraindicated, despite the fact that the most recent large randomized trial at the time had found worse outcomes for AMI patients treated with aspirin.

Subsequent to ISIS-2, overall rates of use of aspirin have increased, to 62 percent of AMI patients in 1990 and 75 percent by 1995 (table 5.2). Because rates of treatment with aspirin at leading academic centers were already high, much of this subsequent diffusion appears to be the result of community physicians “catching up” with the academic center practices following the publication of the trial. Aspirin use among general practitioners has remained lower than use among the most experienced cardiologists (see, e.g., Pashos et al., 1994), suggesting that clinical trial results alone were not enough to alter practices in many cases even for a treatment as simple as aspirin. The continued steady growth in the use of aspirin in recent years may reflect the impact of intervention programs targeted at community physicians that have emphasized aspirin use as an indicator of high-quality care (e.g., Marciniak et al., 1998).

Other studixes have also found significant trends in aspirin use that predated the publication of ISIS-2 (e.g., Lamas et al., 1992). In a detailed analysis of trends in aspirin use, Col et al. (1996) report 1985 and 1990 levels of use similar to those in table 5.2. However, they found that use was rising at the beginning of their study period (early 1986) and that no significant break in the upward trend occurred around the time that the ISIS-2 results became known.

Thrombolytic Drugs

The same biomedical insights that suggested use of agents like aspirin that inhibit further clot formation also suggested that agents that could break down the clots responsible for the AMI could improve outcomes. The use of thrombolytic agents might be regarded as an ideal situation for clinical trials to have an impact on practice. Unlike aspirin, which is unlikely to cause any significant adverse outcomes in patients who do not have clear contraindications, this treatment involves a risk of serious side effects. Thrombolytic drugs inhibit the body's ability to form clots, which can lead to major bleeding complications elsewhere (e.g., hemorrhagic strokes) that offset their favorable impact on the heart. Moreover, the effect of thrombolytics was expected to be highly time dependent, with less favorable effects anticipated when thrombolysis was initiated longer after the AMI began.

Thus, it is not surprising that more than 30 randomized clinical trials of the effects of thrombolytic drugs on acute outcomes after AMI were conducted prior to 1990. (The first small trials of streptokinase, the earliest thrombolytic, were reported by the early 1960s.) In a careful review of all trials of thrombolytic therapy in AMI reported prior to 1992, Lau et al. (1992) report that pooling the results of these trials through metanalysis could have led to the detection of a statistically significant reduction in total mortality by the mid-1970s.[5] Even though this exact result depends on a somewhat strong assumption of a fixed treatment effect, the fact that about four-fifths of the trials showed lower point estimates of mortality in the treatment group while only one-fifth achieved statistical significance indicates a preponderant weight in favor of thrombolytic treatment that could potentially have influenced practice. However, the trials reported prior to 1986 were very small (typically a few hundred patients), did not use standardized protocols, and were not widely recognized among cardiology experts. Two notable, very large trials were conducted in the 1980s—the Gruppo Italiano per lo Studio della Streptochinasi nell'Infarto Miocardico (GISSI, 1986) and ISIS-2 (1988). Both of these trials showed significantly lower mortality in the streptokinase groups, results consistent with (though somewhat more modest than) those obtained in the smaller previous trials.

With the question of thrombolytic benefits resolved, trials since the late 1980s have focused on the differential effects of newer thrombolytic agents that are still under patent, particularly tissue plasminogen activator (tPA), in comparison to "generic" thrombolytics, particularly streptokinase. Previous biomedical studies have suggested that the effects of t-PA and similar new agents on outcomes for AMI patients may be more favorable because the new agents are more fibrin-selective than streptokinase, resulting in more rapid opening of occluded coronary arteries. Early trials of tPA versus streptokinase detected no difference in effects. However, more recent trials in the 1990s have evaluated more rapid and sophisticated delivery protocols suggested by clinical experts, and have shown a small advantage of t-PA in restoring coronary blood flow and in long-term survival as well. In particular, the GUSTO trial (1993) observed a one-percentage-point difference in risk of short-term death—6.3 percent at 30 days with tPA compared to a 7.3 percent risk of death for patients treated with streptokinase ($p < 0.05$)—that persisted at 1 year. More recent trials involving t-PA have evaluated alternative ways and adjuvant treatments for delivering the drug (e.g., Jang et al., 1999). Below, we review the formal evidence comparing thrombolytics to an alternative, more intensive approach to restoring blood flow to the heart, immediate angioplasty.

Table 5.2 shows that, despite the fact that clinical experts could in principle have known of their substantial effects on mortality as early as the 1970s, thrombolytic agents were used rarely before 1980 and in less than 10 percent of AMI patients in 1985, prior to the large randomized trials that provided relatively "definitive" evidence of the benefit of thrombolytics. Use increased more rapidly around the time of publication of the large trials, to around 25 percent of patients by 1990. It has increased further since then (to 31 percent by 1995), but appears to have plateaued in recent years (Goldberg et al., 1999; McClellan et al., 2002). The plateau has occurred despite many studies suggesting that thrombolytic therapy is significantly underused (e.g., Barron et al. [1998] suggested that one-fourth of patients eligible for reperfusion do not receive it) as well as policy efforts to encourage physicians to use thrombolytics.

Slower diffusion of thrombolytics compared to other technologies shown to be effective in AMI care may be the result of more substantial uncertainty about whether the treatment has net benefits for many common types of AMI patients, that is, those presenting for treatment more than a few hours after AMI symptoms began, those who might conceivably have bleeding problems, those with mild heart attacks being treated at smaller hospitals that have limited ability to deal with hemorrhagic complications, and elderly patients. But there are at least two other potential differences from the other technologies we review. First, physicians may be more reluctant to adopt treatments like thrombolytics that can lead to serious, obvious complications that would not have occurred otherwise even if their net benefits are positive in large populations of patients. Second, in contrast to aspirin and the other treatments we review, thrombolytics have not become a mainstay of treatment at leading medical centers in the United States. Teaching hospitals and other large health care facilities have relied increasingly on primary angioplasty to restore blood flow after AMI. Thus, it is likely that academic centers have not developed as much experience with thrombolytics, and do not provide as much guidance on appropriate use in community hospitals, where primary angioplasty is not feasible.

One aspect of thrombolytic use in which academic physicians and other influences such as drug detailing may have had a more important role involves the type of thrombolytic agent employed. Most thrombolytic use in the United States involves tPA (see, e.g., Pashos et al., 1994) despite the fact that tPA costs approximately $1,000 more per dose. Streptokinase is used much more commonly in most other developed countries (McClellan and Kessler, 2002).

Beta-Blockers

Oral beta-blockers were first introduced in the 1960s. They were expected to be beneficial for the long-term management of patients with ischemic heart disease because they block the particular type of sympathetic nerve activity that increases the workload of the heart and can lead to certain irregular heart rhythms. As familiarity with these drugs increased, leading cardiologists hypothesized that beginning treatment with an intravenous beta-blocker immediately after AMI might reduce the damage from the AMI for similar reasons. They also suspected that beta-blockers might reduce the occurrence of fatal irregular heart rhythms (ventricular fibrillation) that are a serious risk in the immediate post-AMI period. Trials of beta-blockers begun after AMI (e.g., by 28 days) showed significant reductions in long-term AMI mortality by the late 1970s (Multicenter International Study, 1977; Norwegian Multicenter Study Group, 1981; and Beta Blocker Heart Attack Trial Research Group, 1982). Trials of beta-blockers *during* AMI generally began somewhat later, with the first positive result reported in 1981 (Hjalmarson et al., 1981) in a Swedish trial involving only 1,400 patients. Larger trials were reported in 1985 and 1986 (MIAMI Trial Research Group, 1985; ISIS-1, 1986). Even though only one of these trials detected a statistically significant reduction in mortality, and even though one arm of a later trial (TIMI-2B: TIMI Study Group, 1989) found no difference in mortality, expert consensus clearly supports the use of beta-blockers soon after AMI in all patients able to tolerate them. This too may be a reflection of "implicit metanalysis" influencing expert opinions; Lau et al. (1992) estimate that the pooled trial results reached statistical significance and remained so with the publication of ISIS-1.[6]

Table 5.2 shows that widespread use of beta-blockers also led the publication of the relevant trial results. By 1980, around 42 percent of AMI patients were receiving beta-blockers soon after their AMI. This percentage increased only modestly by 1995, despite the interim publication of clinical trials. According to Kizer et al. (1999), acute use of beta-blockers among academic cardiologists was common by 1980, prior to publication of any trial results, and has increased rather modestly since the "definitive" trials were published.

ACE Inhibitors

ACE inhibitors have been used for some time for hypertension control. More recently, trials in the late 1980s and early 1990s documented a protective effect of ACE inhibitors for patients with heart failure and left ventricular dysfunction (particularly diabetic patients). The use of ACE inhibitors in the immediate post-AMI period is an even more recent phenomenon; leading cardiologists reasoned that the protective effect against heart failure might also exist in the immediate post-AMI setting. Clinical trials to explore this possibility were first reported in 1992 (Swedberg, 1992), but the first statistically significant demonstration of a benefit in a major trial did not occur until ISIS-4 (1995). While we could find few formal metanalyses of the ACE inhibitor trials (one was included in the ISIS-4 report), it is unlikely that it would imply an earlier date of formal demonstration of a clear benefit. The only previous trials to find a protective point-estimate effect were GISSI-3 (1994), which reached a significance level of only $p < .08$ despite having over 19,000 patients enrolled, and SMILE (Ambrosioni et al., 1995), which was published only two months before ISIS-4.

Table 5.2 shows that, while virtually no use of ACE inhibitors in acute management had occurred by 1985, around 13 percent of patients were being treated by 1990. This percentage had increased to about 21 percent of patients by 1995, the same year that clinical trials documented a significant effect on mortality. Only limited evidence exists on trends in the use of ACE inhibitors since 1995. But available evidence does not suggest dramatic growth in the acute treatment of heart attacks since the relevant trials were published. For example, according to data from hospitals participating in the National Registry of Myocardial Infarctions, acute ACE inhibitor use increased by only 3.3 percent between 1994 and 1996 (Michaels et al., 1999). Acute ACE inhibitor use is viewed as appropriate for patients presenting with heart failure symptoms in the setting of AMI who do not have contraindications; this is likely a minority of the total AMI population. Thus, acute ACE inhibitor use may also have achieved much of its diffusion prior to the completion of the clinical trials.

Primary Angioplasty

Immediate, or primary, angioplasty is a relatively new, intensive treatment in the acute setting for AMI. Angioplasty, which involves the use of a catheter to remove a specific blockage or blockages in the coronary arteries without a major cardiac operation, was first developed in the 1970s and along with catheterization and bypass surgery became common in the treatment of patients after AMI in the 1980s (see, e.g., McClellan and Noguchi, 1998, and Cutler et al., 1999). These intensive procedures, typically done days to weeks after AMI, do not alter the acute course of the AMI; rather, they are intended to prevent progression and further events in patients who have recently experienced AMI (secondary prevention). In contrast, primary angioplasty is intended to restore blood flow to the heart *before* the heart muscle affected by the coronary artery blockage has died. Like thrombolysis, the principal alternative to primary angioplasty, it is an attempt to fend off the bulk of the damage from the AMI. Cardiac catheterization, angioplasty, and bypass surgery all require substantial specialized resources; indeed, diffusion of these procedures accounted for most of the growth in hospital expenditures for elderly AMI patients between 1984 and the early 1990s. The specialized resource requirements for primary angioplasty are in many respects even greater. Not only must the hospital have the capacity to perform catheterization and angioplasty; it must have the capacity to do so quickly and (at least ideally) at all times of the day or night.

Trials of primary angioplasty have generally compared it to thrombolysis, which (as noted above) was documented to reduce mortality substantially just a few years before primary angioplasty began to be used frequently. Most of the early trials did not find significantly lower mortality or complications in the primary angioplasty groups. Indeed, the first three trials published actually found a harmful trend associated with the procedure. In the early study by O'Neill et al. (1986), 30-day mortality was 3.7 percent for eligible patients randomized to thrombolysis compared with 6.8 percent for angioplasty (not significant difference, given small study size). Two subsequent small studies involving fewer than 150 patients each also found insignificantly worse 30-day mortality when primary angioplasty was compared with intravenous streptokinase (Ribeiro et al., 1993) and duteplase (a newer thrombolytic: Gibbons et al., 1993).

However, these studies were soon followed by four reports between 1993 and 1997 (Grines et al., 1993; Zijlstra et al., 1993; de Boer et al., 1994;

GUSTO IIb Investigators, 1997), all showing significantly greater reductions in cardiac events (death or reinfarction) with angioplasty. When all results including the 1997 study are pooled in a metanalysis (Gibson, 1999), there is a clear benefit of angioplasty in reducing reinfarction (7.2 percent in thrombolysis vs. 3.7 percent with PTCA, $p = 0.001$) and probably in reducing 30-day mortality (6.4 percent in thrombolysis vs 4.5 percent for PTCA, $p = 0.056$). Thus, the most recent cardiology practice guidelines in the United States tend to favor primary angioplasty over thrombolysis, with the caveats that this approach is likely to be significantly more costly and that it requires the hospital to provide more intensive and experienced support.

Table 5.2 shows that primary angioplasty was used in approximately 3 percent of AMI patients by 1990; this rate had increased to around 10 percent by 1995, prior to the publication of GUSTO IIb results showing a clearer benefit over thrombolysis. Figure 5.3, which shows procedure use rates by year in California (data on nonelderly patients are available only beginning in 1991), indicates steady growth after 1990, with essentially no impact of the mixed trial results in 1993 and 1994.[7] This pattern is typical of the diffusion of intensive cardiac procedures in AMI patients more generally. In previous research, we have documented steady and relatively consistent growth rates for a decade or longer in the use of cardiac catheterization, angioplasty, and bypass surgery following heart attacks (see, e.g., Cutler et al., 1999). Such trends are consistent with the importance of incremental improvements in practice and "learning by doing." Thus, biomedical knowledge related to intensive procedures that require considerable technical skill is probably even less dependent on formal research studies than is biomedical knowledge related to pharmaceuticals.

More recent studies and medical claims data suggest that steady growth in primary angioplasty has continued since 1995, so that the procedure was well established by the time a preponderance of studies documented net benefits. The procedure is particularly common in teaching hospitals and other leading medical centers. It has diffused much less widely in other countries, which have less favorable systems for new capital investment and reimbursement for intensive procedures. For example, in Canada and the UK, the procedure is essentially not used (McClellan and Kessler, 2002).

For all the technologies described thus far, clinical practice in general (and especially the practices of "leading" clinicians) substantially predated favorable results in clinical trials. However, clinical trials have not always confirmed expert expectations. To the extent clinicians are overly confident about new innovations, welfare losses will occur compared with treatment

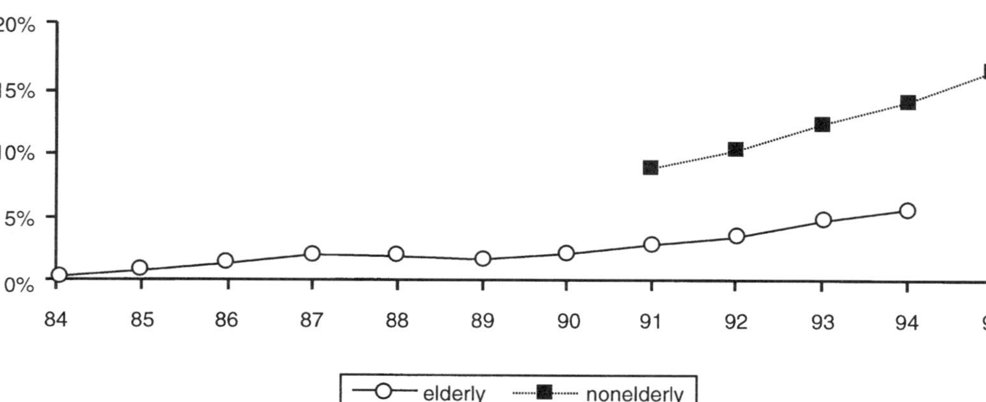

FIGURE 5.3: Primary angioplasty rates for elderly and nonelderly ami patients in California

practices that changed only in response to clinical trials. This appears to have occurred for two AMI treatments.

Lidocaine

Lidocaine is a drug that stabilizes cardiac cell membrane potentials and through this mechanism was expected to reduce the occurrence of ventricular tachycardia (VT) and fibrillation, potentially fatal irregular heart rhythms that occur after AMI. However, better understanding of lidocaine's mechanism of action and growing clinical experience suggested that, while potentially beneficial in a subset of AMI patients at high risk for these arrhythmias, it carried risks of other irregular heart rhythms and disruption in heart function that might lead to net harmful effects in routine AMI use. Trials beginning in 1970 were conducted to determine whether this was the case; in their metanalysis of 19 trials conducted between 1970 and the early 1990s, Lau et al. (1992) concluded that the trials collectively suggested an insignificant trend toward worse outcomes for most patients treated with lidocaine.

Despite the absence of clear evidence from trials, lidocaine use grew and then fell over the past 25 years, presumably in conjunction with the accumulation of clinical experience outside of trials. As table 5.2 shows, use of lidocaine peaked around 1980–85, when close to half of all AMI patients received it. But more recently, use has steadily declined, to around 16 percent of patients by 1995. This treatment rate is probably consistent with the idea of using lidocaine only in the small fraction of AMI cases at very high risk for ventricular tachycardia and fibrillation (e.g. patients who have experienced a short episode of VT).

Calcium Channel Blockers

Calcium channel blockers were approved by the FDA and first marketed in the late 1970s for use in the management of hypertension and chronic ischemic heart disease. Because of their apparently favorable side effect profile, they diffused quickly for these indications. However, no clinical trials have documented a significant mortality reduction associated with their use in acute management of heart attacks; indeed, the point estimates of the major trials (DAVIT-I, 1984; TRENT, 1986; MDPT, 1988; and SPRINT-21, 1993) generally suggest a modest harmful effect. Very recently, new trials have suggested that the slightly worse outcomes were the result of using immediate-release forms of the calcium channel blockers soon after AMI, and that certain calcium channel blockers might be beneficial in certain patients when given somewhat later in the course of acute management (e.g. Hansen et al., 1997). Thus, further trials are ongoing, and some clinicians advocate use of calcium channel blockers in certain cases (Jespersen, 1999).

Table 5.2 shows the use of calcium channel blockers in AMI management over time. The table shows that the drugs initially diffused very widely, presumably as a result of expectations of a significant effect on outcomes. By 1995, however, the treatment rate had fallen by more than half. The decline was largely an incremental process. For example, Col et al. (1996) found an incremental downward shift in the use of calcium channel blockers of only 6 percentage points in the year surrounding the publication of the MDPT trial, with a similar rate of gradual decline both before and after. Whether the most recent beliefs about potentially more beneficial effects of long-acting calcium channel blockers are affecting clinical practice is not yet clear.

Other Acute Treatments

Many other treatments are also used in acute management of AMI. But these technologies, including improved monitoring equipment, systems to reduce the time to reperfusion by thrombolysis and angioplasty, and others, have not been evaluated as extensively in formal research trials as the treatments described here. Thus, clinical practices are even less closely related to the results of formal evidence for these treatments.

Differences in Treatment Trends for Patients Less Frequently Evaluated in Clinical Trials

In our review of treatment trends, we found significantly lower treatment rates in all periods for women and the elderly than for nonelderly males. This finding may simply reflect the fact that more patients in these groups have contraindications to treatment. For example, Canto and colleagues (2000) reported that apparent differences between elderly nonblack men and women in bypass and angioplasty rates after AMI could be explained by differences in comorbid diseases and severity of illness. However, other studies have documented lower rates of use of the AMI treatments described here in female and elderly patients who do not have any contraindications to treatment (e.g. McLaughlin et al., 1996). These differences suggest that formal research studies may play a significant role in increasing clinical confidence in medical practices for the types of patients involved in trials, leading to at least an important incremental effect on practices. The clinical trials just reviewed have provided extensive evidence of the effects of AMI treatments, but for the most part these effects have been estimated for nonelderly, male subjects having few complicating conditions (Gurwitz, Col, and Avorn, 1992), although recent trials have attempted to address this limitation. Unfortunately, evidence is limited on differences in practice trends by sex, age, comorbidity, and other factors that might influence physicians' judgments about the relevance of formal evidence.

Evidence of the Value of Additional Funding for Applied Research

Funding of Formal Trials

For most of the clinical trials reviewed in the previous section, we were able to obtain information on funding sources. Appendix table 5A.1 provides details on the funding of each trial, and table 5.3 summarizes our findings. Table 5.3 is divided into four components: drugs that were off patent for the entire period of our analysis (1975–99; aspirin and generic thrombolytics such as streptokinase); drugs that were on patent for the first part of this period (beta-blockers[8] and lidocaine); drugs that were on patent for the entire period (ACE inhibitors and tPA); and a procedure (primary angioplasty). The table implies that the importance of public funding for formal research studies increases with the extent to which the treatments involve exclusive property rights; a much larger share of the trials for off-patent drugs were funded by public or joint public-private sources. Funding for primary angioplasty trials was also mixed, as might be suspected. While

Table 5.3 Funding Sources for Randomized Controlled Trials (Formal Applied Research) on Heart Attack Treatments

Treatment	Number of Trials Reviewed for Funding Source	Number Reporting Funding Source	Share of Trials with Public Funding (%)
Generic Drugs during Entire Period			
Aspirin	10	8	62
Thrombolytics—Streptokinase	2*	2*	100
Drugs on Patent during Part of Period			
Beta-blockers	7	6	50
Lidocaine	19	13	31
Drugs on Patent during Entire Period			
Thrombolytics—tPA	2*	2*	0
ACE Inhibitors	12	11	44
Calcium Antagonists	6	6	0
Procedure			
Primary angioplasty	7	4	50

*Review of studies involving thrombolytics is still in progress. Estimate incomplete.

medical procedures themselves cannot be patented, biomedical companies hold patents on many drugs (e.g. agents to prevent reblockage) and devices (e.g. stents) that are used in conjunction with this procedure.

The importance of public funding for trials involving drugs and processes that are not fully protected by patents is hardly surprising. But table 5.3 also suggests that the marginal value of additional trials may differ for treatments that do and do not involve patented agents and processes. For both aspirin and generic thrombolytics like streptokinase, there was a substantial delay between the time when clinical mechanisms were well understood and when large formal trials provided convincing evidence that physicians' experience in using the drugs had been justified. The importance of the delay was particularly great for the thrombolytics. As we noted above, thrombolytic use did not increase substantially until after publication of two major trials in the late 1980s. In principle, such trials could have been performed a decade earlier. For aspirin, although there was a long delay between the development of physician experience and confidence in using the treatment and the publication of a clinical trial supporting the evidence, use of the treatment was already fairly widespread by the time of the trial's publication.

For the drugs under patent protection, tPA and calcium antagonists, a number of formal trials on AMI patients were performed soon after the drugs began to be used in clinical practice. When the initial trials of both drugs failed to demonstrate a benefit over alternative therapies, further formal trials were funded. In the case of tPA, the further studies relying on modified methods of using the drug (which in turn had been derived from clinical experience) demonstrated a modest survival benefit. In contrast, fewer trials have been performed to test formally whether refinements in the delivery of streptokinase may also have benefits. In the case of calcium antagonists, the "second round" of formal trials also showed no benefit. However, more recent trials (also based on clinical experience suggesting that giving the drug later in the course of acute treatment might not have adverse effects and that certain types of AMI patients would be more likely to benefit from the drug) have shown a survival benefit. While this evidence only applies to the case of innovations in AMI treatment, it suggests that the marginal value of trials for treatments that are not under patent is relatively high. In the case of streptokinase, earlier funding of a large trial could have led to significantly more patients receiving thrombolytic drugs sooner. However, the value of additional or more rapid trials is limited by the fact that treatments other than thrombolytics were diffusing widely into clinical practice before the trials were reported.

Funding for Informal Research and Development

Unfortunately, despite the importance of "informal" influences on changes in medical practice that is evident from the trends in AMI treatment, little is known about how ideas for practice innovation are generated outside of formal research studies. While considerable research has been directed toward understanding the diffusion of medical practices through conferences, research publications, and other activities, it is unlikely that such diffusion is responsible for the initial development of incremental practice innovations. In the case of acute treatment of AMI, programs to encourage effective medical practice have primarily focused on encouraging the use of treatments that have been justified in convincing randomized clinical trials. Such initiatives to improve quality of care have probably not had much impact yet. To the extent that they do, such "evidence-based medicine" initiatives may retard the worthwhile development and use of treatment innovations that are likely to prove valuable eventually but that have not yet been proven so.

Because there are few explicit channels for explicit funding of "informal" innovation, much of the support for informal innovation presumably comes from payments related to the actual delivery of care. Thus, it seems likely that informal innovations are encouraged primarily by "downstream" economic and regulatory incentives. For example, the relatively favorable reimbursement in many health insurance plans for angioplasty may be an important cause of the notable innovations in acute angioplasty that have occurred over the past decade. But it seems plausible that they may also be more likely to develop in practice settings in which leading clinicians have opportunities to reflect upon and discuss biochemical mechanisms, case reports, and their experiences with patient management.

V. Discussion and Policy Implications

We have analyzed the relationship of formal clinical trials to technological change in the care of heart attacks in the United States from 1975 to 1995. While some previous studies have evaluated the impact of particular clinical trials on medical practice, to our knowledge this is the first comprehensive analysis of the relationship of applied biomedical research to the actual treatment of a common illness. We found some evidence that randomized trials have an important impact on clinical practice. The strongest evidence of a relationship exists for thrombolytic drugs, which are distinguished by the fact that their use leads to significant new medical complications. Thus, firm evidence that the benefits of treatment outweigh the complications seems to have been particularly important for clinicians to support widespread use. Thrombolytics are also distinguished by the fact that they are not the treatment of choice for heading off a heart attack at most leading academic medical centers, which instead are relying increasingly on primary angioplasty.

We found evidence of a more limited impact of clinical trials on medical practice involving most other drug therapies that have been shown to be effective in AMI care, at least in the years surrounding completion of the clinical trials. However, negative trials showing the absence of a beneficial effect in most patients (for lidocaine and calcium channel blockers) had significant if gradual effects on clinical practice. In the case of primary angioplasty, an intensive procedure that is highly dependent on clinical expertise and which has been subject to many incremental improvements over time (e.g. stents and associated anticlotting drugs), we documented a gradual and steady pattern of diffusion that was largely independent of the results of formal research studies.

For all the technologies that were shown to be effective in formal applied research, we found that clinical practices substantially led the results of the trials. This was particularly true for clinicians practicing at academic centers, which were often involved in conducting the clinical trials. But the lead effects were generally widespread enough to encompass a substantial portion of community practice. These informal sources of changes in clinical practice were not always justified or appropriate; informal innovation, just like clinical trials, involves type I and type II errors. But our previous work (Heidenreich and McClellan, 2000) suggests that the health benefits resulting from the informal development of medical practices far outweighed their costs.

We have developed detailed evidence only for the acute treatment of heart attacks. This particular aspect of medical care is unusual, in that most heart attack treatments have been the subject of multiple clinical trials. Far fewer randomized trials have been conducted for innovations expected to influence outcomes of more chronic diseases and combinations of diseases. Our preliminary analyses of primary and secondary prevention of heart disease show substantial "leading" and "trailing" effects around the publication of important research studies; they also show a relatively weaker base of formal evidence for treatment decisions. Thus, it is likely that AMI treatment is a relatively favorable case for the impact of applied biomedical research. We conclude that the informal, incremental developments in clinical "know-how" that occur beyond the setting of formal biomedical research studies are major contributors to growth in the biomedical knowledge base and to the resulting improvements in population health.

Our results show that measures of health care R&D that focus only on formal research studies are missing a major component of innovation in the health care sector. Although health care is clearly one of the most dynamic sectors of the entire economy, it appears only slightly above the national average in terms of its outlays for innovation (Murphy and Topel, this volume). Including informal components of innovation in health care would probably result in a more plausible estimate of health care R&D spending. Obviously, it is not easy to measure the time that academic clinicians spend working out improved protocols for patient care and modifying existing devices and procedures, and that typical clinicians spend in determining how to apply new ideas in their own practice. But our results suggest that these efforts are likely to add up to as much as is currently spent on formal R&D. Thus, health care R&D properly measured may well be on par with or exceed other "high-tech" industries.

This conclusion does not imply that formal biomedical research studies are unimportant contributors to technological change. In the case of heart attacks, with the possible exception of intensive procedures, supportive results from clinical trials appear to be a notable if not essential contributor to the long-term and widespread adoption of valuable innovations in clinical practice. None of the drug treatments we evaluated achieved widespread, lasting diffusion until after the expectation of a net benefit had been confirmed in formal clinical trials. And the trials are also a critical part of the gradual "reverse diffusion" of treatments whose initial promise of better outcomes is not borne out in actual use, and which cannot be rescued by incremental improvements in practice.

Additional support for such formal trials, so that they could be performed sooner and for a more diverse range of patient types and conditions, would appear to have some social value, particularly in the case of nonpatented drugs. Our impression from reviewing the AMI experience is that funding for formal research studies involving patented drugs for which the developers can capture much of the value of innovation is adequate. Indeed, the repeat studies of tPA and calcium channel blockers suggest that patent owners will continue to fund research as long as there is some chance, based on informal clinical evidence, that incrementally modified uses of the treatment will show a benefit. However, it is possible that greater and more responsive public research funding for large, well-done trials involving new uses of generic drugs would have significant benefits. In the case of streptokinase, the state of informal clinical knowledge in the 1970s trial appears to have been adequate to make a large thrombolytic trial like GISSI or ISIS-2 feasible. In part because these trials were not performed for another decade, diffusion of thrombolytic therapy occurred later.

Recommendations about the best use of additional R&D funding should also take into account the important role of informal innovation in health care. Given the limited explicit funding support for informal R&D activities, the marginal value of much of this innovation may be relatively high. Between fiscal year 1996 and fiscal year 2000, federal funding for formal health care R&D increased by over $5 billion in real terms, primarily through increased budgetary authority to the NIH (AAAS, 1999). This funding growth is widely expected to continue. Historically, the bulk of NIH funding has been directed toward supporting formal research studies, including clinical trials. If the additional research support is directed toward the development of better evidence of effective uses of nonpatented drugs and processes, it should help alleviate some of the delays in developing formal evidence to support informal practices; this could speed up the pace of worthwhile innovation in medical practice. At a minimum, the recent "experiment" of rapid funding growth should permit further studies like that performed here, to determine whether the lag time has been reduced between the informal development of innovative practices and the formal demonstration of their value.

The support for informal innovation appears to be waning. Much informal innovation occurs in teaching hospitals: many of the studies we reviewed documented early use of effective new practices and the impetus for new ideas for clinical trials coming from the actual experience of leading clinicians in these institutions. The only direct federal funding source for "informal" R&D, supplemental Medicare payments to teaching hospitals for "graduate medical education," increased significantly from the late 1980s through 1996 but subsequently declined back to about the same real level of spending as in 1992—around $6 billion.[9] To the extent that informal innovation in clinical practices does not reduce costs or improve outcomes for current teaching hospital patients, but does eventually increase the value of medical care after the informal ideas are refined, confirmed in formal trials, and diffused into clinical practice, it is a public good like formal R&D and so is also likely to be underprovided. Recent competitive changes in the health care industry and in government financing seem likely to reduce opportunities for academic clinicians to pursue this type of innovation.

Clearly, evidence is needed on the impact of these recent changes on the extent to which teaching hospitals develop new innovations in practice. One approach, building on the methods developed here, would involve an analysis of the extent to which innovative and initially costly practices adopted at academic centers diffuse into nonacademic settings, and are eventually shown to be worthwhile innovations. Different academic centers have faced more or less difficult financial and competitive pressures in recent years as a result of the changes in federal funding policy and in their competitive environment. An analysis of whether these differential pressures reduce the extent to which teaching hospitals "lead" the development of innovative new practices that are eventually formally demonstrated to be worthwhile could provide a test whether incremental reductions in informal research support have consequences for innovation. More quantitative, "micro" versions of the analysis of technological change for a specific condition, like we have presented here, provide a specific method for implementing this empirical test.

Finally, while informal research support to encourage adoption of effective practices by community health care providers has increased in recent years, the level of funding for such activities is far below the level of funding of formal research support. Since relatively few studies have evaluated informal R&D, the marginal benefits of funding for informal R&D activities and for programs to enhance the effectiveness of informal R&D—for example, by supporting better shared information networks among leading centers—may be relatively high.

Appendix

TABLE 5A.1 Funding Sources for Randomized Controlled Trials of AMI Treatments

Trial Name	Type of Funding	Funding Source
Aspirin		
ISIS-2	Public/private	Hoechst; British Heart Foundation; Sterling Drugs provided aspirin and placebo
Cardiff-1	Private	M.R.I. Epidemiology Unit (Cardiff); Nicholas Research Laboratories
CDPA	Public	NHLBI
Micristin (GDR)	Not reported	
Cardiff-2	Not reported	
AMIS	Public	NHLBI
PARIS-1	Private	GmbH Pharmaceuticals
PARIS-2	Private	GmbH Pharmaceuticals

continued

TABLE 5A.1 *continued*

Trial Name	Type of Funding	Funding Source
TIMI-1	Public	NHLBI
TIMI-2	Public	NHLBI
Thrombolytics		
GISSI (streptokinase)	Public/private	Italian Institutes: ANMCO; Instituto di Ricerche Farmacologiche "Mario Negri"; Consiglio Nazionale delle Ricerche, Ufficio Studi of Ministry of Health; Tonolli Foundation; Casa di Risparmio delle Provincie Lombarde
GUSTO (tPA)	Private	Bayer; CIBA-Corning; Genentech; ICI Pharmaceuticals; Sanofi Pharmaceuticals
Beta-Blockers		
Göteborg	Public	Department of Medicine at Sahlgren's and Östra Hospitals, University of Göteborg, Sweden
MIAMI	Public/Private	MIAMI Trial Research Group; drugs provided by Pharmacy of Östra Hospital (Göteborg)
ISIS-1	Private	ICI Pharmaceuticals Ltd.; British Heart Foundation
TIMI-2B	Public	NHLBI
MDPT	Private	ICI, Ltd. Pharmaceutical Division
Norwegian	Private	Merck Sharp and Dohme Research Lab.
BHAT	Public	NHLBI
ACE Inhibitors		
CONSENSUS-II	Private	Study reports research was supported by Depts. of Medicine and Family and Community Medicine at University of Massachusetts Medical School; Dept. of Ambulatory Care and Prevention at Harvard Medical School; research proposal information suggests Merck, Sharp, and Dohme
GISSI-3	Private	Zeneca Pharmaceutical; Schwarz Pharma
CATS	Private	Bristol-Myers Squibb Inst. For Pharmaceutical Research
SMILE	Private	Bristol-Myers Squibb Inst. For Pharmaceutical Research
ISIS-4	Private	Bristol-Myers Squibb; Astra-Hassle; Hoechst donated drugs

Table 5A.1 *continued*

Trial Name	Type of Funding	Funding Source
CCS-1	Public/Private	Squibb Pharmaceuticals; Fu Wai Hospital, Beijing; University of Oxford, England
CONSENSUS-I	Private	Merck, Sharp, and Dohme Research Lab.
SOLVD(Rx)	Public/Private	NHLBI; Merck Sharp, and Dohme
V-HeFT-II	Public	Cooperative Studies Program of Medical Research Service, Dept. of Veterans Affairs Central Office, Washington, D.C.
SAVE	Private	Bristol-Myers Squibb Institute for Pharmaceutical Research
AIRE	Private	Hoechst
Calcium Antagonists		
DAVIT-I	Private	Knoll AG, Ludwigshafen for drugs
TRENT	Private	Bayer UK Ltd. for drugs
SPRINT-21	Private	ICI Pharmaceuticals Ltd.
MDPT	Private	International private laboratories (Germany, Canada, United States, Spain, others)
SPRINT-1	Private	Bayer AG
DAVIT-II	Private	Knoll Aktiengesellshaft Ludwigshafen, Federal Republic of Germany
Primary Angioplasty		
O'Neil et al. 1986	Public/Private	Dept. of Medicine, Division of Cardiology at University of Michigan at Ann Arbor; Dept. of Medicine, Division of Cardiology at William Beaumont Hospital, Royal Oak, Mich.; Squibb provided materials
Grines et al. 1993	Not reported	Primary Angioplasty in Myocardial Infarction Study Group
Zijlstra 1993	Public	Netherlands: Depts. Of Cardiology and Nuclear Medicine at Ziekenhuis de Weezenlanden, Zwolle; Lab for Clinical Experimental Image Processing, Dept. of Diagnostic Radiation and Nuclear Medicine at University Hospital (Leiden)
de Boer et al. 1994	Public	Netherlands Heart Foundation
GUSTO IIb 1997	Private	Guidant Corporation; Ciba-Geigy

continued

TABLE 5A.1 *continued*

Trial Name	Type of Funding	Funding Source
Ribeiro et al. 1993	Not reported	Unicór Hospital, Interventional Cardiology (Sao Paulo, Brazil); Dept. of Cardiology at Cleveland Clinic Foundation (Cleveland, Ohio)
Gibbons et al. 1993	Private	Burroughs Wellcome Company; E.I. du Pont de Nemours and Company; C.R. Bard, Inc.
Lidocaine		
Pitt 1971	Private	Astra Chemicals Pty. Ltd.; Alfred Hospital (Melbourne, Australia)
Lie 1974	Private	Astra
Mogensen 1970	Public/Private	Astra Pharmaceuticals; Swedish National Association against Heart and Chest Diseases; Karolinska Institutet; Wessén Foundation
Chopra 1971	Private	Pharmaceutical Manufacturing Co. Ltd.
Bleifeld 1973	Private	Amt für Forschung des Landes Nordthein-Westfalen
Darby 1972	Public	General Hospital, Birmingham, England
Bennett 1970	Public/Private	Astra Chemicals, Ltd.; Dept. of Health and Social Security (England)
O'Brien 1973	Public	Cardiology Department of Auckland Hospital (New Zealand)
Koster 1985	Public	Netherlands Heart Foundation
Dunn 1985	Public	Royal Victoria Hospital Research Fellowship (England)
Valentine 1974	Private	Astra Pharmaceuticals; Royal College of General Practitioners, London
Wennerblom 1982	Public	Dept. of Cardiology, Sahlgrenska Hospital in Göteborg (Sweden)
Lie 1978	Public	Dept. of Cardiology and Clinical Physiology and Interuniversity Cardiological Institute at the University Hospital of Amsterdam
Hargareten 1986	Private	Dept. of Trauma and Emergency Medicine at the Medical College of Wisconsin, Milwaukee
Kostuk 1969	Public	Dept. of Medicine at the University of Toronto, Canada; Toronto Western Hospital
Baker 1971	Public	Guy's Hospital London

TABLE 5A.1 *continued*

Trial Name	Type of Funding	Funding Source
Wyse 1988	Public	Alberta Heart and Stroke Foundation; Medical Research Council of Canada; University of Calgary
Sandler 1976	Private	Drugs by Astra
Singh 1976	Private	Astra; St. Vincent Hospital, Worcester; University of Massachusetts School of Medicine

Notes

1. See the other papers prepared for this conference for a more detailed discussion of the heart disease trends.

2. The common estimates of biomedical research expenditures do not include some additional sources of "formal" research expenditures, such as spending by the Veterans Administration and Department of Defense. However, the additional sources are not that substantial.

3. We also reviewed the more limited evidence of other sources of improvement in acute mortality over time. For example, although changes in monitoring methods appear to have been relatively important sources of mortality improvements in the 1960s and early 1970s (Goldman and Cook, 1984), coronary care units with close cardiac monitoring of heart attack patients had largely diffused by the mid-1970s. These coronary care unit (CCU) technologies support rapid detection and treatment of irregular heart rhythms and other serious complications. But because the vast majority of cardiac patients were being monitored by 1975, CCU monitoring has probably not played a major role in the acute mortality improvements since that time. The use of right-heart (pulmonary artery) catheterization for functional assessment in CCUs increased between 1975 and the late 1980s, and then appears to have declined modestly after 1990. Use of these devices is controversial, and there is no clear evidence that they improve survival. Thus, changes in cardiac monitoring have probably not resulted in any significant mortality improvements between 1975 and 1995. Changes in prehospital care, including the implementation of enhanced 911 systems and programs to reduce the "time to needle" of heart attack treatment, have probably had a minor effect on improvements in heart disease outcomes over the past 20 years.

4. Further, it is likely that the secondary-prevention treatments have important interactions with the changes in acute treatment of AMI. For example, AMI patients are now more likely to have blood flow to the heart restored acutely through thrombolytic drugs or primary angioplasty, and then are less likely to have subsequent blockages develop in the same or different coronary blood vessels because of use of cholesterol-lowering drugs and aspirin. Identifying these "interaction effects" is also difficult.

5. See also Stampfer et al. (1982), Yusuf et al. (1985), and Naylor and Jaglal (1990) for reviews of this "early" period in thrombolytic trials.

6. One reason that the effect of acute beta-blocker use has been hard to confirm is the likely modest—though clinically important—size of the effect. In all of the trials, it is on the order of a 10% or less reduction in mortality.

7. As the figure implies, detailed data on nonelderly California patients are available beginning in 1991. Intensive procedure rates in California are somewhat higher than in the rest of the nation; thus, primary angioplasty rates in the figure are greater than national rates for 1990 and 1995 reported in the table.

8. Some beta-blockers remain on patent even today. However, the earliest beta-blockers went off patent relatively early in our study period.

9. Recent legislation added back about $600 million in teaching hospital payments over the next few years, and also rationalized the distribution of these payments across hospitals. Relative to the growth in formal research support, these additions appear to be quite modest. The federal government does provide some additional funding related to enhancing the diffusion of effective practices. Most of the these activities occur through the Agency for Healthcare Research and Quality (AHRQ) and through HCFA's quality initiatives. Total funding for these programs in FY00 is expected to be less than $300 million.

References

Ambrosioni, E., C. Borghi, and B. Magnani, for the Survival of Myocardial Infarction Long-term Evaluation (SMILE) Study Investigators. 1995. "The Effect of the Angiotensin-Converting-Enzyme Inhibitor Zofenopril on Mortality and Morbidity after Anterior Myocardial Infarction." *New England Journal of Medicine* 332:80–85.

Aspirin Myocardial Infarction Study Research Group. 1980. "A Randomized Controlled Trial of Aspirin in Persons Recovered from Myocardial Infarction." *Journal of the American Medical Association* 243:661–69.

Barron, H. V., L. J. Bowlby, T. Breen, W. J. Rogers, J. G. Canto, Y. Zhang, A. J. Tiefenbrunn, and W. D. Weaver. 1998. "Use of Reperfusion Therapy for Acute Myocardial Infarction in the United States: Data from the National Registry of Myocardial Infarction 2." *Circulation* 97, no. 12:1150–56.

Beta Blocker Heart Attack Trial Registry Group. 1982. "A Randomized Trial of Propranolol in Patients with Acute Myocardial Infarction. I. Mortality Results." *Journal of the American Medical Association* 247:1707–14.

Braunwald, E. M. 1997. "Shattuck Lecture—Cardiovascular Medicine at the Turn of the Millenium." *New England Journal of Medicine* 337, no. 19:1360–69.

Canto, J. G., J. J. Allison, C. I. Kiefe, C. Fincher, R. Farmer, P. Sekar, S. Person, and N. W. Weissman. 2000. "Relation of Race and Sex to the Use of Reperfusion Therapy in Medicare Beneficiaries with Acute Myocardial Infarction." *New England Journal of Medicine* 342:1094–100.

Chalmers, T. C. 1974. "The Impact of Controlled Trials on the Practice of Medicine." *Mt. Sinai Journal of Medicine* 41:753–59.

Col, C. N., T. J. McLaughlin, S. B. Soumerai, D. W. Hosmer, J. Yarzebski, J. H. Gurwitz, et al. 1996. "The Impact of Clinical Trials on the Use of Medications for Acute Myocardial Infarction." *Archives of Internal Medicine* 156:54–60.

Coronary Drug Project Research Group. 1976. "Aspirin in Coronary Heart Disease." *Journal of Chronic Diseases* 29:629–42.

Costa, D. L. 2000. "Long-Term Declines in Disability among Older Men: Medical Care, Public Health, and Occupational Change." NBER Working Paper no. 7605.

Cutler, D. M., M. B. McClellan, J. P. Newhouse, and D. Remler. 1999. "Are Medical Prices Declining?" *Quarterly Journal of Economics* 113, no. 4:991–1024.

Cutler, D. M., and E. Richardson. 1997. "Measuring the Health of the US Population." *Brookings Papers on Economic Activity: Microeconomics,* 217–71. Washington, D.C.: Brookings.

Danish Study Group on Verapamil in Myocardial Infarction. 1984. "Effects of Verapamil on Mortality and Major Events after Acute Myocardial Infarction." *European Heart Journal* 5:516–28.

de Boer, M. J., J. C. Hoorntje, J. P. Ottervanger, S. Reiffers, H. Suryapranata, and F. Zijlstra. 1994. "Immediate Coronary Angioplasty versus Intravenous Streptokinase in Acute Myocardial Infarction: Left Ventricular Ejection Fraction, Hospital Mortality and Reinfarction." *Journal of the American College of Cardiology* 23, no. 5:1004–8.

Eddy, D. M. 1996. "Clinical Decision Making: From Theory to Practice. Benefit Language: Criteria That Will Improve Quality while Reducing Costs." *Journal of the American Medical Association* 275:650–57.

Elwood, P. C., A. L. Cochrane, M. L. Burr, P. M. Sweetnam, G. Williams, E. Welsby, et al. 1974. "A Randomized Controlled Trial of Acetyl Salicylic Acid in the Secondary Prevention of Mortality from Myocardial Infarction." *British Medical Journal* 1:436–40.

Elwood, P. C., and P. M. Sweetnam. 1979. "Aspirin and Secondary Mortality after Myocardial Infarction." *Lancet* 2:1313–15.

Fineberg, H. V. 1987. "Clinical Evaluation: How Does It Influence Medical Practice?" *Bulletins on Cancer* 74:333–46.

Fogel, R. 1994. "Economic Growth, Population Theory, and Physiology: The Bearing of Long-Term Processes on the Making of Economic Policy." *American Economic Review,* June.

Friedman, L., N. K. Wenger, and G. L. Knatterud. 1983. "Impact of the Coronary Drug Project Findings on Clinical Practice." *Controlled Clinical Trials* 4:513–22.

Geljins, A., and N. Rosenberg. 1994. "The Dynamics of Technological Change in Medicine." *Health Affairs* suppl.: 24–46.

Gibbons, R. J., D. R. Holmes, G. S. Reeder, K. R. Bailey, M. R. Hopfenspirger, and B. J. Gersh. 1993. "Immediate Angioplasty Compared with the Administration of a Thrombolytic Agent Followed by Conservative Treatment for Myocardial Infarction: The Mayo Coronary Care Unit and Catheterization Laboratory Groups." *New England Journal of Medicine* 328, no. 10:685–91.

Gibson, M. C. 1999. "Primary Angioplasty, Rescue Angioplasty and New Devices." In *Clinical Trials in Cardiovascular Disease,* edited by C. Hennekens, 185–97. Philadelphia: W. B. Saunders Company.

Goldberg, R. J., J. Yarzebski, D. Lessard, and J. M. A. Gore. 1999. "Two-Decades (1975 to 1995) Long Experience in the Incidence, In-Hospital and Long-Term Case-Fatality Rates of Acute Myocardial Infarction: A Community-Wide Perspective." *Journal of the American College of Cardiology* 33:1533–39.

Goldman, L., and E. F. Cook. 1984. "The Decline in Ischemic Heart Disease Mortality Rates. An Analysis of the Comparative Effects of Medical Interventions and Changes in Lifestyle." *Ann Intern Med.* 101, no. 6:825–36.

Goldman L, F. Cook, B. Hashimotso, P. Stone, J. Muller, and A. Loscalzo. 1982. "Evidence That Hospital Care for Acute Myocardial Infarction Has Not Contributed to the Decline in Coronary Mortality between 1973–1974 and 1978–1979." *Circulation* 65, no. 5:936–42.

Grines, C. L., K. F. Browne, J. Marco, D. Rothbaum, G. W. Stone, J. O'Keefe, P. Overlie, B. Donohue, N. Chelliah, G. C. Timmis, et al. 1993, "A Comparison of Immediate Angioplasty with Thrombolytic Therapy for Acute Myocardial Infarction. The Primary Angioplasty in Myocardial Infarction Study Group." *New England Journal of Medicine* 328, no. 10:673–79.

Gruppo Italiano per lo Studio della Streptochinasi nell'Infarto Myocardico (GISSI). 1986. "Effectiveness of Intravenous Thrombolytic Treatment in Acute Myocardial Infarction." *Lancet* 1:397–402.

———. 1994. "GISSI-3 Effects of Lisinopril and Transdermal Glyceryl Trinitrate Singly and Together on 6-Week Mortality and Ventricular Function after Acute Myocardial Infarction." *Lancet* 343:1115–22.

Gurwitz, J. H., N. F. Col, and J. Avorn. 1992. "The Exclusion of the Elderly and Women from Clinical Trials in Acute Myocardial Infarction." *Journal of the American Medical Association* 268:1460–67.

GUSTO (Global Use of Strategies to Open Occluded Coronary Arteries in Acute Coronary Syndromes) Investigators. 1993. "An International Randomized Trial Comparing Four Thrombolytic Strategies for Acute Myocardial Infarction." *New England Journal of Medicine* 329, no. 10:673–82.

GUSTO IIb (Global Use of Strategies to Open Occluded Coronary Arteries in Acute Coronary Syndromes Angioplasty Substudy) Investigators. 1997. "A Clinical Trial Comparing Primary Coronary Angioplasty with Tissue Plasminogen Activator for Acute Myocardial Infarction." *New England Journal of Medicine* 336, no. 23:1621–28.

Hansen, J. F., L. Hagerup, B. Sigurd, F. Pedersen, et al. 1997. "Cardiac Event Rates after Acute Myocardial Infarction in Patients Treated with Verapamil and Trandolapril versus Trandolapril Alone: Danish Verapamil Infarction Trial (DAVIT) Study Group." *American Journal of Cardiology* 79, no. 6:738–41.

Heidenreich, P., and M. B. McClellan. 2000. "Trends in Heart Attack Treatments and Outcomes, 1975–1995: A Literature Review and Synthesis." In *Medical Care Output and Productivity,* edited by E. Berndt and D. Cutler. Chicago: Chicago University Press.

Hjalmarson, A., D. Elmfeldt, J. Herlitz, S. Holmberg, I. Malek, G. Nyberg, L. Ryden, K. Swedberg, A. Vedin, F. Waagstein, A. Waldenstrom, J. Waldenstrom, H. Wedel, L. Wilhelmsen, and C. Wilhelmsson. 1981. "Effect on Mortality of Metoprolol in Acute Myocardial Infarction. A Double-Blind Randomised Trial." *Lancet* 2:823–27.

Hunink, M. G., L. Goldman, A. N. Tosteson, M. A. Mittleman, P. A. Goldman, L. W. Williams, et al. 1997. "The Recent Decline in Mortality from Coronary Heart Disease, 1980–1990: The Effect of Secular Trends in Risk Factors and Treatment." *Journal of the American Medical Association* 277, no. 7:535–42.

ISIS-1 (First International Study of Infarct Survival) Collaborative Group. 1986. "Randomised Trial of Intravenous Atenolol among 16,027 Cases of Suspected Acute Myocardial Infarction." *Lancet* 2:57–66.

ISIS-2 (Second International Study of Infarct Survival) Collaborative Group. 1988. "Randomized Trial of Intravenous Streptokinase, Oral Aspirin, Both, or Neither among 17,187 Cases of Acute Myocardial Infarction." *Lancet* 2:349–60.

ISIS-4 (Fourth International Study of Infarct Survival) Collaborative Group. 1995. "ISIS-4: A Randomised Factorial Trial Assessing Early Oral Captopril, Oral Mononitrate, and Intravenous Magnesium Sulphate in 58,050 Patients with Suspected Acute Myocardial Infarction." *Lancet* 345, no. 8951:669–85.

Israeli SPRINT Study Group. 1993. "Secondary Prevention Reinfarction Israeli Nifedipine Trial (SPRINT) 21: A Randomized Intervention Trial of Nifedipine in Patients with Acute Myocardial Infarction." *European Heart Journal* 9:354–64.

Jang, I. K., D. F. Brown, R. P. Giugliano, H. V. Anderson, et al. 1999. "A Multicenter, Randomized Study of Argatroban versus Heparin As Adjunct to Tissue Plasminogen Activator (TPA) in Acute Myocardial Infarction: Myocardial Infarction with Novastan and TPA (MINT) Study." *Journal of the American College of Cardiology* 33, no. 7:1879–85.

Jespersen, C. M. 1999. "Verapamil in Acute Myocardial Infarction: The Rationales of the VAMI and DAVIT III Trials." *Cardiovascular Drugs and Therapeutics* 13, no. 4:301–7.

Ketley, D., and J. L. Woods. 1993. "Impact of Clinical Trials on Clinical Practice: Example of Thrombolysis for Acute Myocardial Infarction." *Lancet* 342:891–94.

Kizer, J. R., C. P. Cannon, C. H. McCabe, H. S. Mueller, M. J. Schweiger, et al. 1999. "Trends in the Use of Pharmacotherapies for Acute Myocardial Infarction among Physicians Who Design and/or Implement Randomized Trials versus Physicians in Routine Clinical Practice: The MILIS-TIMI Experience." *American Heart Journal* 137:79–92.

Klimt, C. R., G. L. Knatterud, J. Stamler, and P. Meier. 1986. "Persantine-Aspirin Reinfarction Study, Part II. Secondary Prevention with Persantine and Aspirin." *Journal of the American College of Cardiology* 7:251–69.

Lamas, G. A., M. A. Pfeffer, P. Hamm, J. Wertheimer, J. L. Rouleau, and E. Braunwald. 1992. "Do the Results of Randomized Clinical Trials Influence Medical Practice?" *New England Journal of Medicine* 327:241–47.

Lau, J., E. M. Antman, J. Jiminez-Silva, B. Kupelnick, F. Mosteller, and T. C. Chalmers. 1992. "Cumulative Meta-Analysis of Therapeutic Trials for Myocardial Infarction." *New England Journal of Medicine* 327:248–54.

Manton, K., L. S. Corder, and E. Stallard. 1997. "Chronic Disability Trends in the Elderly U.S. Population: 1982–94." *Proceedings of the National Academy of Sciences* 94:2593–98.

Marciniak, T. A., et al. 1998 "Improving the Quality of Care for Medicare Patients with Acute Myocardial Infarction: A Randomized Controlled Trial." *Journal of the American Medical Association* 279:1358–63.

McClellan, M. B., et al. 2002. "Determinants and Consequences of Technological Change in AMI Care in the United States." In *Technological Change in Health Care: A Global Analysis of Heart Attack,* edited by M. B. McClellan and D. P. Kessler. Ann Arbor: University of Michigan Press.

McClellan, M. B., and D. P. Kessler, eds. 2002. *Technological Change in Health Care: A Global Analysis of Heart Attack.* Ann Arbor: University of Michigan Press.

McClellan, M. B., and H. Noguchi. 1998. "Technological Change in Heart Disease Treatment: Does High-Tech Mean Low Value?" *American Economic Review, Papers and Proceedings* 88, no. 2: 90–96.

McLaughlin, T. J., S. B. Soumerai, D. J. Willison, J. H. Gurwitz, C. Borbas, et al. 1996. "Adherence to National Guidelines for Drug Treatment of Suspected Acute Myocardial Infarction: Evidence for Undertreatment in Women and the Elderly." *Archives of Internal Medicine* 156:799–805.

MDPT (Multicenter Diltiazem Postinfarction Trial) Research Group. 1988. "The Effect of Diltiazem on Mortality and Reinfarction after Acute Myocardial Infarction." *New England Journal of Medicine* 319:385–92.

MIAMI Trial Research Group. 1985. "Metoprolol in Acute Myocardial Infarction (MIAMI): A Randomised Placebo-Controlled International Trial." *European Heart Journal* 6:199–226.

Michaels, A. D., C. Maynard, N. R. Every, and H. V. Barron. 1999. "Early Use of ACE Inhibitors in the Treatment of Acute Myocardial Infarction in the United States: Experience from the National Registry of Myocardial Infarction 2." *American Journal of Cardiology* 84, no. 10:1176–81.

Multicenter International Study. 1977. "Improvement in Prognosis of Myocardial Infarction by Long-Term Beta-Adrenoreceptor Blockade Using Practolol." *British Medical Journal* 3: 735–40.

Naylor, C. D., and S. B. Jaglal. 1990. "Impact of Intravenous Thrombolysis on Short-Term Coronary Revascularization Rates: A Meta-Analysis." *Journal of the American Medical Association* 264:697–702.

NCHS (National Center for Health Statistics). 1999. Mortality series. <http://www.cdc/gov/~nchs>.

Norwegian Multicenter Study Group. 1981. "Timolol-Induced Reduction in Mortality and Reinfarction in Patients Surviving Acute Myocardial Infarction." *New England Journal of Medicine* 304:801–7.

O'Neill, W., G. C. Timmis, P. D. Bourdillon, P. Lai, V. Ganghadarhan, J. Walton Jr., R. Ramos, N. Laufer, S. Gordon, M. A. Schork, et al. 1986. "A Prospective Randomized Clinical Trial of Intracoronary Streptokinase versus Coronary Angioplasty for Acute Myocardial Infarction." *New England Journal of Medicine* 314, no. 13:812–18.

Pashos, C. L., S. L. Normand, J. B. Garfinkle, J. P. Newhouse, A. M. Epstein, and B. J. McNeil. 1994. "Trends in the Use of Drug Therapies in Patients with Acute Myocardial Infarction, 1988 to 1992." *Journal of the American College of Cardiology* 23:1023–30.

Persantine-Aspirin Reinfarction Study Research Group. 1980. "Persantine and Aspirin in Coronary Heart Disease." *Circulation* 62:449–61.

Ribeiro, E. E., L. A. Silva, R. Carneiro, L. G. D'Oliveira, A. Gasquez, J. G. Amino, J. R. Tavares, A. Petrizzo, S. Torossian, R. Duprat Filho, et al. 1993. "Randomized Trial of Direct Coronary Angioplasty versus Intravenous Streptokinase in Acute Myocardial Infarction." *Journal of the American College of Cardiology* 22, no. 2:376–80.

Rosenberg, Nathan. 1994. *Exploring the Black Box*. Cambridge: Cambridge University Press. See esp. chap. 1.

Stampfer, M. J., S. Z. Goldhaber, S. Yusuf, R. Peto, and C. H. Hennekens. 1982. "Effect of Intravenous Streptokinase on Acute Myocardial Infarction: Pooled Results from Randomized Trials." *New England Journal of Medicine* 307:1180–82.

Swedberg, K., P. Held, J. Kjekshus, K. Rasmussen, L. Ryden, and H. Wedel. 1992. "Effects of the Early Administration of Enalapril on Mortality in Patients with Acute Myocardial Infarction. Results of the Cooperative New Scandinavian Enalapril Survival Study II (CONSENSUS II)." *New England Jouranl of Medicine* 327:678–84.

TIMI Study Group. 1989. "Comparison of Invasive and Conservative Strategies after Treatment with Intravenous Tissue Plasminogen Activator in Acute Myocardial Infarction: Results of the Thombolysis in Myocardial Infarction (TIMI) Phase II Trial." *New England Journal of Medicine* 320:618–27.

U.S. Congress Office of Technology Assessment. 1983. *The Impact of Randomized Controlled Trials on Health Policy and Medical Practice.* OTA Report BP-H-22. Washington, D.C.: U.S. Government Printing Office.

Vogel, G., C. Fischer, and R. Huyke. 1979. "Reinfarktprophylaxe mit azetylsalizylsaure." *Folia Heamatologica* (Leipzig) 106:797–803.

Weinstein, M. C., P. G. Coxson, L. W. Williams, T. M. Pass, W. B. Stason, and L. Goldman. 1987. "Forecasting Coronary Heart Disease Incidence, Mortality, and Cost: The Coronary Heart Disease Policy Model." *American Journal of Public Health* 77, no. 11:1417–26.

Wilcox, R. G., J. R. Hampton, D. C. Banks, J. S. Birkhead, I. A. Brooksby, C. J. Burns-Cox, et al. 1986. "Trial of Early Nifedipine in Acute Myocardial Infarction: The TRENT Study." *British Medical Journal* 293:1204–8.

Yusuf, S., R. Collins, R. Peto, et al. 1985. "Intravenous and Intracoronary Fibrinolytic Therapy in Acute Myocardial Infarction: Overview of Results on Mortality, Reinfarction, and Side Effects from 33 Randomized Controlled Trials." *European Heart Journal* 6:556–85.

Zijlstra, F., M. J. de Boer, J. C. Hoorntje, S. Reiffers, J. H. Reiber, and H. Suryapranata. 1993. "A Comparison of Immediate Coronary Angioplasty with Intravenous Streptokinase in Acute Myocardial Infarction." *New England Journal of Medicine* 328, no. 10:680–84.

CHAPTER SIX

Can Medical Cost-Effectiveness Analysis Identify the Value of Research?

David Meltzer

I. Introduction

Over the past several decades, the remarkable and unprecedented increase in health care expenditures throughout the world, but especially in the United States, has prompted increasing concerns that current levels of health care expenditures are excessive. Indeed, it has been suggested that medical care has been provided not only beyond where its marginal benefits exceed its costs, but often into ranges where there is little or no benefit. Examples of such "flat of the curve" medical care (Enthoven, 1980), and concerns that in some instances medical interventions may even have been applied to the point of doing harm, have provided key motivation for the growth of efforts to identify when specific medical treatments are beneficial and worth their costs.

The importance of determining when specific medical technologies are worthwhile has been intensified in recent years with the growing recognition that increases in health care costs have been largely driven by the development and diffusion of new medical technologies. Analysis of the sources of medical cost growth suggest that, of the 2.5 percent annual growth in medical expenditures in the United States since 1960 relative to the rest of the economy, 1.6 percent stemmed from growth in the relative quantity of health care, while only 0.9 percent was caused by growth in the relative price of health care (Fuchs, 1990). However, work by Joseph Newhouse and

David Meltzer is associate professor in the Section of General Internal Medicine, Department of Economics, and Harris Graduate School of Public Policy at the University of Chicago and a faculty research fellow of the National Bureau of Economic Research.

This chapter was initially prepared for "The Economic Value of Medical Research," a conference organized by Funding First and the Lasker Foundation. The author would also like to acknowledge financial support from The John M. Olin Foundation, The Robert Wood Johnson Foundation, and the National Institute of Aging.

colleagues (Newhouse, 1992; Cutler, McClellan, Newhouse et al., 1998) has suggested that much of the apparent growth in the medical consumer price index is itself due to unmeasured improvements in quality. This implies that growth in medical technology is the primary, if not sole, reason for growth in health expenditures.

The immediate implication of this finding is that controlling health care costs will ultimately require controlling the development and diffusion of medical technology. In accomplishing this goal, reimbursement systems that provide both developers and users of technologies with the appropriate incentives both to control costs and to produce quality health care are essential. Nevertheless, they are not sufficient, since they do not provide the tools to figure out how to accomplish those objectives through specific decisions about individual technologies. It is interesting in that regard that there is no convincing evidence that the costs within managed care plans have grown at any lesser rate than costs outside of managed care plans (Smith et al., 1998). Moreover, it appears that often little of the savings of managed care plans is due to lower utilization but is instead due to more effective bargaining with providers (Lindrooth, Norton, and Dickey, 1998). These findings suggest that managed care plans have had difficulty in addressing the problem of technology assessment. On the patient side, patient incentives for cost containment (such as copayments) may play some role (Manning et al., 1987). However, their effectiveness is constrained by the fact that the majority of health expenditures are consumed by a small fraction of the population with very high costs (Berk, Monheit, and Hagan, 1988), and the willingness of most people to face financial risks of such magnitude is limited. This again reinforces the position that decisions to limit the use of specific medical technologies are likely crucial if costs are to be contained.

However, many of these new technologies have substantial health benefits and, as many of the papers to be discussed here suggest, people appear to place high valuations on the improvements in health that have taken place in recent decades (Cutler and Richardson, 1997; Murphy and Topel, this volume; Nordhaus, this volume). This suggests that indiscriminate reductions in the provision of health care could easily result in losses in welfare. Nevertheless, the high average benefit of medical technology does not appear to be matched by high marginal benefit in many instances. This has been evident in many empirical analyses of the expansion of access to medical care among people who already have fairly good access to medical care. In experiments such as the RAND health insurance experiment (Manning et al., 1987), and in observational studies in which quasi-experimental techniques have been used to look at "exogenous" increases in access (McClellan, McNeil, and Newhouse, 1994), it has not been possible to show any significant improvement in health outcomes. Thus, a central challenge in ensuring the efficient allocation of resources for health care and for health care research is to identify technologies whose incremental benefits are worth their costs. It is in response to this that the field of medical technology assessment has arisen, with the majority of analyses performed using the techniques of one particular approach: medical cost-effectiveness analysis.

Likewise, as people have questioned when medical treatments are "worth it," they have also understandably asked when medical care research is likely to be worthwhile. Are current levels of spending too little or too great? Are we spending our research dollars on the right opportunities? The papers to be discussed here suggest that the value of improvements in health that have arisen over the past several decades is likely to far exceed the costs of the medical care and medical care research that have been devoted to accomplishing such gains. To the extent one believes that these gains in health have resulted from medical expenditure and medical research, this work suggests that these expenditures have been not only "worth it," but actually major contributors to increasing welfare. If this is accepted, then it is in turn tempting to conclude that additional increases are justified. It is absolutely possible that this is the case. However, even if such expenditures have been worthwhile on average, it is another set of questions what their value is at the margin, and whether research funds are being allocated to the correct opportunities. Indeed, both Congress and the National Institutes of Health (NIH) have faced increasing pressures from disease-specific interest groups in recent years to justify their decisions about resource allocation, and questions such as these have been of sufficient concern to Congress that they have played a role in recent discussions about increased funding for research, and led Congress to request the advice of the Institute of Medicine on whether priorities for the allocation of funds at NIH have been appropriate (IOM, 1998). Indeed, while the resulting IOM report did not conclude that medical expenditures to date have been allocated incorrectly, it did conclude that NIH should pay greater attention to the burden of illness in assessing priorities for research. Following on this, others have suggested that NIH could better identify the most promising projects if it took greater advantage of formal approaches to assess the burden of illness and opportunities for research to lessen the burden of illness (Tengs, 1998). In a similar vein, but with a different perspective on current approaches to resource allocation, a recent article in the *New England Journal of Medicine* has argued that in fact NIH funds have been allocated in a manner largely consistent with certain broad measures of the burden of illness (Gross, Anderson, and Powe, 1999). In commenting on this, NIH Director Harold Varmus has reasonably asked to what extent such measures of the burden of illness either capture the true burden of illness or should factor in the setting of priorities for research as opposed to scientific opportunity, especially given the importance of basic research in the advancement of medicine and the difficulty of predicting where the products of basic research will be of value (Varmus, 1999).

This chapter builds on recent work in the theoretical foundations of cost-effectiveness analysis to examine the potential for formal technology assessment to help identify the value of specific medical technologies and the most promising avenues for future research. In analyzing this issue, the emphasis is placed on the tools of medical cost-effectiveness analysis because it has been the most widely used approach to assess the value of specific medical technologies. The key message is that, just as medical cost-effectiveness analysis can provide insight into the value of medical interventions in specific contexts, it may have the potential to provide important insights into the value of biomedical research if applied in the right settings with methodological rigor and a thoughtful understanding of its strengths and limitations.

The chapter begins with a critical review of the methodological foundations of medical cost-effectiveness analysis. This suggests both the potential of these tools as well as a series of important challenges that must be addressed in any effort to use them, whether to value specific medical technologies or to value research opportunities. The paper then examines the prospects for harnessing the tools of medical cost-effectiveness to assess the expected value of research using a value of information framework. Though the theoretical and technical barriers to performing such calculations are formidable and essentially preclude the application of these approaches to the study of basic research, value of information calculations may be useful for assessing the value of research in a range of specific clinical contexts, including clinical trial design. Though the application of such techniques, even in these circumscribed areas, is in its infancy, these calculations may have the potential to become an important tool to identify and maximize the value of research. Realizing this potential will require renewed attention to the methodological foundations of cost-effectiveness analysis and the rigorous application of those principles. Even so, rational allocation of funds for research will require an understanding of the intrinsic limitations of these approaches and a continued reliance on the type of sound scientific judgment that has shaped the resource allocation process to date.

II. Cost-Effectiveness Analysis of Medical Interventions

As a first step in understanding the potential for the tools of medical technology assessment to inform priorities for biomedical research, it is important to understand the strengths and limitations of the tools in assessing the value of medical care. Because medical technology assessment is a large and active area of research, a comprehensive review is not possible here. Nevertheless, a general knowledge of the approach and some of its key limitations, and the potential for addressing those limitations, is important to understanding the potential of applying the methods to help identify the value of research.

Scope and Origins of Cost-Effectiveness Analysis

Since its origins with a handful of publications in the academic medical literature in the 1960s, medical technology assessment has grown at an accelerating rate, reaching nearly 1,000 publications annually in recent years and covering an immense range of specific applications within medicine (Elixhauser et al., 1998). Interestingly, although the pioneering studies in medical cost-effectiveness analysis were done in the United States (Weinstein and Stason, 1976), the greatest interest in the field over the past several decades has been in European countries and former British colonies, including Canada, Australia, and New Zealand. This greater level of interest in these countries compared with the United States can likely be traced to the greater role played by national health systems in those countries and a variety of challenges to the idea of technology assessment in the United States, driven particularly by certain medical professional societies and pharmaceutical and medical device producers attempting to avoid regulation (Perry and Thamer, 1999). Nevertheless, there has recently been increasing interest in technology assessment in the United States. This has been largely driven by private payers seeking to identify approaches to cost containment and, not surprisingly, pharmaceutical and medical device manufacturers attempting to market their products. In this context, interest in these techniques from within the pharmaceutical industry has been particularly intense. However, the high financial stakes for companies have led to concerns that what the industry has called "pharmacoeconomics" may not consistently provide objective evaluations, as well as to Food and Drug Administration attempts to develop guidelines for pharmacoeconomic evaluation (Neumann, Zinner, and Paltiel, 1996).

This problem is clearly complicated by a series of important deficiencies in the methodological foundations of medical technology assessment. While some methods familiar to economists with clearly developed theoretical foundations, such as willingness-to-pay approaches to contingent valuation, have played some role in the field, they have been used in by far the minority of studies. The most commonly cited reasons that contingent valuation methods have not been more widely used are a reluctance to directly place a dollar value on health, concerns that such analyses will result in less attention to the health problems of the poor, and basic methodological concerns about the ability to measure people's actual willingness to pay (Gold et al., 1996). Instead, reflecting the origins of these analyses in medical decision analysis and quantitative psychology, the predominant approach has been that of cost-effectiveness analysis. Following this approach, interventions are ranked in terms of their cost per unit of benefit, and those that offer the lowest cost per unit of benefit at the margin are selected. Application of this procedure generates cost-effectiveness ratios for a broad set of interventions that can then be listed in order of decreasing cost-effectiveness from top to bottom. Such a "league table," listed in this case in terms of cost per life-year saved, is illustrated by table 6.1. Exactly where to draw the line in such a table between what is considered cost-effective and what is not considered cost-effective is not clear. Many papers in the literature seem to adopt thresholds in the $50,000 to $100,000 per life-year or quality-adjusted life-year (QALY) range (Goldman et al., 1992), but regardless of where the line is drawn, such rankings are useful because they suggest that one should always engage in activities at the top of the list before moving further down the list.

An Example of an Important Application of Cost-Effectiveness Analysis: Pap Smears

A brief example of the application of cost-effectiveness analysis to a particular medical technology, Pap smears, may serve to illustrate the value of the approach. Because of their ability to detect cervical cancer while it is still easily treatable, regular Pap smears have become a key component of preventive health care for women, and indeed mortality from cervical cancer has fallen substantially in countries when cervical cancer screening has been implemented. Moreover, the test is relatively inexpensive and has few risks. It may not be surprising, therefore, that a cost-effectiveness analysis by Eddy (1981) estimated an annual Pap smear to extend life at a cost of only $1,535 per year of life saved. This example is consistent with the general impression, emphasized by many of the papers to be presented here, that the average value of medical care is high. However, cervical cancer generally progresses quite slowly, with 8 years on average passing from the time a lesion is first detectable to when it is no longer easily treated;

Table 6.1 Cost-Effectiveness of Common Medical Interventions

Intervention	Cost/QALY
Neonatal PKU screening	< 0
Secondary prevention of hypercholesterolemia in men aged 55–64 years	2,000
Secondary prevention of hypercholesterolemia in men aged 65–74 years	13,000
Pap smear every 3 years after 4 negative annual Pap smears	17,000
Treatment of severe hypertension	17,000
Annual breast exam 55–74	14,000–30,000
Secondary prevention of hypercholesterolemia in men aged 75–84 years	19,000
Annual breast exam 40–50	25,000–58,000
One-time physical exam for abdominal aortic aneurism	29,000
Treatment of mild hypertension	34,000
One-time ultrasound for abdominal aortic aneurism	42,000
Mammography 65–74 compared to breast examination	45,000–163,000
Mammography 40–50 compared to breast examination	52,000–237,000
Primary prevention of hypercholesterolemia in men ages 55–64	60,000–99,000
Screening exercise test in asymptomatic 40 year-old males	124,000
Pap smear every 2 years after 3 negative annual Pap smears vs. every 3 years	258,000
Physical exam every 5 years for abdominal aortic aneurism	747,000
Pap smear every year after 3 negative annual Pap smears vs. every 3 years	833,000
Ultrasound every 5 years for abdominal aortic aneurism	907,000

Source: Meltzer, 1997.

and for this reason it is important to consider the incremental value of annual Pap smears relative to less frequent ones. In Eddy's analysis, the results are striking: a Pap smear done every 3, 2, and 1 year—compared to no Pap smear—increased life expectancy by 70 days, 71 days, and 71 days and 8 hours. Thus the marginal gains from increasing the frequency from 3 to 2 years and from 2 to 1 year are only 1 day, and 8 hours, respectively. In terms of marginal cost per year of life saved, performing the Pap smear every third year costs $521 per year of life saved, while moving from 3 to 2 years and from 2 to 1 year cost $18,250 and $165,909 per year of life saved, respectively. In a more recent analysis with somewhat improved epidemiological data (Eddy, 1990) and updated to 1996 dollars, the marginal cost of the annual Pap smear compared with one done every 2 years was $833,000 per year of life saved (Meltzer, 1997). Based on this, most people would agree that the marginal value of an annual Pap smear relative to its cost is low. Based on these analyses, women who have a history of normal Pap smears and no other risk factors are now recommended to have a Pap smear only every third year (U.S. Preventive Services Task Force, 1996). Similarly, increased efforts have been put into identifying women who have not recently had a Pap smear. Results of these screening initiatives suggest that they detect cancers that would otherwise have likely progressed shortly to generate both serious illness and high costs, and thus save both lives and money (Mandelblatt and Fahs, 1988). Thus the cost-effectiveness analysis of Pap smears provides a prime example of how medical technology assessment can be used to shape the efficient use of technology.

Though not unique, the Pap smear example is certainly one of the more striking applications of these technology assessment techniques by virtue of the large magnitude of the differences in average and marginal cost-effectiveness of the intervention and the relative simplicity of the measure of benefit as years of life saved. But most medical technology assessments do not yield such striking results, and this makes attention to a variety of methodological and measurement issues in cost-effectiveness analysis crucial in determining the potential for these approaches to assist in the allocation of funds for biomedical research. Some of these key issues concern what perspective to take in performing cost-effectiveness analysis, how to measure both costs and benefits, and what to do when there is uncertainty about those costs and benefits. Complicating the discussion of nearly all these issues from the perspective of economic theory is that, although solid microeconomic principles provide the central justification for this approach (Weinstein and Zeckhauser, 1972; Weinstein, 1995; Gold et al., 1996), researchers working on cost-effectiveness analysis have rarely returned to these first principles in addressing methodological issues. Indeed, despite involvement by some European economists, U.S. economists have paid very little attention to the field; while medical journals and health economics specialty journals commonly publish articles on medical cost-effectiveness analysis, in the 14 major economics journals catalogued by JSTOR dating to the 1960s,[1] there is only one reference to medical cost-effectiveness analysis. Whether greater attention to the questions raised in medical cost-effectiveness by mainstream economists could help advance the methods of cost-effectiveness analysis is not certain, but the current state of research in the area suggests that there are likely to be meaningful opportunities to advance the field. Nevertheless, understanding these important unresolved issues concerning the methodological foundations of cost-effectiveness analysis is essential to developing a realistic assessment of the potential to apply these techniques to assess opportunities for research.

Perspective

Some of the most fundamental ambiguities concerning the measurement of costs and benefits for cost-effectiveness analysis relate to the choice of perspective. This could be the perspective of a specific entity, such as an individual, family, HMO, or Medicare, or a societal perspective that incorporates all costs and benefits regardless of to whom they accrue. Though more narrow, the perspectives of individual entities may be particularly useful in understanding the incentives faced by those entities. For example, the out-of-pocket cost of a prescribed treatment for a patient is likely to be a better predictor of that patient's compliance with a regimen than the full price (or cost) of a drug. In contrast, the societal perspective is generally adopted when the goal is to identify interventions that may offer benefits to society as a whole. For this reason, the societal perspective has received increasing favor for use in cost-effectiveness analysis, including the recommendation of the Panel on Cost-Effectiveness in Health and Medicine, which was convened by the Public Health Service to develop consensus on methods for cost-effectiveness analysis (Gold et al., 1996).

From the perspective of neoclassical economic analysis, the issues raised by this societal perspective are particularly challenging. In particular, the set of issues raised by the Arrow Impossibility Theorem suggest that, if the choice being analyzed is one that implies a distribution of outcomes across different members of society, there can be no nondictatorial allocation algorithm that simultaneously satisfies a minimal set of assumptions concerning Pareto optimality, unrestrictedness of domain to individual preference orderings, and independence of irrelevant alternatives (Arrow, 1951). Surely this result, which seems to have in general diminished the enthusiasm of economists for the field of social choice (see Sen [1999] for a discussion of this), must have diminished the interest in evaluating alternative allocations of social resources in health care through cost-effectiveness analysis as well.

Nevertheless, there are ways in which the choices analyzed through medical cost-effectiveness analysis may be seen as more consistent with neoclassical economic theory. For example, much as Harsanyi (1955) argued that if individuals in society are uncertain about their future utilities and maximize expected utility it may be possible to construct a social welfare function respecting their individual preferences, recent attempts to place cost-effectiveness analysis in a welfare-economic framework have relied on expected utility models that can also be understood as the result of expected utility maximization of a representative consumer (Garber and Phelps, 1997; Meltzer, 1997). Whether or not one finds such arguments convincing, or indeed accepts the idea that the Arrow Theorem fundamentally undermines the concept of social welfare (Sen, 1999), it seems that the area of health care evaluation is one of the most important areas for the ongoing debate about the possibility of meaningful representations of social choice.

Even once a choice of perspective is adopted, however, there remain crucial questions of how to measure costs and benefits that must also be answered in order to use these tools to help inform priorities for biomedical research.

Measuring the Benefits of Medical Interventions

In order to apply the principles of cost-effectiveness analysis across a range of medical interventions, it is necessary to develop a single metric that can capture the benefits of a broad class of medical interventions. This has been and remains a key challenge for cost-effectiveness analysis. Compared with disease-specific measures such as the number of cancers detected or cured, effects on mortality, as measured by life-years saved, have the advantage of comparability across diseases, but unfortunately do not capture the important effects of medical care on quality of life. Recognition of this has led to the development of the concept of quality-adjusted life years (QALYs), which was first applied in the context of evaluating the cost-effectiveness of the treatment of hypertension (Weinstein and Stason, 1976).

Following this approach, each year of life is weighted by a factor between 0 and 1 intended to reflect the quality of life in that year, where 0 is equivalent to death and 1 to perfect health. These quality-of-life weights are most commonly derived by psychometric techniques based on responses to hypothetical choices. Some of these approaches have no discernable connection to theory whatsoever, but two common approaches can be fairly readily connected to neoclassical economic theory (Gold et al., 1996). Specifically, these describe (1) choices between life with a given illness and a gamble involving life in perfect health and death with some probability (the standard gamble approach) or (2) choices between longer life with illness and a shorter life in full health (the time tradeoff technique).

Despite the potential connection of these measures to economic theory, QALYs have been controversial. Indeed, while practitioners of cost-effectiveness analysis have often been surprisingly willing to proceed in the absence of evidence of validity of these measures, many economists have often been equally unwilling to consider whether these measures may be of value, especially given the known limitations of alternative approaches, such as contingent valuation approaches to willingness-to-pay (Pauly, 1995). Nevertheless, quality-adjusted life expectancy has become the dominant outcome measure used in medical technology assessment and is used in the majority of the 1,000 or so papers in medical technology assessment published annually. Moreover, QALYs were recently endorsed as the preferred measure of health benefits by the Panel on Cost-Effectiveness in Health and Medicine that was convened by the Public Health Service to provide advice on techniques for the performance of medical technology assessment in the United States (Gold et al., 1996).

However, despite their popularity, serious questions about the validity of QALYs remain. A sampling of the more important of these questions include their basic ability to capture the dimensions of health that people value, and to reflect how people value risk, prefer the present relative to the future, adapt to health limitations, or express variations in preferences. To date, the research that has examined the validity of QALYs as a measure of patient preferences has most commonly compared the results of using different methods of quality-of-life assessment, for example the time tradeoff versus the standard gamble (e.g. Blumenschein and Johannesson, 1998). These studies have tended to find some correlation among these measures. However, the problem with this approach to the validation of QALYs is that it only implies that these different techniques are measuring something in common, and not that they reflect what people value in making health care decisions. At its essence, the problem is the absence of a "gold standard" that reflects what people value with respect to their health and health care.

This problem of identifying what people desire in seeking health care in fact arises far more broadly than in cost-effectiveness analysis. Indeed, it is faced daily by patients and clinicians alike and is generally addressed by clinicians' attempts to inform patients of their options and then help them make the choice that best reflects their preferences. While this mode of medical decision making may be chosen to some extent because of a belief in autonomy as of intrinsic value, the emphasis among both patients and physicians on informed consent also places a great deal of emphasis on individual variation in preferences, and the belief that informed choice is the most reliable way to identify those preferences. Even if they are not a perfect measure of individual preferences, however, informed choices are certainly a compelling standard by which to assess possible measures of patient preferences. This suggests that one way to assess the validity of quality-of-life measures is their ability to predict patient choices.

In recent work, colleagues and I have collected data on the stated and revealed preferences of patients with diabetes for intensive therapy to attempt to assess the validity of quality-of-life measures (Meltzer and Polonsky, 1998). Intensive therapy for diabetes, which involves increased frequency of glucose checks and insulin dosing, has been shown to decrease long-term complications of the disease such as blindness, amputation, and renal failure, but also requires greater effort by patients and can cause increased frequency of hypoglycemic events (Diabetes Control and Complications Trial Research Group, 1993). As a result, intensive therapy would be expected to have effects on both the length and quality of life, and therefore is a natural context in which to look for effects on quality-adjusted life expectancy. In the study, we asked patients all the questions necessary, following currently accepted techniques, to assess their perceived gain in quality-adjusted life expectancy with intensive versus conventional therapy. These included time tradeoff questions to elicit their beliefs about the quality of life associated with intensive versus conventional therapy and the complications associated with diabetes; questions about their beliefs concerning the effects of intensive therapy on the probability of complications; and questions designed to elicit their rate of time preference. We then used a published model of the effects of intensive therapy to calculate their predicted gain (or loss) in quality-adjusted life expectancy from intensive therapy (Diabetes Control and Complications Trial Research Group, 1996).

Our results suggest that patients who believe that current quality of life would not be harmed by intensive therapy and patients who believe that intensive therapy is likely to be effective in reducing complications are more likely to choose intensive therapy. However, patients who believe that complications would more severely harm quality of life and patients who have lesser preference for the present over the future are not more likely to pursue intensive therapy. Thus the effects of these individual elements that go into the QALY calculation are only partially consistent with the predictions underlying the QALY model. Nevertheless, when these factors are combined to calculate the change in QALYs with intensive therapy, that change is found to be highly predictive of who chooses intensive therapy (just less than about 75 percent sensitive and 75 percent specific).[2] One might conclude from this that despite reasonable theoretical concerns about their validity, QALYs appear to do a fairly good job of reflecting people's preferences.

However, the fact that people are reporting their answers to these questions knowing their choice of treatment suggests the possibility that their answers may be shaped by the decisions they have made (Festinger, 1957). In particular, people who have chosen intensive therapy may minimize its negative effects on quality of life while people on conventional therapy may minimize the predicted reduction in complications compared with intensive therapy. Similarly, people who believe that the benefits of intensive therapy are large and who believe that the impositions required by the therapy are minor may be more likely to report themselves as following intensive therapy even when they actually follow conventional therapy. Indeed, we find evidence that this is the case. Moreover, when we use the gain in QALYs to predict actual therapy as defined by the frequency of glucose checks and insulin doses according to the DCCT, we find that QALYs do an extremely poor job of predicting actual therapy, with a sensitivity and specificity of less than 60 percent. This suggests that much of the apparent ability of the change in QALYs to predict choice reflects attempts to minimize cognitive dissonance.

To address the possibility that any correlation between a gain in QALYs lived and choices reflects cognitive dissonance, what is needed are prospective studies of the ability of QALYs to predict choice. These studies would examine whether patients' beliefs about the quality of life and likelihood of specific health outcomes related to medical interventions prior to facing decisions about those interventions predict the choices that they actually make. It will also be important to compare these measures to measures based on willingness to pay, which have been favored by economists. While it seems likely that that current measures based on quality-adjusted life expectancy will do very poorly, it seems equally likely that measures based on willingness to pay may do no better. Even such negative results would serve several goals. First, they would provide some solid information about the validity of current quality-of-life measures, and, in so doing, generate appropriate concern among those using those measures. Second, they would provide some concrete evidence about the relative merits of these measures and perhaps suggest when one or the other measure might be of more value. Third, and most important, they would propose a criterion, the ability to predict choices, by which improved quality-of-life measures might be generated and validated. Until such exercises have been completed, it is difficult to know whether the tools of quality-of-life measurement for cost-effectiveness analysis have much ability to represent the factors that patients most value in seeking medical care. Nevertheless, the basic assumption behind QALYs—that the benefits of medical care cannot be fully measured by reductions in mortality and must also strive to reflect the value of improvements in morbidity—must nevertheless be correct.

Measuring the Costs of Medical Interventions

Though perhaps to a lesser extent than with the measurement of benefits, the measurement of costs in cost-effectiveness analysis has also generated controversies with potentially important implications for the use of the tools of cost-effectiveness analysis to inform priorities for biomedical research. Perhaps not surprisingly, some of these controversies can be traced to the lack of a solid theoretical foundation for medical cost-effectiveness analysis. Among the most long lasting of these controversies is a set of issues surrounding the treatment of future medical and nonmedical costs related to medical interventions.

Indeed, for almost 25 years, there has been ongoing debate among researchers working in medical cost-effectiveness analysis about how to account for costs that occur following a medical intervention. For example, when a person has coronary artery bypass surgery and this averts the cost of a heart attack that would otherwise have occurred, should this be counted as a saving? Beyond these costs for "related" illnesses, if a person who would otherwise have died of a heart attack lives on to develop some other "unrelated" illness such as Alzheimer's disease, should the costs of that be counted? What about consumption or earnings in added years of life?

Most commonly, cost-effectiveness analyses have tended to count only effects on costs for "related" illness, but without any rigorous justification for excluding other costs. One reason for this lack of rigor has been the absence of a clear theoretical framework in which to consider cost-effectiveness analysis. In 1995, Alan Garber and Charles Phelps made an important contribution toward developing such a framework in a National Bureau of Economic Research working paper that analyzed this question in the context of a model of lifetime utility maximization (Garber and Phelps, 1995). Surprisingly, they found that the relative rankings of interventions were not affected if one included or excluded these future unrelated costs, so long as they were truly unrelated (as defined by a conditional independence assumption) and they were consistently either included or excluded.

However, more complete analysis of this issue in the context of a more general lifetime utility maximization model that permits resources to be allocated over the life cycle so that there can be net borrowing or lending at different ages, suggests that the Garber and Phelps results are in fact an artifact of an implicit assumption that future costs are zero (Meltzer, 1997;

Meltzer, in press). Indeed, the results of the analysis imply that in fact all future costs must be included: both medical—for related and unrelated illness—and nonmedical (Meltzer, 1997). Moreover, analyses that exclude future costs are generally biased to favor interventions that extend life over interventions that improve the quality of life, especially in the elderly.

To understand the effects of including future costs, it is useful to consider the following approximation of the cost-effectiveness ratio in terms of cost per QALY that includes future costs, where C is the average annual net resource use over the remainder of a person's life after treatment:

$$\begin{aligned}\text{Cost Effectivness}_{\text{future costs}} &= (\Delta \text{ present costs})/(\Delta \text{ QALY}) \\ &\quad + (\Delta \text{ future costs})/(\Delta \text{ QALY}) \\ &= (\Delta \text{ present costs})/(\Delta \text{ QALY}) \\ &\quad + C^{*}(\Delta \text{ life expectancy})/(\Delta \text{ QALY})\end{aligned}$$

For elderly persons, among whom consumption generally exceeds production so that C is positive, the effect of including future costs is to increase the cost-effectiveness ratio in proportion to the cost per year of life lived and the ratio of changes in life expectancy to quality-adjusted life expectancy. Thus analyses of interventions for the elderly that omit future costs favor interventions that extend life over interventions that improve quality of life.

For young adults, however, C is often negative, since the expected present value of a young person's lifetime earnings is often greater than the expected present value of the person's lifetime medical and nonmedical consumption. Studies that exclude such future costs would overestimate the true societal costs of treating young people whose net resource use over their remaining lifetime is negative.

Since few studies to date have examined the effects of including all future costs in cost-effectiveness analyses, the above approximation is useful for developing estimates and intuition concerning how including future costs may affect the cost-effectiveness of medical interventions. Such estimates can be developed by combining age-specific estimates of future net resource use (e.g. consumption plus medical expenditures minus earnings) with estimates of the effects of interventions on life expectancy and quality-adjusted life expectancy from published studies. An example of such an exercise is illustrated in table 6.2, which is reprinted from Meltzer (1997), and clearly shows the potential for including future costs to change both the absolute and relative cost-effectiveness of medical interventions, especially when an intervention has much larger effects on length of life than quality of life. Even if one adopts a $100,000 per QALY threshold for cost-effectiveness, the effects on the cost-effectiveness of the treatment

TABLE 6.2 Effect of Future "Unrelated" Costs on the Cost per Quality-Adjusted Life Year

Intervention	Change in LE	Change in QALE	Change in LE/QALE	Annual Future Cost ⓒ	Bias due to Future Cost	Reported Cost/QALY	Actual Cost/QALY
Adjuvant chemotherapy for Duke's C colon cancer age 55 years Smith et al. (1993)	2.4 yr	0.4 yr	6.00	3,000	18,000	16,700	34,700
Treatment of severe hypertension, men aged 40[a] years Stason and Weinstein (1977)	4 yr	3.9 yr	1.03	–5,000	–5,200	18,000	12,800
Adjuvant chemotherapy for node-negative breast cancer age 45 years Hillner and Smith (1991)	11 mo	5.1 mo	2.16	–4000	–8700	18,000	9300
Adjuvant chemotherapy for node-negative breast cancer age 60 years Hillner and Smith (1991)	7.7 mo	4.0 mo	1.93	8,000	15,400	21,000	36,400
Treatment of severe hypertension, men aged 50[a] years Stason and Weinstein (1977)	2.6 yr	2.5 yr	1.04	0	0	25,000	25,000
Coronary artery bypass 3-vessel disease, mild angina aged 55 Wong et al. (1990)	0.6 yr	0.7 yr	0.86	3,000	2,600	31,000	33,600
Coronary artery bypass 3-vessel disease, severe angina age 55 Wong et al. (1990)	1.4 yr	1.4 yr	1.00	3,000	3,300	45,000	48,300

continued

TABLE 6.2 *continued*

Intervention	Change in LE	Change in QALE	Change in LE/QALE	Annual Future Cost (c)	Bias due to Future Cost	Reported Cost/QALY	Actual Cost/QALY
Adjuvant chemotherapy for node-negative breast cancer age 75 Desch et al. (1993)	2.9 mo	1.8 mo	1.61	20,000	32,200	54,000	86,200
Hormone replacement therapy ages 55–65 Tosteson and Weinstein (1991)	0.0458 yr	.0387 yr	1.18	8,000	9,400	54,200	63,600
Treatment of severe hypertension, men aged 60[a] years Stason and Weinstein (1977)	1.5 yr	1.4 yr	1.07	8,000	8,500	60,000	68,500
Adjuvant chemotherapy for Duke's C colon cancer age 60 Estimated based on Smith et al. (1993)[b]	1,8 yr	0.1 yr	18.00	8,000	144,000	67,000	211,000
Hemodialysis for end-stage renal disease (ESRD) men aged 30 years Estimated based on Garner and Dardis (1987) and Hornberger et al. (1992)[c]	—	—	1.50	0	0	117,000	117,000
Hemodialysis for ESRD men aged 60 Estimated based on Garner and Dardis (1987) and Hornberger et al. (1992)[c]	—	—	1.50	8,000	12,000	117,000	129,000

Costs converted to 1993 dollars using the medical CPI (Monthly Labor Review, Bureau of Labor Statistics, 1994).
[a]Stason and Weinstein already include future unrelated medical costs, so the additional future costs here refer only to consumption net of earnings.
[b]Estimates made for 60-year-olds assuming life expectancy of 16 years at age 60 as opposed to 20 years at age 55 used to calculate the cost-effectiveness at age 55.
[c]Cost-effectiveness estimates based on Garner and Dardis (1987) using quality-of-life estimates from Hornberger et al. (1992).

of hypertension, adjuvant chemotherapy for Duke's C colon cancer, and end-stage renal disease for hemodialysis for 60-year-old men reported at the bottom of the table suggest that these effects can be quantitatively significant.

Although the estimates based on the above approximation may provide some indication of the effects of including future costs on the cost-effectiveness of medical interventions, the accuracy of such approximations is not clear. One important reason that such approximations may be poor is that they implicitly assume that all mortality reductions resulting from a medical intervention occur immediately, which is certainly not the case for some (if not most) medical interventions. For example, less than 2 percent of the benefits of intensive therapy for diabetes among young adults in terms of increased life expectancy occur in the first two decades that intensive therapy is followed (Meltzer et al., 2000). This suggests the importance of developing estimates of the cost-effectiveness of medical interventions that directly incorporate future costs. Although the number of such estimates remains extremely limited and does not yet include interventions that would be expected to have the largest effects on length of life relative to quality of life, a growing number of such estimates are now available (table 6.3), and again suggest the potential for changes in the relative cost-effectiveness of medical interventions when future costs are included. Thus, as with the issues surrounding perspective and the measurement of benefits, the issues surrounding measurement of costs demonstrate some of the important measurement issues the must be addressed if the tools of cost-effectiveness analysis are to provide a comprehensive framework with which to assess the value of opportunities for research.

TABLE 6.3 Effect of Directly Incorporating Future Costs on Cost-Effectiveness

	Without Future Costs	With Future Costs
Hip replacement women aged 60 years (Meltzer et al., 1998)	Cost-Saving	Cost-Saving
Treatment mild HTN men aged > 70 years (Johanesson, Meltzer, and O'Conor, 1997)	\$5,000/QALY	\$30,000/QALY
Hip replacement men aged 85 years (Meltzer et al., 1998)	\$9,177/QALY	\$9,042/QALY
Intensive therapy IDDM starting ages 13–39 years (Meltzer et al., 2000)	\$30,000/QALY	\$15,000/QALY

III. Using Cost-Effectiveness to Inform Priorities for Research

In addition to the methodological challenges discussed above, one of the main challenges faced by medical cost-effectiveness analysis concerns how to perform sensitivity analyses to address uncertainty about the benefits and costs of medical interventions. It is through this set of methods that cost-effectiveness analysis can be used to inform priorities for research.

Although there have been many proposals about how to address uncertainty in cost-effectiveness analyses, it has probably not been adequately recognized that there may be multiple reasons to perform sensitivity analysis. These include (1) to help a decision maker to make the best decision in the presence of uncertainty, (2) to identify the sources of uncertainty to guide decisions for individuals or subgroups having characteristics that differ from a base case, and (3) to set priorities for the collection of additional information. Meltzer (2001) studies these problems by examining the implications of an expected utility maximization model for the optimal choice of medical interventions or the acquisition of additional information when there is uncertainty about the costs and benefits of the interventions. The results indicate that if the objective is to maximize expected utility given available information—as is implied, for example, by maximization of quality-adjusted life expectancy—and if financial risk is effectively diversified through either public or private insurance, then the optimal decision for any group is determined by the ratio of the expected cost divided by the expected benefit. However, if the objective of sensitivity analysis is to set priorities for the acquisition of additional information, the appropriate measure of benefit is the incremental increase in expected utility with additional information. It is through this latter approach that the tools of medical cost-effectiveness analysis and the vast literature on the cost-effectiveness of specific medical interventions (Elixhauser et al., 1998) can potentially be used to help better identify the value of medical research. The sections that follow develop the basic framework for performing such calculations; describe the challenges involved in performing them; and illustrate some of their possible implications for the value of research. Though ideal value of information calculations may be difficult to perform, certain simpler approaches to sensitivity analysis are identified that may provide bounds on the value of information with less stringent data requirements. Together, these approaches suggest not only a theoretically grounded approach through which the tools of medical decision analysis can be extended to inform priorities for research, but also the important limitations of such approaches.

Methods for Sensitivity Analysis

Before illustrating the derivation and application of methods for performing sensitivity analysis, it is useful to discuss the existing methods.

The oldest and most commonly used forms of sensitivity analyses are univariate or multivariate sensitivity analyses. These approaches vary the parameters of the model individually across a range of possible outcomes to see how the cost-effectiveness of an intervention changes. In some instances, the parameter values are varied over the range of all possible values, while in other cases they are varied across confidence intervals identified from the literature, or until some specified threshold for cost-effectiveness is reached. Advantages of these analyses are that they demonstrate the effects of individual parameters or of groups of parameters on the analysis and that their results can be easily calculated and reported. However, the major problems with these sorts of analyses are that they do not clearly delineate either what range of parameter values to consider or what to do when some of those parameter values would change the optimal decision, and that they are very likely to lead to indeterminate results while providing little perspective on the likelihood and welfare consequences of those outcomes.

More recently, population-based sampling approaches to estimating costs, effectiveness and cost-effectiveness ratios, sometimes termed stochastic cost-effectiveness analysis, appear to be receiving increasing attention in the field (O'Brien et al., 1994; Gold et al., 1996; Polsky et al., 1997). However, these analyses still do not address the question of the optimal decision in the presence of uncertainty because they do not suggest what to do when the set of possible costs and outcomes include ones that would make the cost-effectiveness ratio fail to meet the chosen threshold for cost-effectiveness.

In assessing these methods, it is interesting to note that while all of them appear to have some significance for the objectives described in the preceding section, none of them are explicitly linked to that set of objectives. To address this, we now summarize the approach described in Meltzer (2001) by which an expected utility maximization model can be used to examine optimal decisions about treatment and the acquisition of additional information under uncertainty. We begin by describing a model of optimal decision making under uncertainty and then extend that model to calculate the expected value of information gained by research.

A Deterministic Model of Health Outcomes with Uncertainty about Effectiveness

To focus our analysis of uncertainty, we assume that there is uncertainty about the effectiveness ($\theta \in \Theta$) of a medical intervention (m) but that the outcome of a medical intervention given θ is certain. By making this assumption, we put aside the issues related to uncertainty in outcome for an individual, and focus instead on uncertainty for a "representative consumer"; but the basic results are easily extended to the more general case (Meltzer, 2001). To model uncertainty in the costs and benefits of an intervention, we allow both utility (U) and the costs of the medical intervention (c) to depend directly on θ. In addition, we let utility depend on nonmedical consumption (x) and medical expenditure so that $U = U(m, \theta, x(\theta))$ and $c = c(m, \theta)$. Here x is written as $x(\theta)$ to denote the fact that x will vary with θ for any m to satisfy the budget constraint $c(m, \theta) + x(\theta) - I = 0$ for each level of effectiveness. To model cost-effectiveness, we assume that people maximize expected utility[3] and study the example of a representative consumer who maximizes expected utility subject to a budget constraint conditional on each level of effectiveness:

$$(1)\quad \max_m \int p(\theta)U(m, \theta, x(\theta))d\theta \text{ such that } c(m, \theta) + x(\theta) - I = 0 \text{ for all } \theta$$

Meltzer (2000) describes how this can then be rewritten as a LaGrange multiplier problem* in which the $\lambda(\theta)$ is the multiplier for the budget constraint for each level of θ, and optimized over the set of possible expenditures on medical intervention to generate the following first order condition for medical expenditure:

$$(2)\quad \int p(\theta)\frac{\partial U(m, \theta, x(\theta))}{\partial m}d\theta + \int \lambda(\theta)p(\theta)\frac{\partial c(m, \theta)}{\partial m}d\theta = 0$$

This condition implies that investment in a medical intervention should occur to the point at which its expected marginal benefit (utility) equals the expected value of the marginal-utility-of-income-weighted marginal cost. Allowing the marginal utility of income to depend on θ reflects the possibility that changes in the utility function or costs with θ might alter the marginal utility of income.

It is not difficult to imagine how these effects of uncertainty about the costs and effectiveness of medical interventions might meaningfully alter the marginal utility of income for an individual. For example, if a person

*Specifically: $\underset{m,\lambda(\theta)}{\text{Max}} \int p(\theta)U(m, \theta, x(\theta))d\theta + \int \lambda(\theta)p(\theta)\,[I - c(m, \theta) - x(\theta)]\, d\theta$

of working age undergoes joint replacement for arthritis and then suffers a severe complication, is forced into early retirement, and requires continuous care, both their utility and medical costs will be affected and their marginal utility of income could change substantially. In a population, however, such effects are less compelling to the extent that insurance can equate the marginal utility of income across health states unless an intervention leads to an extraordinarily large change in either population health or costs. Thinking from a population perspective in which most extremely expensive medical interventions affect a relatively small number of persons and most common medical interventions are relatively modest in cost, it is much less likely that the (aggregate) marginal utility of income will change substantially with uncertainty about the costs or benefits of a single intervention.[4] If this is the case, then $\lim \lambda(\theta) \rightarrow \lambda$ and the first order condition for medical expenditures can be simplified to solve for the cost-effectiveness ratio:

$$(3) \qquad \frac{\displaystyle\int p(\theta)\frac{\partial c(m, \theta)}{\partial m}d\theta}{\displaystyle\int p(\theta)\frac{\partial U(m, x(\theta))}{\partial m}d\theta} = \frac{1}{\lambda}$$

Thus it follows from expected utility maximization that the optimum cost-effectiveness ratio of an intervention under uncertainty is closely approximated by the ratio of expected costs to expected benefits. Interestingly, a similar "ratio of means" approach is suggested by Stinnett and Paltiel (1997) as the solution to a constrained optimization problem in a linear programming context, and by Claxton (1999) in a Bayesian discrete choice decision theoretic context. However, neither analysis derives the result directly from a formal utility maximization model or addresses the possible dependency of the marginal utility of income on θ.

While this argument about the dependence of the marginal utility of income on θ has not been made previously within the context of medical cost-effectiveness analysis, a very similar argument is made by Arrow and Lind (1970) concerning the evaluation of risk in public investment decisions. In that article, the authors argue that the large scale of the public sector allows it to effectively eliminate any welfare loss associated with the riskiness of investments by spreading the risk across a sufficiently large population. The relevance of this reasoning here relies both on this diversification effect and the relatively modest magnitude of almost any single public health care decision in the context of overall health and health expenditures.

Sensitivity Analysis to Guide Individual or Subgroup Decisions

This same basic approach can be applied when sensitivity analysis is done to guide decisions for individuals or subgroups. In this case, the only difference is that some of the parameters in the parameter vector θ have a different probability distribution $p'(\theta)$ than in the overall population. Thus the optimal decision for individuals or subgroups is again the ratio of the expected value of costs to the expected value of benefits, only using the relevant prior probability distribution for the subgroup or individual.

Application to a Stylized Decision concerning a Treatment of Uncertain Benefit

Figure 6.1 describes a stylized decision concerning an intervention known to cost $10,000 but of uncertain benefit. Specifically, the example assumes that there is a 90 percent chance that the benefit is 0.1 life-year, but also a 5 percent chance each that the benefit is 0.01 or 1 life-year.

Taking these three possibilities individually, the cost-effectiveness ratios are $100,000, $1,000,000, or $10,000 respectively. Using a cutoff of $100,000 per life-year, a traditional sensitivity analysis would be indeterminate. Such indeterminacy is extremely common in cost-effectiveness analyses.

Other common approaches to sensitivity analysis might interpret the same data differently. For example, the stochastic cost-effectiveness approach might conclude that since there is only a 5 percent chance that the intervention is not cost-effective, it should be selected. On the other hand, the same approach could be used to argue that the project should not be selected, since there is only a 5 percent chance that the intervention will

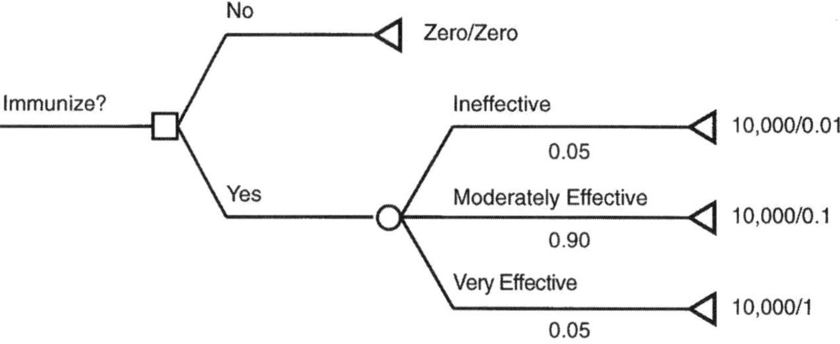

Figure 6.1: Simplified decision concerning a treatment of uncertain benefit
Note: Cost ($)/Effectiveness (Life-Years)

provide a benefit in excess of its cost. The problem with this perspective is that it does not reflect the magnitude of potential benefits relative to costs. Similar problems exist with other standard approaches (e.g. threshold analyses), the general problem being that the approaches do not have a way to systematically incorporate information on both the likelihood and magnitude of benefits relative to costs.

Following the ratio of means approach described above, the expected cost is \$10,000 and the expected benefit is: $0.05*0.01 + 0.9*0.1 + 0.05*1.0 = 0.0005 + 0.09 + 0.05 = 0.1405$ life-years. Thus the cost-effectiveness ratio is \$10,000/0.1405 life-years = \$71,174/life-year saved, which is clearly cost-effective by the \$100,000 per life-year standard. What is striking about this example is that, even though the chance that the intervention is highly beneficial is only 5 percent, more than one-third ($0.05/0.1405 = 36\%$) of the expected benefit comes from the unlikely event that it is highly effective, and this benefit is enough to make the intervention cost-effective from an expected value perspective. It is this ability to incorporate both the magnitude and likelihood of benefits and costs into a single statistic that can be used to guide decision making that is the primary advantage of the expected value approach over the traditional approaches that incorporate only one or the other dimension, and often generate indeterminate conclusions that do not provide much guidance for decision making.

Sensitivity Analysis to Guide Information collection

Having identified the implications of this expected utility approach for the optimal decision under uncertainty given available information, we now extend the approach to determine when collecting additional information is likely to be worthwhile. When a study is done to improve information concerning parameters in a decision model, the value of information is the change in expected utility that comes from a change in uncertainty about the parameters. Although this basic approach dates at least to the pioneers of statistical decision theory (e.g. Raiffa and Schlaifer, 1961; Pratt, Raiffa, and Schlaifer, 1965), it has not been commonly used in developing techniques for sensitivity analysis in medical decision analysis. Indeed, when formal techniques for clinical trial design have been implemented (e.g. O'Brien et al., 1994; Al et al., 1998; Briggs and Gray, 1998), they have often been based on criteria for decision making such as confidence intervals around the cost-effectiveness ratio, which generate suboptimal results for the same reasons as the problems with threshold approaches to sensitivity analysis that are described above. Two exceptions to this are Claxton and Posnett (1996) and Hornberger (1998), which attempt to identify optimal sample size for a clinical trial from a cost-effectiveness perspective using a full Bayesian approach.

Adopting the expected utility approach, assume that for any information set describing the parameter distribution, $p(\theta)$, there is an optimal choice of m as described above. Call this $m^*(p(\theta))$. This implies an expected utility with existing information (EU_0) of

$$(4) \quad \int p(\theta)U(m^*(p(\theta)), \theta, x(\theta))d\theta$$

Now consider the possibility that we can conduct research to acquire additional information about θ at cost c_r. Though the analysis is easily generalized to permit an infinite number of possible outcomes of the experiment,[5] assume for simplicity that only two outcomes are possible: with probability q that the distribution of θ is found to be $p'(\theta)$ and with probability $(1 - q)$ that it is found to be $p''(\theta)$, where, for consistency with the initial prior distribution, $q^* p'(\theta) + (1 - q)^* p''(\theta) = p(\theta)$. In these cases, the optimal level of medical expenditure will be $m^*(p'(\theta))$ and $m^*(p''(\theta))$, which yield an expected utility of

$$(5) \quad q \int p'(\theta)U(m^*(p'(\theta)), \theta, x^{*\prime}(\theta))d\theta + (1 - q) \int p''(\theta)U(m^*(p''(\theta)), \theta, x^{*\prime\prime}(\theta))d\theta$$

Where $x^{*\prime}(\theta)$ and $x^{*\prime\prime}(\theta)$ are determined from the budget constraint net of research costs c_r (i.e. $c(m, \theta) + x(\theta) + c_r - I = 0$ for all θ). It follows that the change in expected utility with the collection of information, or expected value of information (EVI), is

$$(6) \quad q \int p'(\theta)U(m^*(p'(\theta)), \theta, x(\theta))d\theta + (1 - q) \int p''(\theta)U(m^*(p''(\theta)), \theta, x(\theta))d\theta - \mathrm{EU}_0$$

If this is positive, then the study is worth performing; if not, then it is not worth performing.

Although this value of information calculation is easily described theoretically, implementing it requires meaningful information on the prior probabilities of the parameters required for the calculation, and these may be very difficult to obtain. When the available data permits, these may be estimated based on published studies that report means and confidence intervals that may then be used to describe the full distribution of parameter values. In other instances, primary data collection may be required.

Nevertheless, there may still be a significant number of cases in which it will not be possible to identify much information that will inform priors. Moreover, it may be quite difficult to characterize how an experiment is likely to affect the posterior distributions of the parameters.

These empirical challenges suggest that techniques for assessing the value of information that do not rely on this data concerning prior or posterior distributions would be highly useful. When such information on priors is available, one possibility is the expected value of perfect information: $EVPI = \int p(\theta)U(m^*(\theta))d\theta - EU_0$, where $m^*(\theta)$ is the optimal choice of m if θ is known. Since the expected value of information is always positive,[6] this provides an upper bound on the ideal value of information described above while having the advantage of being independent of the posteriors. Indeed, this is probably one reason that the EVPI approach has been used in the cost-effectiveness literature (e.g. Felli and Hazen, 1998).[7]

Although EVPI is simpler to determine than EVI, it still depends on the priors, so that an alternative measure that did not depend on this might also be useful. One such measure is the maximal value of information (MVI) over all possible values of $\theta \in \Theta$, $MVB = \underset{\theta \in \Theta}{\text{Max}}\, U(m^*(\theta))$. Although this will also only be an upper bound on EVPI and, therefore, EVI, it depends only on knowledge of the value function conditional on θ. Although this may be a relatively crude upper bound, it is worthwhile to note that this criterion in fact corresponds to that implied by a threshold analysis in which the bounds are determined by the extreme values of the parameter (assuming, as is usually done, that the value function is monotonic with respect to the parameters). Thus, application of the threshold technique based on the full range of possible values of a parameter can be considered a bound on the more general value of information calculation, only with less rigorous information requirements. Thus, like EVPI, the threshold technique based on the full range of possible values a parameter might take can be considered a method for placing an upper bound on the more complex EVI calculation. When these calculations suggest the MVI or EVPI is low, the full EVI calculation is not necessary. It is worth noting that, in contrast, the common practices of assessing cost-effectiveness at a 95 percent confidence interval for a parameter or calculating stochastic cost-effectiveness intervals have no apparent theoretical justification.

Going even further, if Θ is enlarged to include any possible conceivable value of θ, even if those values are excluded under current technology, this type of reasoning can be extended to consider any possible research relating to the parameter in question. For example, if the probability of cure with the best current treatment for a disease is between 20 percent and 40 percent and the treatment is found not to be cost-effective, one could calculate whether treatment would be cost-effective if the cure rate were 100 percent. This might be called the maximum value of research (MVR), and can be used to generate an upper bound on MVI that does not require any data at all concerning the parameter in question. The MVR concept could also be expanded to consider innovative approaches to the diagnosis or treatment of disease that led to fundamental changes in the structure of the decision tree, and not just the effects of changes in its parameters.

Application to a Stylized Model of the Decision whether to Treat Prostate Cancer

In order to illustrate the approaches described above, Meltzer (2001) examines a highly stylized model of the decision to treat prostate cancer. In this simplified model (fig. 6.2), the decision to treat prostate cancer is presented as a decision between radical prostatectomy (surgical removal of the prostate) and "watchful waiting" (no intervention unless the disease is found to spread). This decision is represented by the two decision nodes in figure 6.2. In this simplified model, radical prostatectomy is assumed to be curative, so that the patient lives out a normal life expectancy of 25 years. Radical prostatectomy is major surgery, however, and carries the risk of immediate death, which is assumed to occur in 5 percent of patients undergoing treatment. The outcome of watchful waiting will depend on how quickly the prostate cancer progresses. Many cancers will progress slowly enough that men die of other causes before they die of prostate cancer and thus live a "normal" life expectancy (assumed here to be 25 years). Other men will progress rapidly and die of prostate cancer (assumed here to occur at 10 years). For simplicity, we assume that quality of life is not a concern in prostate cancer treatment so that outcomes are measured in life-years, which are the same as quality-adjusted life-years. Radical prostatectomy is assumed to cost $10,000, and the "unrelated" future costs associated with the extension of life are assumed to be $20,000 per year.

However, there is substantial uncertainty about the natural history of prostate cancer that is not captured by these assumptions. In fact, there is a great deal of uncertainty even about average rates of progression to death from prostate cancer—that is, how aggressive the disease is on average. This is the dimension of uncertainty focused on in this example. It is captured in a stylized way in figure 6.2 by the upper and lower decision trees that differ in the fraction of tumors that will progress rapidly (0.085 in the

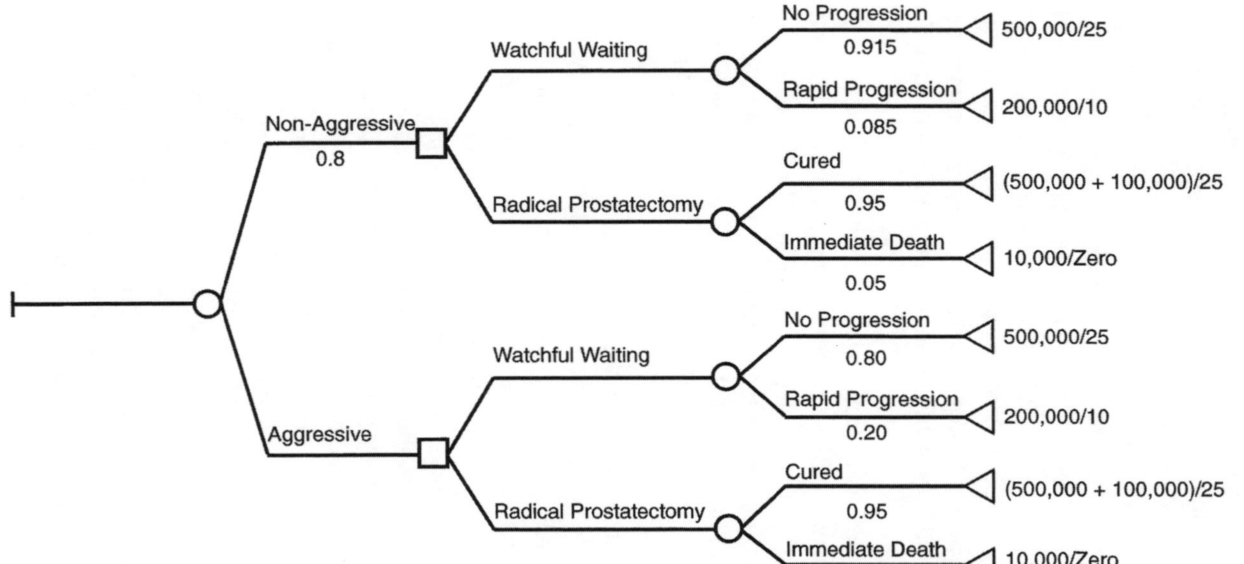

FIGURE 6.2: Simplified cost-effectiveness model for screening for prostrate cancer with uncertainty about progression rates
NOTE: Cost ($)/Effectiveness (Life-Years)

"nonaggressive" case, and 0.2 in the "aggressive" case). Though of course some other fraction in between or near these two might be imagined to be correct, it is assumed here for simplicity that one or the other of these values is precisely correct.

Panels 1 and 2 of table 6.4 show the results of a cost-effectiveness analysis of the treatment decision in the nonaggressive and aggressive cases. In both cases, treatment provides a benefit, but in the first case it is a small benefit, with a cost per QALY of $420,000; in the second case it is a much larger benefit, with a cost per QALY of only $26,000. If we assume that the cutoff for cost-effectiveness is $100,000 per QALY, then the optimal decision in the first case would be watchful waiting, while in the second case it would be treatment.

The leftmost part of the decision tree describes the possibility that either of these cases might hold and places some prior probabilities on the two arms (0.2 aggressive, 0.8 nonaggressive). Panel 3 of table 6.4 reports the expected benefits and costs of the screening decision when these priors are held. In that case, the ratio of the expected costs to expected benefits is $47,000, which would be cost-effective by the $100,000/QALY standard. This might be considered surprising because the assumption was that there was an 80 percent chance that the progression was not aggressive, and treatment is clearly not cost-effective by the $100,000/QALY standard in that case. The result is driven by the 20 percent chance of a much larger benefit, despite the fact that that possibility is not very likely. As with the example above, this points out the potential for the ratio of the expected value approach to generate different results from approaches that do not account for both the magnitude and likelihood of the potential benefits.

The remainder of the example addresses whether the collection of additional information would be of value. Following the approach described above, we begin with calculation of the maximum value of information. This calculation can be done in a variety of ways, requiring progressively more information. To take an extreme example, assume that we knew nothing about the probability that prostate cancer is aggressive, but only the life expectancy of patients with aggressive cancers who are treated or not treated, and the price of prostatectomy. In the absence of knowledge about the probability that cancers would progress rapidly, there is no clear guidance about whether watchful waiting or prostatectomy dominates, so we consider both cases as reference cases. Assume initially that no treatment will be the reference point. To identify an upper bound on the value of information, one could assume that all patients have aggressive cancers. Specifically, assuming that all men who have prostate cancer but are not treated

TABLE 6.4 Value of Information for Cost-Effectiveness of Screening for Prostate Cancer

Panel 1: Prostate Cancer Known Non-Aggressive: Fraction Rapidly Progressing = 0.085

Strategy	Cost (K$)	ΔCost (K$)	QALY	ΔQALY	ΔC/ΔQALY (K$/QALY)	Value ΔQALY (K$)*	Net Increm. Benefit (K$)
Watchful waiting	475	.	23.725	.	.	.	.
Radical prostatectomy	485	11	23.75	0.025	420	2.5	−8.5

Panel 2: Prostate Cancer Known Aggressive: Fraction Rapidly Progressing = 0.2

Strategy	Cost (K$)	ΔCost (K$)	QALY	ΔQALY	ΔC/ΔQALY (K$/QALY)	Value ΔQALY (K$)*	Net Increm. Benefit (K$)
Watchful waiting	440	.	22	.	.	.	.
Radical prostatectomy	485	45	23.75	1.75	26	175	130

Panel 3: Aggressiveness of Prostate Cancer Not Known: Prob. Aggressive (as in Panel 2) = .2

Strategy	Cost (K$)	ΔCost (K$)	QALY	ΔQALY	ΔC/ΔQALY (K$/QALY)	Value ΔQALY (K$)*	Net Increm. Benefit (K$)
Watchful waiting	467.6	.	23.38	.	.	.	.
Radical prostatectomy	485	17.4	23.75	0.37	47	37	19.6

continued

TABLE 6.4 *continued*

Panel 4: Expected Value with Perfect Information: Prob. Aggressive (as in Panel 2) = 0.2							
Strategy	Cost (K$)	ΔCost (K$)	QALY	ΔQALY	ΔC/ΔQALY (K$/QALY)	Value ΔQALY (K$)*	Net Increm. Benefit (K$)
Watchful waiting	467.6		23.38	.	.	.	.
Optimal w/ perfect info.	476.6	9	23.73	0.35	26	35	26
Radical prostatectomy	485	8.4	23.75	0.02	420	2	−6.4

Panel 5: Expected Value w/ Improved Info.: 50% Chance Study ⇒ Prob. Agg. = 0.05; 50% chance study ⇒ Prob. Agg. = 0.35							
Strategy	Cost (K$)	ΔCost (K$)	QALY	ΔQALY	ΔC/ΔQALY (K$/QALY)	Value ΔQALY (K$)*	Net Increm. Benefit (K$)
Prob. aggressive = 0.05							
Watchful waiting	473.3		23.64				
Radical prostatectomy	485	11.7	23.75	0.11	106	11.1	−0.6
Prob. aggressive = 0.35							
Watchful waiting	462.8		23.12	.	.	.	.
Radical prostatectomy	485	22.2	23.75	0.63	35	62.9	40.6
Expected Value of Info. (vs. expected value of optimal decision with initial info. (Prostatectomy)) = 0.5*0.6 =							0.3

*1QALY = $100K

live 10 years (QALYs), while those who are treated live 25 years (QALYs), the value of treatment per patient would be 15 QALYs*$100,000/QALY = $1.5 million per patient. Alternatively, we could assume that that treatment would be the reference case, in which case the benefit of determining that treatment was not cost-effective would be the cost savings from avoiding prostatectomy ($10,000/patient) and avoidance of treatment-related mortality (0.05 mortality*25 years maximum life expectancy*$100,000/QALY = $125,000/patient), which sum to $135,000 per patient.

If one were then to use this knowledge of the maximum value of information for a patient to decide whether investment in a study to resolve the ambiguity about the aggressiveness of prostate cancer would be worthwhile, one might multiply these numbers by the number of men who are found to have prostate cancer annually (100,000) and divide by some real interest rate (0.03) to reflect the discounted value of the value of that information over time, thereby obtaining the maximum value of information (MVI): $1.5 million*100,000/0.03 = $5 trillion if the baseline strategy is watchful waiting and $0.135 million*100,000/0.03 = $450 billion if the baseline strategy is prostatectomy. The extremely large magnitude of these estimates of the MVI suggest the potential for information of immense value to come from knowledge about the efficacy of prostate cancer treatment. This value of information is large relative to the cost of any conceivable clinical trial.

Of course, these MVI calculations represent an upper bound, and a fair interpretation of these findings is that the MVI approach is simply not informative in this case, despite its analytical simplicity and independence of assumptions about the probabilities that cancers are aggressive. This suggests that it is worthwhile to pursue the expected value of perfect information (EVPI) approach.

The EVPI approach is described in panel 4 of table 6.4. The panel describes the expected value of three strategies: watchful waiting, radical prostatectomy, and the optimal decision with perfect knowledge of the actual average progression rate (EVPI). The last two columns calculate the value of the change in QALYs (assuming $100,000 per QALY for illustration) and the net incremental benefit of the policy choice compared with the strategy immediately above it in the table.

The first point to note is that if a decision were made based on the most likely cost-effectiveness ratio ($420,000), watchful waiting would be chosen; but if a decision were made based on the ratio of the expected values, radical prostatectomy would be chosen, which yields a net benefit of ($26,000 – $6,400) = $19,600 per patient relative to watchful waiting.

This quantifies the expected gain from the improvement in decision making by using the mean of the expected values as opposed to basing the decision on the most likely cost-effectiveness ratio, as is generally done in the "base case" reported by most cost-effectiveness analyses.

The second point to note is that the expected value of the gain versus watchful waiting with perfect information is even higher at $26,000 per patient. This implies an additional gain of $6,400 per patient from perfect information compared with the best possible decision with the initial information. Converting this patient level estimate of the value of research into a population level estimate as above suggests an EVPI of $6,400*100,000/0.03 = $21 billion. As with the MVPI, the large magnitude of the EVPI suggests that the expected value of perfect information about the efficacy of prostate cancer treatment would indeed be quite large relative to the cost of almost any conceivable clinical trial.

Of course, this too is an upper bound on the expected value of information that would come from any actual clinical trial, since any clinical trial is likely to provide less than perfect information. Panel 5 of table 6.4 examines one such case, in which an experiment is conducted that has two possible outcomes: a 50 percent probability of an outcome that suggests that the probability that prostate cancer is aggressive is 0.05 and a 50 percent probability of an outcome that suggests that the probability that prostate cancer is aggressive is 0.35. (Note this preserves the prior that the probability that prostate cancer is aggressive is 0.2, since 0.5*0.05 + 0.5*0.35 = 0.2.) The expected value of outcomes from watchful waiting and radical prostatectomy given these two possible outcomes of the experiment are reported in the upper and lower parts of panel 5. In the first case, the optimal decision switches to watchful waiting as compared with prostatectomy with the initial information, which yields a net surplus of $600 per patient. In the second case, prostatectomy remains the optimal choice, so there is no additional benefit to having done the study. Thus the expected net benefit is 0.5*$600 = $300 per patient. A decision about the study might be made by comparing its cost with the expected value of the information (EVI): $300*100,000/0.03 = $1 billion. Therefore, the value of this study would be quite large, although substantially less than the upper bound suggested by the EVPI.

→

FIGURE 6.3: Decision tree model
NOTES: Pos = Positive, Neg = Negative, TURP = Transurethral Resection of the Prostate, MWU = Metastatic Workup, Palp Ext = Palpable Extension, Clin = Clinical Stage, Comp = Complications

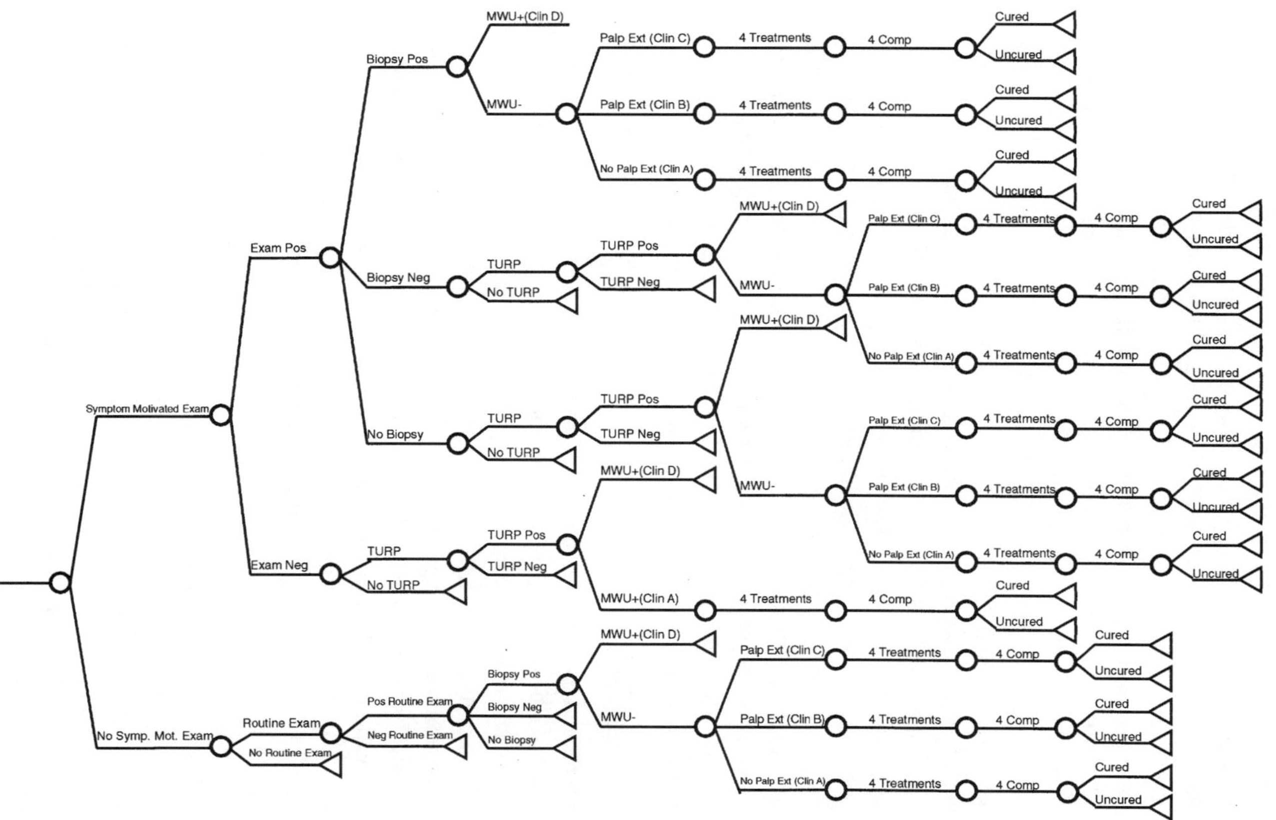

Symptom Motivated Exam
No Symp. Mot. Exam
Exam Pos
Exam Neg
Biopsy Pos
Biopsy Neg
No Biopsy
MWU+(Clin D)
MWU-
Palp Ext (Clin C)
Palp Ext (Clin B)
No Palp Ext (Clin A)
4 Treatments
4 Comp
Cured
Uncured
TURP
No TURP
TURP Pos
TURP Neg
MWU+(Clin A)
Routine Exam
No Routine Exam
Pos Routine Exam
Neg Routine Exam

In theory, in a similar manner, all possible experiments concerning all other dimensions of the model might be examined to determine whether they would be worthwhile. In this way, it might be determined how much could be gained by improved sensitivity and specificity of screening tests, decreased complications of treatment, improved risk stratification prior to treatment, and so on. To meaningfully model prostate cancer screening and treatment for such an exercise, the model one would have to construct would need to be vastly more complex than the simplified example described here (fig. 6.3). Both the data and computational demands of such an exercise would be formidable, especially in the construction of priors, and this would certainly require reliance on some of the approaches to bound the actual value of information, as suggested above. Clearly, there has been no attempt in this example to suggest that a comprehensive attempt to perform a precise calculation of the type described would generate results anywhere resembling these in magnitude. However, these simplified calculations do illustrate the types of calculations that might be performed to assess the value of research, including more simple calculations such as the EVPI that require less information. How informative such calculations would be in practice is an unresolved empirical question.

IV. Conclusion

This paper has reviewed the tools of medical cost-effectiveness analysis and examined the potential to use those tools to inform priorities for biomedical research. As suggested by some recent policy analysts, it is possible in principle to construct measures of the value of information that can describe the benefits of investing in research. The work required to move from what is theoretically possible to the actual application of these principles to produce valid and reliable estimates of the value of research involves a series of methodological and empirical challenges. We have already discussed many of these methodological challenges above, including issues related to perspective, the measurement of benefits, and the measurement of costs. Additional issues include ambiguities about how costs of illness may affect quality-of-life measurements and the implications of such effects for the measurement of productivity costs (Meltzer and Johannesson, 1999), and basic issues, about how risk at the individual level may affect welfare, that are essentially ignored by the assumptions that perfect insurance is available and that people maximize expected utility (Kahneman and Tversky, 1979).[8]

At an empirical level, there are important challenges in developing meaningful priors concerning the parameters of decision models (e.g.

probabilities, quality-of-life values, discount rates, etc.). As discussed above, this may often require extensive review of existing data, primary data collection, or even sometimes analyses based on a variety of arbitrary priors. It may also be very difficult to determine priors for the likelihood that a research project will find a meaningful result. Whether it is possible to adequately address these challenges will be resolved only through efforts to apply these ideas empirically. While some of the empirical challenges can be addressed by bounding the calculations using concepts such as the expected value of perfect information and maximum value of information, it is possible that such bounds may not be very informative, as suggested by our example in which the maximum value of information is $5 trillion, while the expected value of information is only $1 billion, or 0.02 percent of the total.

To apply these approaches to assess the value of research, there are also a variety of additional challenges. These include the interdependence of the benefits of research projects on related topics; the possibility that the research might become less (or more) valuable over time if other technological or demographic changes arise that alter the management, frequency, or natural history of the disease; and the unpredictability of how the results of research (particularly basic research) might be useful in areas outside the initial areas of inquiry. The difficulty of these issues implies that the sort of formal analyses suggested here are more likely to be of use for evaluating clinical research than for evaluating basic research.

Despite the theoretical and empirical issues raised by this work, the importance of making good decisions about the allocation of resources to medical interventions and medical research suggests that work in this area should be made an important priority. In considering whether formal approaches based on the tools of cost-effectiveness analysis are likely to have much influence on priority setting, it is encouraging that the recent report of the Institute of Medicine on improving priority setting at the NIH recommended that "[i]n setting priorities, NIH should strengthen its analysis and use of health data, such as burdens and costs of diseases, and on data on the impact of research on the health of the public" (IOM, 1998: 11). Nevertheless, it is essential that efforts to improve the process by which research funds are allocated and better understand the value of research accurately reflect the considerable difficulty of those tasks. In that context, it is encouraging that, with papers such as those presented here, economists are beginning to turn their attention toward understanding the value of medical research. As this work continues, it will be important to keep in mind that—even with evidence that some treatments may have little value at the margin and limited evidence about the connection between research and gains in health—health is a domain that people value very highly and in which great strides have been made in recent decades.

Notes

1. *Econometrica, Economic Journal, Journal of Applied Econometrics, Journal of Economic History, Journal of Economic Literature, Journal of Economic Abstracts, Journal of Economic Perspectives, Journal of Industrial Economics, Journal of Money, Credit and Banking, Journal of Political Economy, Quarterly Journal of Economics, Review of Economic Studies, Review of Economics and Statistics.*

2. Technically this is just one of the possible thresholds at which a criterion for preference could be drawn. To fully reflect the predictive power of a diagnostic test, one can plot a full receiver operating characteristic (ROC) curve, which shows all possible combinations of sensitivity and specificity for a diagnostic test at varying thresholds for defining a positive test. We do not do that here because the additional information does not substantially alter the perception of the accuracy of QALYs for predicting overall preference.

3. While individual preferences may in fact be inconsistent with expected utility maximization, QALYs implicitly assume that people maximize expected utility. While the relaxation of this assumption might be desirable, doing so would therefore involve a substantial reformulation of the way in which health benefits are assessed even in the absence of uncertainty. This is discussed further in the conclusion of this chapter.

4. Note that even if changes in health status were to lead to substantial changes in income or the need for nonmedical assistance holding income constant across individuals in different health states, optimal insurance could still equate the marginal utility of income across states. In practice, of course, insurance will generally fall short of this ideal, but this is nevertheless a useful point of reference.

5. In the general case, we wish to compare the expected utility resulting from the optimal decision m^* given the original budget constraint in the absence of information with the expected utility resulting from the optimal decision in the presence of the new information subject to a budget constraint that includes the cost of collecting information (Cr). Thus we compare the expected utility resulting from the solution to

$$\operatorname*{Max}_{m,\lambda(\theta)} \int p(\theta)U(m,\theta,x(\theta))d\theta + \int \lambda(\theta)p(\theta)[c(m,\theta)+x(\theta)-I]\,d\theta$$

with the expected utility of the solutions to the optimal decision problems for the j possible outcomes of the experiment as individually given by

$$\operatorname*{Max}_{m,\lambda(\theta)} \int p_j(\theta)U(m,\theta,x(\theta))d\theta + \int \lambda(\theta)p_j(\theta)[c(m,\theta)+x(\theta)+c_r-I]d\theta$$

$$\text{where} \int_{j\in J} p_j(\theta)p(j)dj = p(\theta).$$

See Meltzer (2001) for details.

6. To see this, note that if research costs are 0, the fact that $m^*(p'(\theta))$ and $m^*(p''(\theta))$ are optimal implies that the first two terms in this equation are greater than

$$(11) \quad q\int p'(\theta)U(m^*(p(\theta)),\theta,x(\theta))d\theta + (1-q)\int p''(\theta)U(m^*(p(\theta)),\theta,x(\theta))\,d\theta = \int p(\theta)U(m^*(p(\theta)),\theta,x(\theta))d\theta,$$

which is the expected utility from the optimal expenditure level in the absence of information. This implies that the expected value of free information is greater than zero. For completeness, it should be noted that this result applies only to public information. When information is private, there is no guarantee that its expected value will be positive (e.g. Rothschild and Stiglitz [1976]).

7. It should be noted, however, that Felli and Hazen (1998) consider the expected value of perfect information, relative to the expected value of an optimal decision that they specify, as one that maximizes the expected payoff given parameter values that the investigator feels are "most likely to obtain" (p. 100). This seems to suggest the modal value(s) of the parameter(s). Nevertheless, in their applications they tend to choose the mean values of their parameters. Regardless, since neither of these is generally the optimal decision given available information, this calculation will overstate the actual expected value of perfect information relative to an optimal decision given imperfect information. In this sense, the calculation by Hazen and Felli can be viewed as an upper bound on the true EVPI. The only advantage of this approach over the theoretically correct approach is that it avoids the need to determine the decision that maximizes the expected value with existing information. This is not a substantial advantage, however, because if the value of information is small, then collecting additional information is presumably not worthwhile; therefore, knowing the optimal decision with existing information is key. Similarly, if the value of information is large, then one still wants to try to determine the EVPI relative to an optimal decision with existing information in order to see how much that decreases the bound on the EVPI. Thus, in either case, the calculation of EVPI relative to the optimal decision given current information is preferred. It is also generally not an extremely difficult determination to make once it is possible to assess the expected value of outcomes from an arbitrary (optimal or suboptimal) decision.

8. Even though the expected utility maximization assumption is implicit in QALYs, it may not well reflect the way in which people incorporate uncertainty into their preferences (Kahneman and Tversky, 1979). However, while this is clearly an important limitation of QALYs, it is one that needs to be addressed regardless of the issues about aggregate uncertainty that are addressed in sensitivity analysis. As discussed above, concerns about aggregate financial and health risk do seem somewhat less compelling in a social context where the risks associated with decisions about individual technologies are likely to be modest from an aggregate perspective. Nevertheless, the issue of how risk should be assessed in policy decisions is important and deserves further consideration because other assumptions about preferences concerning risk or about insurance would lead to different conclusions about a range of methodological issues in cost-effectiveness analysis, including sensitivity analysis (e.g. Mullahy, 1997).

References

Al, Maiwenn J., Ben A. van Hout, Bowine C. Michel, and Frans F. H. Rutten. 1998. "Sample Size Calculation in Economic Evaluations." *Health Economics* 7:327–35.

Arrow, Kenneth. 1951. *Social Choice and Individual Values.* New Haven, Conn.: Yale University Press.

Arrow, Kenneth, and Robert Lind. 1970. "Uncertainty and the Evaluation of Public Investment Decisions." *American Economic Review* 16, no. 3 (June): 364–78.

Berk, Marc L., Alan C. Monheit, and Michael M. Hagan. 1988. "How the U.S. Spent Its Health Care Dollar: 1929–1980." *Health Affairs* 7, no 4 (fall): 46–60.

Blumenschein, Karen, and Magnus Johannesson. 1998. "Relationship between Quality of Life Instruments, Health State Utilities and Willingness to Pay in Patients with Asthma." *Annals of Allergy, Asthma, and Immunology* 80:189–94.

Briggs, Andrew H., and Alastair M. Gray. 1998. "Power and Significance Calculations for Stochastic Cost-Effectiveness Analysis." *Medical Decision Making* 18 (suppl.): S81–S92.

Brook, Robert H., J. E. Ware, W. H. Rogers, E. B. Keeler, A. R. Davies, C. A. Donald, G. A. Goldberg, et al. 1983. "Does Free Care Improve Adults' Health? Results from a Randomized Controlled Trial." *New England Journal of Medicine* 309, no 24:1426–34.

Claxton, Karl. 1999. "The Irrelevance of Inference: A Decision-Making Approach to the Stochastic Evaluation of Health Care Technologies." *Journal of Health Economics* 18, no. 3 (June): 341–64.

Claxton, Karl, and John Posnett. 1996. "An Economic Approach to Clinical Trial Design and Research Priority-Setting," *Health Economics* 5, no. 6 (November-December): 513–24.

Cutler, D. M., M. McClellan, J. P. Newhouse, et al. 1998. "Are Medical Prices Declining? Evidence From Heart Attack Treatments." *Quarterly Journal of Economics* 113, no. 4 (November): 991–1024.

Cutler, David, and Elizabeth Richardson. 1997. "Measuring the Health of the U.S. Population." *Brookings Papers: Microeconomics*: 217–71.

Diabetes Control and Complications Trial Research Group. 1993. "The Effect of Intensive Treatment of Diabetes on the Development and Progression of Long-Term Complications in Insulin-Dependent Diabetes Mellitus." *New England Journal of Medicine* 329, no. 14:977–86.

———. 1996. "Lifetime Befits and Costs of Intensive Therapy as Practiced in the Diabetes Control and Complications Trial." *Journal of the American Medical Association* 276, no. 17: 1409–15.

Eddy, David. 1981. "The Economics of Cancer Prevention and Detection: Getting More for Less." *Cancer* 47:1200–1209.

———. 1990. "Screening for Cervical Cancer." *Annals of Internal Medicine* 113:214–26.

Elixhauser, Anne, Michael Halpern, Jordana Schmier, and Bryan R Luce. 1998. "Health Care CBA and CEA from 1991 to 1996: An Updated Bibliography." *Medical Care* 36, no. 5:MS1–MS9.

Enthoven, Alain C. 1980. *Health Plan*. Reading, Mass.: Addison-Wesley.

Felli, James C., and Gordon B. Hazen. 1998. "Sensitivity Analysis and the Expected Value of Perfect Information." *Medical Decision Making* 18, no. 1 (January-March): 95–109.

Festinger, Leon. 1957. *A Theory of Cognitive Dissonance*. Stanford, Calif.: Stanford University Press.

Fuchs, Victor. 1990. "The Health Sector's Share of the Gross National Product." *Science* 247:534–38.

Garber, Alan, and Charles Phelps. 1995. "Economic Foundations of Cost-Effectiveness Analysis." NBER Working Paper. Later published in *Journal of Health Economics* 16, no. 1 (1997):1–32.

Gold, Marthe R., Joanna E. Siegel, Louise B. Russel, and Milton C. Weinstein. 1996. *Cost-Effectiveness in Health and Medicine*. Oxford University Press, New York.

Goldman, L., D. J. Gordon, B. M. Rifkind, S. B. Hulley, A. S. Detsky, D. S. Goodman, B. Kinosian, and M. C. Weinstein. 1992. "Cost and Health Implications of Cholesterol Lowering." *Circulation* 85: 1960–68.

Gross, Cary P., Gerald F. Anderson, and Neil R. Powe. 1999. "The Relationship between Funding by the National Institutes of Health and the Burden of Disease." *New England Journal of Medicine* 340, no. 24:1881–87.

Harsanyi, J. C. 1955. "Cardinal Welfare, Indivividualistic Ethics, and Interpersonal Comparisions of Utility." *Journal of Political Economy* 63:309–21.

Hornberger, John. 1998. "A Cost-Benefit Analysis of a Cardiovascular Disease Prevention Trial, Using Folate Supplementation as an Example." *American Journal of Public Health* 88, no. 1: 61–67.

IOM (Institute of Medicine). 1998. *Scientific Opportunities and Public Needs: Improving Priority Setting and Public Input at the National Institutes of Health.* Washington, D.C.: National Academy Press.

Johannesson, Magnus, David Meltzer, and Richard O'Conor. 1997. "Incorporating Future Costs in Medical Cost-Effectiveness Analysis: Implications for the Cost-Effectiveness of the Treatment of Hypertension." *Medical Decision Making* 17:382–89.

Kahneman, Daniel, and Amos Tversky. 1979. "Prospect Theory: An Analysis of Decision under Risk." Econometrica 47, no. 2:263–91.

La Puma, J., and E. F. Lawlor. 1990. "Quality-Adjusted Life Years: Ethical Implications for Physicians and Policy Makers." *Journal of the American Medical Association* 263:2917–21.

Lindrooth, Richard C., Edward C. Norton, and Barbara Dickey. 1998. "Selective Contracting and Utilization Management." Unpublished manuscript, Northwestern University.

Mandelblatt, Jeanne, and Marianne Fahs. 1988. "The Cost-Effectiveness of Cervical Cancer Screening for Low-Income Elderly Women." *Journal of the American Medical Association* 259, no. 16:2409–13.

Manning, Willard, Joseph Newhouse, Naihua Duan, et al. 1987. "Health Insurance and the Demand for Medical Care: Evidence from a Randomized Experiment." *American Economic Review* 77, no. 3:251–77.

McClellan, Mark, Barbara J. McNeil, and Joseph P. Newhouse. 1994. "Does More Intensive Treatment of Acute Myocardial Infarction in the Elderly Reduce Mortality?" *Journal of the American Medical Association* 272, no. 11 (21 September): 859–66.

Meltzer, David. 1997. "Accounting for Future Costs in Medical Cost-Effectiveness Analysis." *Journal of Health Economics* 16, no. 1:33–64.

———. 2001. "Addressing Uncertainty in Medical Cost-Effectiveness Analysis: Implications of Expected Utility Maximization for Methods to Perform Sensitivity Analysis and the Use of Cost-Effectiveness Analysis to Set Priorities for Medical Research." *Journal of Health Economics* 20, no. 1:109–29.

———. In press. "Theoretical Issues in Accounting for Future Costs in Medical Cost-Effectiveness Analysis." In *Policy Issues in Pharmaceutical Cost-Effectiveness Analysis*. Washington, D.C.: AEI Press.

Meltzer, David, Brian Egleston, David Stoffel, and Erik Dasbach. 2000. "The Effect of Future Costs on the Cost-Effectiveness of Medical Interventions among Young Adults: The Example of Intensive Therapy for Type-1 Diabetes." *Medical Care* 38, no. 6:679–85.

Meltzer, David, G. Hazen, M. Johannesson, I. Abdalla, R. Chang, A. Elstein, and A. Schwartz. "Effect of Future Costs on the Cost-Effectiveness of Life Extension and Quality of Life Improvement among the Elderly." *Medical Decision Making* 18:475 (October).

Meltzer, David, and Magnus Johannesson, 1999. "Inconsistencies in the 'Societal Perspective' on Costs of the Panel on Cost-Effectiveness in Health and Medicine." *Medical Decision Making* 19 (October): 371–77.

Meltzer, David, and Tamar Polonsky. 1998. "Do Quality-Adjusted Life Life Years Reflect Patient Preferences? Validation Using Revealed Preference for Intensive Treatment of IDDM." *Journal of General Internal Medicine* 13, no. 33 (April).

Mullahy, John. 1997. "Which Cost-Effectiveness Ratio? Evaluating Health Policies and Medical Technologies in Stochastic Contexts." Unpublished manuscript, University of Wisconsin, Madison.

Neumann, P. J., D. E. Zinner, and A. D. Paltiel. 1996. "The FDA and Regulation of Cost-Effectiveness Claims." *Health Affairs* 15, no. 3 (fall): 54–71.

Newhouse, Joseph P. 1992. "Medical Care Costs: How Much Welfare Loss." *Journal of Economic Perspectives* 6:3–21.

O'Brien, Bernie J., Michael F. Drummond, Roberta J. Labelle, and Andrew Willian. 1994. "In Search of Power and Significance: Issues in the Design and Analysis of Stochastic Cost-Effectiveness Studies in Health Care." *Medical Care* 32, no. 2:150–63.

Pauly, Mark. 1995. "Valuing Health Care Benefits in Money Terms." In *Valuing Health Care: Costs, Benefits and Effectiveness of Pharmaceuticals and Other Medical Technologies,* by Frank Sloan. New York: Cambridge University Press.

Perry, Seymour, and Mae Thamer. 1999. "Medical Innovation and the Critical Role of Health Technology Assessment." *Journal of the American Medical Association* 282, no. 19 (17 November): 1869–72.

Polsky, Daniel, Henry A. Glick, Richard Willke, and Kevin Shulman. 1997. "Confidence Intervals for Cost-Effectiveness Analysis: A Comparison of Four Methods." *Health Economics* 6:243–52.

Pratt, John W., Howard Raiffa, and Robert Schlaifer. 1965. *Introduction to Statistical Decision Theory*. New York: McGraw-Hill Book Company.

Raiffa, Howard, and Robert Schlaifer. 1961. *Applied Statistical Decision Theory*. Clinton, Mass.: Harvard Business School, Colonial Press.

Rothschild, Michael, and Joseph Stiglitz. 1976. "Equilibrium in Competitive Insurance Markets: An Essay on the Economics of Imperfect Information." *Quarterly Journal of Economics* 90:629–50.

Sen, Amartya. 1999. "The Possibility of Social Choice." *American Economic Review* 89, no. 3:349–78.

Smith, Sheila, M. Freeland, S. Heffler, and D. McKusick. 1998. "The Next Ten Years of Health Spending: What Does the Future Hold?" *Health Affairs* 17, no. 5:128–40.

Stason, William B., and Milton Weinstein. 1977. "Allocation of Resources to Manage Hypertension." *New England Journal of Medicine* 296, no. 13:732–39.

Stinnett, Aaron A., and John Mullahy. 1998. "Net Health Benefits: A New Framework for the Analysis of Uncertainty in Cost-Effectiveness Analysis." *Medical Decision Making* 18, no. 2 (suppl.): S68–80.

Stinnett, Aaron A., and David Paltiel. 1997. "Estimating CE Ratios under Second-Order Uncertainty: The Mean Ratio versus the Ratio of the Means." *Medical Decision Making* 17:483–89.

Tambour, Magnus, Niklas Zethraeus, and Magnus Johannesson. 1998. "A Note on Confidence Intervals in Cost-Effectiveness Analysis." *International Journal of Technology Assessment in Health Care* 14, no. 3 (summer): 467–71.

Tengs, Tammy O. 1998. "Planning for Serendipity: A New Strategy to Prosper from Health Research." Health Priorities Project Policy Report no. 2. Washington, D.C. Progressive Policy Institute.

U.S. Preventive Services Task Force. 1996. *Guide to Clinical Preventive Services (CPS)*, 2d ed. Report of the U.S. Preventive Services Task Force, Stk # 0107-001-00525-8. Washington, D.C.: Government Printing Office.

Varmus, Harold, 1999. "Evaluating the Burden of Disease and Spending the Research Dollars of the National Institutes of Health." *New England Journal of Medicine* 340, no. 24:1914–15.

Weinstein, Milton, 1995. "Theoretical basis of Cost Effectiveness." In *Valuing Health Care: Costs, Benefits and Effectiveness of Pharmaceuticals and Other Medical Technologies,* by Frank Sloan. New York: Cambridge University Press.

Weinstein, Milton, and William B. Stason. 1976. *Hypertension: A Policy Perspective.* Cambridge, Mass.: Harvard University Press.

Weinstein, Milton, and Richard J. Zeckhauser. 1972. "Critical Ratios and Efficient Allocation." *Journal of Public Economics* 2, no. 2:147–57.

CONTRIBUTORS

David M. Cutler
Department of Economics
Harvard University
Cambridge, MA 02138

Paul Heidenreich
Section of Cardiology 111C
Palo Alto Veterans Administration Medical Center
3801 Miranda Avenue
Palo Alto, CA 94304

Srikanth Kadiyala
National Bureau of Economic Research
1050 Massachusetts Avenue
Cambridge, MA 02138

Frank R. Lichtenberg
Columbia University
3022 Broadway, 726 Uris Hall
New York, NY 10027

Mark McClellan
Department of Economics
Stanford University
Stanford, CA 94305

David Meltzer
Department of Medicine
University of Chicago
5841 South Maryland Avenue, MC 2007
Chicago, IL 60637

Kevin M. Murphy
Graduate School of Business
University of Chicago
1101 East 58th Street
Chicago, IL 60637

William D. Nordhaus
P.O. Box 208268 Yale Station
New Haven, CT 06511

Robert H. Topel
Graduate School of Business
University of Chicago
1101 East 58th Street
Chicago, IL 60637

AUTHOR INDEX

SUBJECT INDEX